The Art of
TEACHING ITALIAN

The Art of
TEACHING ITALIAN

GIULIA GUARNIERI
Editor

Foreword by
JANICE ASKI

GEORGETOWN UNIVERSITY PRESS / WASHINGTON, DC

© 2024 Georgetown University Press. All rights reserved. No part of this book may be reproduced or utilized in any form or by any means, electronic or mechanical, including photocopying and recording, or by any information storage and retrieval system, without permission in writing from the publisher.

The publisher is not responsible for third-party websites or their content. URL links were active at time of publication.

Library of Congress Cataloging-in-Publication Data

Names: Guarnieri, Giulia, editor.
Title: The art of teaching Italian / Giulia Guarnieri, editor.
Description: Washington, DC : Georgetown University Press, 2024. | Includes
   bibliographical references and index.
Identifiers: LCCN 2023030834 (print) | LCCN 2023030835 (ebook) |
   ISBN 9781647124168 (hardcover) | ISBN 9781647124175 (paperback) |
   ISBN 9781647124182 (ebook)
Subjects: LCSH: Italian language—Study and teaching—English speakers. |
   Italy—Civilization—Study and teaching.
Classification: LCC PC1065 .A76 2024 (print) | LCC PC1065 (ebook) |
   DDC 458.007—dc23/eng/20231211
LC record available at https://lccn.loc.gov/2023030834
LC ebook record available at https://lccn.loc.gov/2023030835

♾ This paper meets the requirements of ANSI/NISO Z39.48-1992 (Permanence of Paper).

25 24   9 8 7 6 5 4 3 2   First printing

Printed in the United States of America

Cover design by Martha Madrid
Interior design by BookComp, Inc.

*To all those who have been a part of my getting there:
Lucilla, Giancarlo, Renata, Edgardo.*

CONTENTS

Foreword   ix
    Janice Aski

    Introduction   1
       Giulia Guarnieri

1   Meeting the Challenges during the Pandemic: Low-Stakes Pedagogy in the Elementary Italian Classroom   7
       Silvia Carlorosi and Giulia Guarnieri

2   Talking Points: Conversation Courses as Models for Multilevel and Multimodal Curricular Innovation   25
       Julia Cozzarelli and Marella Feltrin-Morris

3   Discovering Italian American Culture through Digital Humanities: Building Language Competencies and Community Engagement in the Italian Curriculum   41
       Domenica Diraviam and Viviana Pezzullo

4   The Capitals of Italian Culture: Teaching, Learning, and New Technologies   60
       Patrizia Palumbo and Alessandra Saggin

5   Experiential Learning Opportunities and High-Impact Practices in Intermediate and Advanced Italian Language Courses   79
       Paola Bernardini and Tatiana Selepiuc

6   Re-Visioning the Linguistics Landscape through a Multiliteracies Framework: Authorizing Learners' Personal Semiotics in a Glocal Space   92
       Barbara Spinelli

7	Audiovisual Translation in Language Learning and Teaching: The "Learn Italian with Subtitles" Project at the University of Liverpool (UK) *Rosalba Biasini and Francesca Raffi*	118
8	Teaching Italian through Podcasting: Pedagogical Rationale, Implementation, and Student Evaluation of the Podcast Project *Dagli Inviati sul Campus* *Elisabetta Ferrari, Riccardo Amorati, and John Hajek*	135
9	A Case Study on Chinese Exchange Students in Italy: Issues, Adaptation Strategies, and a Culture-Shock Management Syllabus *Shuang Liang, Pietro Amadini, Alessandro Macilenti*	153
10	Tandem Learning in an Italian Program: A Study of Perceived and Measured Gains in Language Proficiency and Cultural Competence *Louise Hipwell*	175
11	BLM and ə: Introducing Diversity in the Syllabus Design *Valentina Abbatelli*	197
12	Queering the Italian and Modern Languages Syllabi: Toward a Queer Language Pedagogy and Intersectional Teaching Practices *Luca Malici*	216
13	Adopting and Adapting a Language MOOC: Learning from Students' Experience in Intermediate Italian Blended Courses *Daniela Bartalesi-Graf and Luisa Canuto*	234
14	Teaching Italian Using LMOOCs: The Target Audience and New Operational Models *Matteo La Grassa and Andrea Villarini*	257

List of Contributors 275
Index 283

FOREWORD

Long ago, instruction was all about teaching decontextualized grammatical structures, vocabulary, and text translation. It didn't take long to move on from a model that worked for Latin to a model that shifted focus to speaking modern languages. Unfortunately, the revised goal, motivated by a need/desire to quickly learn to speak a new language, was actually not communication, since the method for developing speaking skills was based on behavioralist techniques that promoted rote memorization with drills and error avoidance. Thanks to research in linguistics, applied linguistics, the burgeoning field of second language acquisition, as well as a variety of other disciplines, language programs refocused again, increasingly taking into account the complexity and intersection of language, culture, communication, and interaction.

Communicative language teaching felt like liberation from constraints—the beginning of a new era of creativity. The doors opened to incorporating instruction in the four skills, teaching culture (broadly defined), and including films, art, music, and so on in the language curriculum. The result was elementary-level language texts bursting with materials that could not all be covered in the language sequence, so instructors had to make strategic choices (while the perceived need to prioritize grammar, however, persisted). Intermediate and advanced coursework moved in parallel, with a shift to topics outside of traditional literary analysis, in order to update, innovate, and/or reinvigorate curricula and attract more students as the enrollment crisis in languages in particular and humanities in general gained momentum. The push to increase enrollments also reinforced the commitment to apply technology to language instruction, such as the development of MOOCs and new applications to facilitate interaction and language use.

This instructional evolution timeline, outlined in broad strokes of change and progress, demonstrates how Italian programs were poised to confront the two events in the spring of 2020 that, together with other sociopolitical developments, changed everything. In early spring (March 2020) the COVID-19 pandemic triggered the sudden move to online instruction, for which few were prepared, and on May 25, 2020, George Floyd was murdered by a police officer in Minneapolis, Minnesota, which generated Black Lives Matter (BLM) protests and an intensification of social justice movements.

Italian language programs have taken a remarkable turn, and this collection brings together some of the best and brightest solutions for adapting instruction to the new reality. Falling enrollments in language courses, which at some institutions has led to department/program closures, continues to be a top concern for most, particularly given the budget crisis triggered by the pandemic and other motivating factors, such as a push for undergraduate "professionalization" and "credentialing" that may drain students from language majors and minors. New technologies, developed in part during the pandemic, are being explored, utilized, and refined for their pedagogical benefits in a new instructional space. Most important, however, BLM has redirected almost everyone's attention to pressing social issues that were not getting the attention they needed and deserved. Many have doubled down on the exploration of race and ethnicity, migration and integration, diversity and communication, identity and intersectionality, to name a few, at all levels of the curriculum, reflecting a similar move in targeted investments, core course requirements, and modified expected goals and outcomes at the college and university level. This collection demonstrates how world language programs are, in a new way, an integral part of conversations in higher education. It is now our job to intensify our messaging as to how our contributions to undergraduate education are not only unique but essential. The concept that unites all types of diversity and inclusion work is *intercultural competence* (IC), which has a variety of definitions. One definition is based on Deardorff's (2006, p. 254) pyramid representation of the attitudes, knowledge(s), skills, and qualities that comprise intercultural competence, and can be expressed as follows: "Intercultural competence is a lifelong process that includes the development of . . . attitudes (respect and valuing of other cultures, openness, curiosity), knowledge (of self, culture, sociolinguistic issues), skills (listen, observe, interpret, analyze, evaluate, and relate), and qualities (adaptability, flexibility, empathy, and cultural decentering) in order to behave and communicate effectively and appropriately to achieve one's goals to some degree."

I dare to propose that intercultural competence cannot be fully achieved without the study of a new language because there are skills that can *only* be developed in courses taught in a language other than the learner's native language. When students interact with their peers and/or native speakers in their imperfect second language, they become mindful and cognitively aware of the process of communication; they learn to manage ambiguity in communication and the anxiety this generates, as well as to adapt to the behavior and expectations of others. They lose their "linguistic superiority," which can lead to heightened awareness of one's "Otherness." These experiences, combined with explicit instruction in the IC attitudes, knowledge(s), skills, and qualities, provide the essential groundwork for the lifelong process of expanding one's intercultural competence.

The contributions to *The Art of Teaching Italian* provide creative solutions to enrollment issues and demonstrate that it is possible to enhance the learning experience despite these obstacles. In addition, they introduce innovative applications of technology that display pedagogical ingenuity, and they exemplify an extraordinary engagement with diversity that makes Italian programs a leader, not a follower, in university initiatives to produce interculturally competent graduates.

Janice M. Aski, The Ohio State University
Professor of Italian and Director of the Center
for Languages Literatures and Cultures

BIBLIOGRAPHY

Aski, J. M., & Weintritt, A. D. (2020). New messaging and intercultural competence training in response to falling enrollments in world languages. *Italica*, *97*(1), 134–54.

Deardorff, D. K. (2006). Identification and assessment of intercultural competence as a student outcome of internationalization. *Journal of Studies in International Education*, *10*(3), 241–66. https://doi.org/10.1177/1028315306287002

INTRODUCTION

Giulia Guarnieri

Effective teaching in any circumstance requires a deep understanding of who students are and, if necessary, adaptation of the lesson plan to respond to the needs that each cohort of students presents. Students' needs vary and instructors must be attentive and empathetic to them, providing an environment for growth that also fosters persistence when obstacles occur. *The Art of Teaching Italian* focuses on the underpinning of Italian language pedagogy, addressing epistemological questions on how learning happens by exploring the interrelationships between the various aspects of teaching paradigms, including epistemology, methodology, and deliveries, while at the same time addressing the basic assumptions of educational research and assessment of learning, making the contributions in this volume pertinent to every foreign language professional who is an engaged researcher and practitioner.

This volume was born during the height of the SARS-CoV-2 (COVID-19) pandemic in 2020, when the world saw unprecedented disruption and turmoil. The devastating impact of this health crisis on education has been amply documented by the Centers for Disease Control and Prevention (CDC) and the American Council on Education, underscoring various aspects of its overall impact. The pedagogical, economic, social, political, and, particularly, the mental health of students impacted each differently. The pandemic exacerbated the mental health status of low-income students, student of color, and LGBTQ+ students (American Council on Education, 2020).[1] This health emergency brought more attention than before to the importance of meaningful and effective teaching and the need to create valuable, deliberate, and intentional pedagogies and praxes to support not only student learning but also in-depth approaches that impact the totality of students' lives. It was in this moment that we all started to rethink teaching and learning Italian from a different perspective, and I felt that we needed to share the good work being done by so many Italian language instructors.

Given the transdisciplinary nature of this volume, this book will appeal to teachers from various parts of the world. It is a great addition to professional development workshops for teachers as well as for Italian language and pedagogy scholars, teacher trainers, world languages faculty coordinators, and graduate students in Italian language, all of whom will gain more teaching knowledge and access to hands-on materials, experiences, and critical pedagogies in each chapter. Throughout the book, the contributors have striven to provide pragmatic examples for faculty to use to reconfigure course syllabuses and teaching approaches. The international group of scholars who contributed to this volume are practitioners with established research backgrounds. Key topics discussed in this book include the challenges of teaching Italian language online during the pandemic and having to reconfigure the curriculum to meet course learning outcomes and deliverables.

The first chapter, by Silvia Carlorosi and myself, describes how Italian language instructors were confronted with several hurdles when the college shut down and courses were forced to be 100% online. One of the most pressing topics was engaging students with writing assignments, which students had always found challenging to complete. Strategically, deconstructing the traditional writing assignments into low-stakes writing activities increased student participation and decreased students' apprehensions about writing compositions in a foreign language. The result, we argue, was an increase in completion rates.

Julia Cozzarelli and Marella Feltrin-Morris also address the challenges brought on by the pandemic and their effect on a program already struggling to maintain stable enrollments in Chapter 2. They focus on the redesign of two conversation and culture courses; initially created as advanced language classes, they are now accessible to lower-proficiency students. These "stacked" courses, with different course numbers and serving different groups of students, but with overlapping content, enabled faculty members to teach students at different levels simultaneously. This chapter not only reveals the success of this innovation but also provides a model for other multilevel courses in language, literature, and culture.

Solutions for future unexpected format changes through the integration of digital humanities into language courses is the focus of Chapter 3 by Domenica Diraviam and Viviana Pezzullo. Students enrolled in lower-level language courses were asked to populate a digital archive on Italian American

Memories, an activity that went beyond the mere learning of the target language to support experiential learning and foster students' agency and professional skills beyond the classroom.

Similarly, Patrizia Palumbo and Alessandra Saggin discuss in Chapter 4 their newly created online platform for intermediate and advanced language courses centered on Italian cities, through which students grow their intercultural competence. The multidimensional online platform, with topics covering music, literature, cuisine, cinema, and artifacts, emphasizes the vastness of modern Italian immigrants' contributions in recent decades. Students interacting with the platform maximize their exposure to L2 in meaningful ways with authentic contexts and audiences.

Another project focusing on cities inspired Paola Bernardini and Tatiana Selepiuc to transform their Italian courses into high-impact educational practices (HIPs) and foster a diversity-oriented and globally focused curriculum where students engage in virtual tours of cities from the present and past, as described in Chapter 5. Besides using cultural productions such as theater, translation, and film subtitles in the classroom, students engage cross-linguistic and cross-cultural comparisons as key elements, which increases students' interactivity through problem-solving and interaction with real-world problems.

In Chapter 6, Barbara Spinelli presents research that also explores urban space. She begins with Piero Bassetti's notion of Italicity, in which people identify with Italian values and behaviors rather than with physical borders, a concept easily replicated in an urban classroom setting, as a theoretical backdrop for her teaching practice. Students accumulate images of artifacts of an urban space, such as graffiti, buildings, statues, and gardens, then reinterpret and assemble them in a digital portfolio reflecting their personal point of view and self-direction. Through gathered data and the concept of imagined communities, Spinelli details the great potential of this pedagogical approach, bridging the gap between theory and tangible language practices and deliveries.

Chapter 7 by Rosalba Biasini and Francesca Raffi focuses on a unique approach to teaching using audiovisual translation, in particular subtitling, as a pedagogical practice. Even during the turn to online learning during the COVID-19 pandemic, Biasini and Raffi's students engaged in different classroom projects through this new medium. By doing so, students improved their communicative and sociolinguistic proficiencies, in addition to acquiring soft skills that, as the authors point out, are highly valuable in the fields of translation and interpretation.

Like Biasini and Raffi's project-based pedagogy, Elisabetta Ferrari, Riccardo Amorati, and John Hajek embedded project-based learning into their intermediate language course in the form of podcasting. Chapter 8 showcases how students produce podcasts on Italian cultural themes, interacting with the local community. The authors also discuss assessment results using a mixed-methods study on students' perception of their learning experience, pointing out how adding podcasting to the curriculum supports the students' sense of agency, problem-solving skills, critical thinking skills, and reflective abilities.

The authentic Italian experience is reserved for students who plan to travel to Italy and study the language *in loco*, and the proposal offered by Shuang Liang, Pietro Amadini, and Alessandro Macilenti in Chapter 9 centers on the study-abroad experience of Chinese students in Italy. The chapter informs the study-abroad communities in Italy of how to mitigate the adverse effects of culture shock and improve the academic experience for future cohorts.

Foreign language partnerships can also be experienced virtually, and this is exactly what Louise Hipwell articulates in Chapter 10. This original contribution explores the results of a data-driven study of a virtual exchange between an American and an Italian university based on a language exchange and monitoring program called Teletandem. Hipwell describes the Teletandem approach, in which native English speakers are paired with native Italian speakers and each student has opportunities to practice their target language. She then explains how other colleges can implement, manage, and assess the same approach in low-intermediate proficiency level courses. In the chapter, Hipwell examines key language-learning outcomes such as confidence building, engagement, intercultural awareness, and personal connections, among others.

Valentina Abbatelli addresses the importance of equity in the Italian curriculum, in particular focusing on diversity, inclusivity, and representation of Black Lives Matter (BLM) themes and exploring the Italian colonial past through an active and intentional pedagogical approach in Chapter 11. The examples and suggestions provided by the author showcase how inclusivity can be successfully embedded in the language curriculum and how lessons on diversity improve linguistic and intercultural competence while stimulating student participation. Luca Malici's thought-provoking Chapter 12 also tackles the topic of diversity, this time focusing on how to embed Queer Language Pedagogy (QLP) in language classes. Malici's pragmatic approach offers the opportunity for instructors to rethink the representations and discourses on women, families, race, and sexuality in commercially available teaching materials.

Chapters 13 and 14 conclude the volume, both dedicated to language massive open online courses (LMOOCs). Both chapters, in dialogue with each other, offer suggestions on how to create efficient and wide-ranging online courses. Chapter 13, by Daniela Bartalesi-Graf and Luisa Canuto, explains the adaptation of an AP Italian Language and Culture course as an LMOOC for intermediate and advanced language courses by using blended and flipped approaches. The data-driven chapter shows how the conversion of this course offers many advantages, such as the affordability of ready-made online material to support students' learning, broadening Italian language program access, and addressing declining enrollments. Chapter 14, by Matteo La Grassa and Andrea Villarini, provides insights into how various people worked together to create an LMOOC in an Italian university. La Grassa and Villarini cite concrete classroom examples and approaches for its implementation. Supported by data gathered through the analysis of participant interactions and course evaluation questionnaires, the authors suggest that LMOOCs can represent a valid teaching resource and a possible model for other institutions to adopt.

The chapters in this volume constitute important current pedagogy. Italian teachers should take special note of the many contributions touching on diversity in the curriculum. As a field, we should continue work to evolve these pedagogies and approaches and to make them permanent features of Italian courses. The book emphasizes that many efforts to include multiculturality have been accomplished but the road ahead is still long. Language practitioners should take the time to explore the relationships of power, culture, and politics present within their schools and programs in order to enact real change.

The Art of Teaching Italian embraces new theories and pedagogies and helps teachers infuse social equity into curricula across campuses. It is my hope that the contributions of this book will offer a blueprint for reshaping and updating language and culture courses in universities across the world and for scholars and instructors to embrace these new theories and practices and refine specific teaching skills. I hope that these chapters inspire practitioners to expand their scholarly and pedagogical horizons by exploring new approaches. It is common to seek refuge in what we know how to do best; nevertheless, we hope that each chapter will prompt readers to explore multidimensionality and welcome different voices and approaches to teaching and learning.

I thank all of the contributors, with whom I enjoyed working. The book would not exist if we did not acknowledge that *The Art of Teaching Italian* was inspired by the most valuable members of our teaching communities, our students, who motivate and guide us every day to provide them with exemplary service.

NOTE

1. American Council on Education. (2020). *Mental health, higher education, & COVID-19: Strategies for leaders to support campus well-being.* Washington, DC.

1

MEETING THE CHALLENGES DURING THE PANDEMIC

Low-Stakes Pedagogy in the Elementary Italian Classroom

Silvia Carlorosi and Giulia Guarnieri

In this chapter we document, via quantitative data, how the creation of mini-writing assignments, or low-stakes compositions, is pivotal in allowing students to view writing in a more positive light and as a less daunting task. The main concern that prompted our investigation was to increase student participation in writing activities in elementary Italian courses at an urban community college. In addition we wanted to find out why students were so reluctant to write. Moreover, we aimed to find effective solutions that would encourage them to feel more at ease in tackling writing tasks. To make writing more attractive we created multicultural-themed assignments that meshed Italian culture with the various cultures relevant to our student population. We also discuss here the anticipated problems of cheating in online writing assignments and provide solutions to prevent them from occurring by embedding a growth mindset approach.[1] This approach has had a much better chance of working, given our student population matrix, than what one would expect using conventional surveillance practices.

    The COVID-19 pandemic (SARS-CoV-2) in 2020 created additional stress for students, whose first instinct was to keep their family safe, maintain an occupation, overcome technical challenges, and navigate the isolation of the online learning environment. For many this took a toll, as reported by the Columbia University Community College Research Center: "As of October 2020, more than 40 percent of households report that a prospective student is cancelling all plans for community college; another 15 percent are either taking fewer classes or switching programs. Community college students are cancelling their plans at more than twice the rate of four-year college students" (Belfield & Brock, 2020). In addition, several *New York Times* articles and other journals documented the impact the pandemic had on student retention and mental health, including increased feelings of loneliness, anxiety, and depression.[2] A recent study analyzing a sample of undergraduate college students found that "stress, anxiety, and depression were the pervasive problems for college student population during the pandemic. . . . These key findings are very concerning considering that mental health is strongly associated with student wellbeing, academic outcomes, and retention" (Lee et al., 2021). Furthermore, additional factors such as student predisposition, lack of steady income, and study habits harshly affected the community college population, which faced additional adverse circumstances (Núñez, 2013; Willenborg, 2016; Yukselturk & Bulut, 2007).

COLLEGE AND PROGRAM BACKGROUND

Bronx Community College (BCC) is a Hispanic-serving institution where 46% of its population are first-generation college students (Bronx Community College, 2022). About 40% of students have a household income of less than $15,000, and 72% of students receive financial aid. In a 2020 college survey, 50% of students reported that "they worry about/worry sometimes about running out of food and losing current housing" (Bronx Community College, 2022). As shown in many investigations (Morgan et al., 2009; VanderStel, 2014), adverse conditions have a greater impact on lower socioeconomic populations in terms of academic outcomes. At our institution, for instance, more than 62% of students need remediation in one or more areas (math, writing, and reading), and this often results in 20% graduation rates in three years.

All of these numbers inform us that Bronx Community College students have many concerns and worries about their personal lives. With this unprecedented health emergency added to the mix, their classroom performance was highly impacted.

ITALIAN PROGRAM BACKGROUND

From spring 2020 to 2022 we observed that it was difficult for our students to make college a priority. They frequently came unprepared to class, did not ask for help, and gave up at the first obstacle they encountered, which often resulted in dropping the class or even dropping out of college.

On average, we offer nine sections each semester of Beginning Italian I and II (first and second semesters); we have three part-time instructors and two full-time professors who regularly teach each year. Among the students' learning outcomes for Beginning Italian, we emphasize that at the end of the course students will "understand, speak, read, and write Italian at a middle-beginning level, in class work and on tests" (Carlorosi, 2022, p. 3) and, in addition, "produce oral and written texts that draw on elements of vocabulary, grammar and culture that [they have] studied and discussed. These texts may take the form of oral presentations, skits, journal or blog entries, or letters" (p. 4).

Although in Italian language elementary courses writing counts for a high percentage of the grade (20%), often students do not complete writing assignments. Several instructors noticed, over the years, that about 30% of the students did not submit their compositions. This situation, which became more severe during the pandemic, prompted some reflection, as we realized that writing, for our college students, was becoming a daunting task. Sometimes the guidelines and rules of these writing tasks take away from the creativity process, as students may feel overwhelmed by them and struggle with writing mechanics and anxiety (Zhang, 2019). Students whose first language is not English may even experience the fear of not being able to express their thoughts coherently and may not know the reasons why they are underperforming. Many students at our college are non-native English speakers (44.1%), and this can impact their confidence in an academic setting.[3]

METHODS

In approaching our methodology, we had to consider additional problems unique to the historical situation the college was facing. Due to the COVID-19 pandemic from spring 2020 to spring 2022, most of the classes at BCC were offered online or with a hybrid modality.[4] Although most faculty underwent preparatory workshops to adapt their pedagogy to the new online modalities with the main objective of enhancing students' engagement, unfortunately many students ended up abandoning their course of study and disenrolling from the college. As a result, BCC has been facing the lowest rate of enrollment and retention of the past few years. In fall 2021 BCC counted 7,265 students enrolled, a number that has been gradually declining from previous years. As a comparison, in fall 2015 the number of new students enrolled was over 10,000.[5] Retention data saw the same declining course, and in 2015 it reached 58.8 percent. The pandemic's challenges impacted higher education or education in general on many platforms, and concern was expressed by various institutions. In March 2021 the Brown Center on Education Policy hosted a webinar to discuss the drawbacks most universities were and still are facing. Recent drops in enrollment rates and the difficulty of engaging students online during the pandemic remain a top priority for most campuses and have a global resonance (Green et al., 2020; Zerbino, 2021).

Our focus as educators, thus, was to enhance the intrinsic engagement of students enrolled in Italian courses and improve the retention rate in such a challenging environment. In order to do so, whatever the modality, instructors need to increase students' affect (enthusiasm, interest, belonging); cognition (deep learning, self-regulation), and behavior (time and effort, interaction, participation) toward the subject (Green et al., 2020; Kahu, 2013), and in this specific case, toward written assignments.

We thus aimed at increasing students' motivation to study Italian, humanizing their learning process while in an online challenging modality. We adapted the relevance of content, strove to create a learning group community, and gave them tools to self-monitor their learning (Dixon, 2010). When instructors become more than just subject matter experts and are able to improve the relevance of the course content to the students' interests, they are implementing humanized learning. This increases students' motivation to attend class after class and makes students feel part of a larger community so that they are more likely to be engaged and achieve the course objectives (Picciano, 2002; Richardson & Swan, 2003; Rovai & Barnum, 2003).

In creating a learning community it is also important to work alongside the program, across all classes, not just within a single course. The first step toward creating a learning community, thus, was to strengthen the connection among all the instructors, both full-time faculty and adjuncts. We implemented frequent online meetings, which enriched our communication with each other and became a channel where we could share challenges and brainstorm solutions. Our communication was a key tool to discuss which topics of interest we should address in class, with the main purpose to increase students' affect toward the subject (Kahu, 2013). However, two aspects of Kahu's categorization may be considered out of the instructors' direct control: students' cognition and their behavior toward the subject. Deep learning, self-regulation, and the time and effort students dedicate to the subject are extremely subjective to each of them. We thus composed quantitative surveys to administer at various times during the semester, which guided us to ameliorate students' affect and helped them to improve their awareness, cognition, and behavior.

SURVEY ANALYSIS

Part of our strategy to find out why students did not complete compositions was to administer anonymous surveys. The design was important since we did not want to overwhelm students; therefore, we opted for short surveys of three to eight questions asked in a multiple-choice format. As documented by Baroutsis, surveys are important to ascertain "likes or dislikes, their progress with the class learning, or elaborate on something that you want more information about" (Baroutsis et al., 2016, p. 135). The first survey we administered, the results of which are shown in Figures 1.1 and 1.2, covered the crucial importance of writing and asked students to reflect on their attitude toward the written text during the very first week of the semester. We asked students to think about how they faced the task of writing a composition, what they feared most, and whether writing a short composition would make them feel more comfortable. In a sample group of sixty students, all enrolled in the first semester of Italian, 54% admitted that they feared the difficulty of the task, 19% its length, and 19% the time it takes them to write. Consistently, 73% confirmed that writing a shorter composition would put them more at ease.

As part of a growth mindset approach, in the second survey we decided to ask students to self-assess their behaviors and reflect on their personal

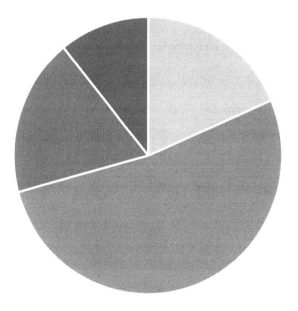

Length = 19%   Difficulty = 54%   Time = 19%   Overwhelming = 11%

FIGURE 1.1. What fears do you have when you write a composition in Italian?

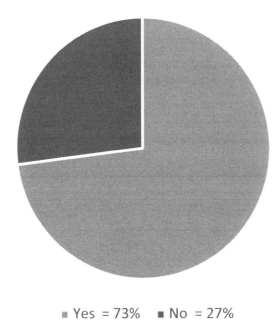

■ Yes = 73%   ■ No = 27%

FIGURE 1.2. Are short writing assignments less scary? (%; $N = 60$)

engagement within the class and with the subject. We asked questions regarding their attendance in class, arriving prepared and on time, and completing assignments. Although the results of such a survey were consistently positive (around 90% affirmed that they came on time, prepared, and engaged, $N = 44$), we should take into consideration that the forty-four students who answered the survey were those who regularly attended class and successfully finished it with a grade higher than B.

We administered this survey three times during the semester, as we strongly believe that our students need supportive tools to help them keep their focus on their learning despite the unprecedented problems surrounding them during the pandemic. With these surveys, we asked students to direct their attention to the importance of dedicating the right amount of time and effort to studying the subject, making sure to interact with other students, and participating in class to improve their behavior and cognition of the class. However, the scope and benefit of such a survey went beyond the actual responses, as it was focused on raising awareness in students and their self-monitoring of their personal engagement. We thought it was important to promote a tool for self-awareness that would force them to take corrective measures if prompted by asking probing questions. A third survey was then administered at the end of the semester aimed at providing instructors and

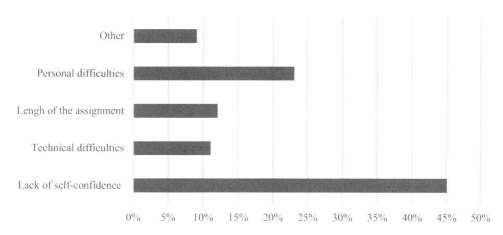

FIGURE 1.3. Student survey on plagiarism.

students with a sense of closure regarding students' attitudes toward writing, as well as their engagement with the topics covered during the course. The data we gathered from fifty-two students was, on the one hand, consistent with previous results in terms of their appreciation of the low-stakes modality and opportunities to write on more relatable topics. On the other hand, we learned new aspects of student behaviors, especially those related to cheating and performance anxiety. Across all sections of Italian, 80% of students reported they had more opportunities to change their perspective and awareness regarding other cultures. In terms of writing, 80% of students indicated their preference for writing shorter compositions instead of longer ones. In return we documented that 90% of the students who passed the course completed the written assignments without delays.

As the emergency transition to online learning during the pandemic also saw an increase in cheating (Supiano, 2020), in the exit survey we asked students about their habits. Results indicated their lack of self-confidence as the first motive for cheating (45%); the second most popular reason was personal difficulties (23%); and the third was the length of the assignment (12%). The analysis of their responses reveals how socioemotional factors are the most relevant reason for academic dishonesty. Because the demographics of our student population often impact students' behaviors, we decided to intervene with measures to combat both cheating and the sense of helplessness students were revealing. As instructors we need to implement a growth mindset environment in our courses and establish supportive relationships with students, which will lead to better academic performance. Scientific literature has often pointed out the strong relationship between self-esteem and student success

(Valentine et al., 2004; Zhang, 2019). Community college students need to feel a sense of belonging and see relevance in what they are studying, in addition to actively participating in providing feedback to the instructor.

LOW-STAKES WRITING ASSIGNMENTS

In response to the writing survey and to support the students' writing needs, we started to implement more frequent but shorter low-stakes writing assignments. Such assignments take the shape of informal, exploratory writing activities aimed at helping students to ease the pressure they feel and at guiding them on the task of composing a higher thinking critical piece, one more apt to nurture their unique voice and agency, while they discover, develop, and clarify their own thinking. Short and spontaneous writings as such offer more opportunities to enrich an equitable curriculum promoting inclusion, global citizenship, and collaboration while challenging bias and stereotyping. It is crucial to assign these short writings on a frequent basis and make them as informal, spontaneous, and explorative as possible so that students are guided to reflect on and elaborate key concepts and ideas presented in class (Bean, 2001). As Bean explains, "What we mean is the kind of exploratory, thinking-on-paper writing we do to discover, develop and clarify our own ideas. Exploratory writing is typically unorganized and tentative, moving off in unanticipated directions as new ideas, complications, and questions strike the writer in the process of thinking and creating" (p. 97). This writing technique lowers the pressure of composing long texts while achieving higher pedagogical results, and it can be applied to any module. Furthermore, it can enhance participation, inclusion, and cultural competence. Often this practice is limited to the last five minutes of class or given as short homework assignments. Although low-stakes writing is relatively well known in English subject classes and writing classes, we strongly believe that it is as just as useful in foreign language classes and can be introduced at any level of learning a second language (L2) from the most elementary to the most advanced.

Many studies encompass the challenges of specifically writing in a foreign language, which is highly affected by the social, cultural, and academic background of students' first language (L1) (Manchón, 2009). Other studies focus on the benefits of writing in an interactive learning environment using an L2 (Norizan et al., 2013; Sun, 2010). More recently, researchers analyzed the challenges of writing in a foreign language and how students feel more prone to overcome them when facing a more creative and amusing assignment, such as writing comics (Aleshchanova et al., 2018).[6] These findings and studies demonstrate that writing creatively, in an online context and possibly in an online community of peers, has been a successful practice (Chamcharatsri & Iida, 2022). However, we advocate for more research that focuses on the benefits of using online miniwriting tasks in an L2 classroom, and in particular in Italian.

As explained above, it is also crucial to increase students' affect in the form of enthusiasm, interest, and belonging in any learning environment, and most importantly in a foreign language class, which by nature is outside their comfortable zone of belonging. To achieve this aim it is essential to keep the topic of writing as close as possible to the students' interests and identities so that they will feel personally involved in the act of writing. The multicultural identity of our students, and arguably of all students, has given us the key to construct relevant and engaging low-stakes writings. Explorative writing in an L2 should in fact be specifically aimed at promoting cultural competence and nurturing students' individual voices and agency, while also building a supportive learning environment. If these assignments are appropriately crafted and delivered, with space for students to talk about themselves and realities close to their identity, students will go beyond the rudimentary concept of learning a linguistic construction; this will increase students' interest in coming to class, their confidence in their ability as writers, and their self-esteem as their ideas are valued more than the form in which they are expressed; while at the same time it will diminish their fears of the writing exercise.

EQUITY-ORIENTED ONLINE ACTIVITIES

With all this in mind, we designed our courses around frequent miniwriting assignments in discussion boards, short journal entries, blogs, and wikis.[7] The two to three regular compositions that students used to write in an ITL 111 and 112 course have been replaced by about six to eight shorter written assignments, and all these short writing assignments were collected in students' personal blogs.[8] Blogs became an online private space for students to upload their assignments and to collect their thoughts, their explorative writings, which would then lead them to deeper reflection.

A common denominator for all the assignments was to always refer to the students' own original culture and somehow compare it with Italian culture, which they were introduced to during the course. One of the main Student Learning Outcomes of both ITL 111 and ITL 112 is precisely related to being able to examine their own culture vis-à-vis Italian culture (Carlorosi, 2022).

Engaging in multicultural education means using educational strategies directly developed to make students aware of their own history and culture, and to bring it into dialogue with that of others (Banks, 2019; Nieto & Bode, 2018). American society, and arguably any contemporary society, is pluralistic, and bringing multiculturality to the surface of teaching allows instructors to promote inclusivity and diversity among students, while at the same time promoting the acquisition of critical thinking and self-reflection in a democratic teaching environment. As James Banks explains in his enduring study of multicultural education, "Diversity presents both challenges and opportunities for nations, schools, and teachers. An important goal of multicultural education is to help educators minimize the problems related to diversity and to maximize its educational opportunities and possibilities" (2019, p. x). It was our goal to capitalize on our students' multicultural backgrounds, thus providing them with an occasion to grow as learners and citizens of a global community.

SAMPLE WRITING ACTIVITIES

We developed our low-stakes writing exercises, then, with these premises in mind. One successful low-stakes writing assignment was presented in the context of a unit focused on Italian food and the simple present tense. Beginning Italian students were asked to contribute to a wiki, where they each had to select a menu from their favorite restaurant, choose some items from the menu, place them in the appropriate Italian category (antipasto, primo, secondo, contorno, dolce, bevande), and finally write a few sentences on how the restaurant's food culture would connect to their own and/or to Italian culture. Students were genuinely engaged in investigating various culinary cultures vis-à-vis their own, and they produced extremely interesting and culturally diverse reviews of various restaurants. As evident from Figure 1.1, grammar accuracy was not the focus of the exercise, although it was something students were asked to work on at a later stage. However, the exercise gave them the option to explore other culinary cultures and compare and contrast them with their own and with Italian culture, as that was the main topic of the module they were studying. For the wiki nature of the exercise, the finished product was a collection of menus and personal reflections displaying different cultural approaches.[9]

Over the four semesters we took into consideration, we noticed that for this assignment the compliance rate was higher than for other, longer compositions students used to write (only 17.6% did not submit the assignment). Therefore, we quickly realized that simple yet compelling writing assignments in which students could express personal details about their likes and dislikes and their specific cultural traits were more effective at engaging them than other tasks in which students were asked to describe topics unrelated to themselves. The grade distribution also reflected the success of this exercise, as 92% of the students enrolled received a grade of C+ or higher, assessed according to a tailored rubric shared across sections.[10]

Another example of a very productive low-stakes writing assignment for elementary students in Italian was a blog entry on their food habits. We asked students to take a photo of the inside of their refrigerator and upload it to their blog. They then had to write a one-paragraph reflection about what they eat and what their food choices tell people about their habits, culture, diet, and cultural values. This exercise was conducted at a later stage of the Italian class when students were studying partitive pronouns and adjectives while using the passato prossimo tense, during a module focused on Italian recipes. Again, the assignment's outcome not only proved interesting to the students, but the completion rate was also successful, increasing by 20% compared to previous, more traditional assignments.

These results demonstrate that students were actively learning the subject and were engaged in the material. The success in completion and interest can be explained not only by the topic, as eating is certainly something everyone can relate to, but also by the playful aspect of each assignment, an element of discovery that helped students see everyday items differently. Most of them are proud to show off their favorite restaurant menu, for example, and the same menu can be seen from different cultural perspectives (as opposed to a main dish, Italian food culture includes several dishes during a meal). The exercise based on the refrigerator highlighted students' awareness of their food habits. They probably had never looked at their refrigerator in that way before, nor had they compared it with other students' refrigerators. It must be noted that ours was not a course on nutrition; we were not interested in elucidating the nutritional values of food. Rather the goal was to exercise, in a practical context, the use of specific grammar items (partitives and the passato prossimo tense, as anticipated) while describing their grocery items. We were also pleasantly surprised by the fact that their writing was not necessarily accurate, which revealed that students were not relying on electronic translations, as they used to do in the previous longer writing compositions we assigned. Students proved to be more interested and focused in drafting their thoughts with the language tools they had, and in a specific context that was previously explored in class, as opposed to crafting their sentences focusing on accuracy and possibly translating from their mother language using some online support.

As a final project, which worked as an outcome of all the previous low-stakes writing assignments, students of ITL 111 prepared a personal reflection describing an object that would represent them, explaining why, and connecting it to their own culture and to Italian culture. The outcomes, once again, were very positive in terms of both completion and engagement. Students provided a picture of an object, a written paragraph combining its description and their thoughts, and an audio recording of their thoughts. Students selected clothing accessories, instruments, books, and other everyday objects, and they were able to look at them beyond their denotative meanings, enhancing their descriptions with cultural connotations that situated their own identity in relation to what they had learned about Italian identity. All of this helped to build their self-esteem and sense of belonging in the classroom and supported the notion that their culture and ethnic background matter (Walton & Cohen, 2011).

CONCLUSIONS

As discussed, the forced online environment for college students created problems in terms of academic success and mental health, among others (Nguyen et al., 2021). For community college students this occurrence exacerbated an already fragile situation in terms of emotional variables such as anxiety, stress, and isolation. The impact on our Italian language program was noticeable and overwhelming for instructors, who saw a decrease in attendance, responsiveness, and preparedness among students that was particularly evident in writing assignments that were rarely completed or resubmitted; thus, the urgency to take action to tackle these issues. Our strategy to combat this situation involved the creation of low-stakes assignments, which, according to our quantitative data, proved to be successful in terms of completion, enjoyability, and stress reduction. To make writing less scary and more enticing, we also designed compositions focused on personal engagement that elicited a sense of belonging (Hass & Osborn, 2007). As a matter of fact, in our chosen sampling, which included Beginning Italian I courses in fall and spring 2021, out of ninety-four students who completed the course, only ten did not submit their written assignments (9.4%).

Our critical thinking project-based writing activities speak to the writing-intensive pedagogy founded on the principle, among others, of "writing to think" (and low-stakes assignments), following Greenstein's theory. According to Greenstein's approach, thinking through writing deepens students' learning (Greenstein, 2013), and by actively engaging in personal writing assignments, students deepen their thinking through the mere act of writing, even in shorter papers.

Additionally, our strategy also involved students' self-monitoring, and through online surveys they voiced an appreciation for the minicomposition modality, which decreased stress and anxiety and gave them a sense that they could complete the writing assignments. However, we must note that cheating remains an unresolved issue. The surveys revealed that students used electronic translators or sought outside help with writing tasks, but most importantly highlighted the reasons behind these choices. The top two justifications were linked to socioemotional variables rather than issues with the writing activity itself. Only 10% of students reported they never cheated; however, 50% answered "I try my best," and 40% indicated they used help from outside sources. These numbers require some reflection; as instructors we must address cheating as an important issue from an ethical, logistical, and social point of view. Moreover, it is equally important to confront the problem by addressing the reasons behind this behavior. We understand that the forced online environment provided the backdrop for cheating to expand; however, students' sense of helplessness and anxiety appear to be the main cause of cheating in our classes. More work is needed on our part to create a classroom space where students acquire strategies to understand how to navigate difficulties by learning from mistakes and seeking help from the instructor and the Italian tutor before going online to find the answers or giving up on an assignment or class.

To conclude, this study strengthens the research for low-stakes writing activities, their implementation, and their impact on Italian language students at an urban community college. Changing the length of compositions was a good strategy to help with compliance and plagiarism, but this alone was not sufficient. As instructors we must encourage students to keep going, even when something gets difficult. These principles, linked to the growth mindset, will increase students' self-esteem and performance when applied consistently within the classroom setting. Better training for full-timers and part-timers in growth mindset practices is paramount in the Italian program and across community colleges to change students' habits and behaviors. Our data show that the implementation of growth mindset principles in our courses increased students' overall academic performance and well-being in terms of completion, engagement, and prevention of apprehension about writing. When students feel supported and included in the class, they tend to do better academically, as revealed in a recent comprehensive study (Yeager & Dweck, 2020). Going forward, not only will we keep implementing low-stakes writing assignments in our classes, but we will also find ways to train more instructors in growth mindset pedagogy given the positive results we received from embedding this approach in terms of student outcomes. Introducing the writing-to-think approach along with low-stakes assignments gave students the opportunity to be active participants in the evaluation of their own learning and by the same token helped increase class attendance and participation.

NOTES

1. The growth mindset approach was first developed thirty years ago by psychologist Dr. Carol Dweck, who studied strategies that led to student success. If students believe they can improve by working hard, putting in extra time, asking for help, and making connections, they can more easily achieve academic success. Both students and instructors play a key role in changing habits and minds when obstacles occur.
2. Several *New York Times* articles have been written on the effect of the pandemic on students, such as these: March 31, 2021; April 3, 2021; July 28, 2021; December 22, 2021. Additionally, other articles from educational platforms such as *Edutopia* reflected on similar issues on April 16, 2021, and October 13, 2022.
3. At Bronx Community College other spoken languages are Spanish, 33.5%; Bengali, 1.8%; Twi-Fante, 1.3%; French, 1.2%; Akan, 0.8%; Arabic, 0.6%; Fula, 0.4% (Office of Institutional Research, Bronx Community College, 2022).
4. A hybrid modality consists of half of the classes offered in person on campus and half synchronously online.
5. You can consult all the official numbers on the Office of Institutional Research web page: https://bcc-cuny.digication.com/oir/Data_Tredn_Reports.
6. "The students of the above specialties participating in the experiment realize their individual difficulties in learning a foreign language in general and developing writing skills in particular, but enjoy the creative writing assignments, since the comics make the writing process amusing and reduce the stress factor" (Aleshchanova et al., 2018, p. 4).
7. Journals, notebooks, and marginal book notes are the most well-known forms of exploratory writings, but in our online language teaching environment we used

chats, wikis, and blogs. Journals, blogs, and chats are student-to-instructor communication tools. Wikis are a sort of collaborative writing that allows every student to write something in a shared online document, review and make changes to what others write, and fully contribute to the final text. In Blackboard, the academic platform we use at BCC, the system keeps track of who wrote what, so that the instructor has a full picture of the students who participated and contributed to the document. The same can be said for any other academic online platform.
8. Common topics for those compositions revolved around the textbook chapter topics and included describing a city, describing themselves or a friend, describing a regular day or their weekend activities, and writing a fairy tale or a movie. Those topics were highly general and didn't seem to be enticing the students' engagement. Generally, during a full semester, about 70% of the students enrolled in a class would successfully complete these writing assignments and less than 30% would dedicate themselves to any kind of writing review.
9. Example of a wiki from a student in our courses: "Il ristorante preferito e' Carmelitas. Mangio un taco con pollo e fagioli, e avocado, a chips. Bevo una birra e un acqua. Prendo dolce, chamuco, tipo messicano. Io sono peruviano e la mia famiglia va a ristorante domenica notte. La cocina italiana e messicana e similare e' colore, e' felice. La famiglia e' muy importante a messico e a Peru."
10. Fifty-one students were enrolled in four consecutive semesters of Italian 111 (spring 2017–spring 2018). Forty-seven students received a grade of C+ or higher and four students a D or lower.

BIBLIOGRAPHY

Aleshchanova, I. V., Frolova, N. A., & Zheltukhina, M. R. (2018). Creative approach to development of competence "writing" in foreign language classes. *SHS Web of Conferences*, *50*, 01025. Accessed February 8, 2022. https://www.researchgate.net/publication/331906520_Teaching_resources_in_professionally_oriented_foreign_language_learning

Banks, J. (2019). *An introduction to multicultural education*. New York: Pearson.

Bean, J. (2001). *Engaging ideas: The professor's guide to integrating writing, critical thinking and active learning in the classroom*. Hoboken, NJ: Jossey-Bass.

Belfield, C., & Brock, T. (2020). Behind the enrollment numbers: How COVID has changed students' plans for community college. *Edutopia*. Accessed January 14, 2022. https://ccrc.tc.columbia.edu/easyblog/covid-enrollment-community-college-plans.html

Baroutsis, A., McGregor, G., & Mills, M. (2016). Pedagogic voice: Student voice in teaching and engagement pedagogies. *Pedagogy, Culture & Society*, *24*(1), 123–40. Accessed January 25, 2022. https://doi.org/10.1080/14681366.2015.1087044

Bronx Community College. *Data trends reports*. Accessed January 8, 2022. https://bcc-cuny.digication.com/oir/Data_Tredn_Reports

Carlorosi, S. (2022). *Beginning Italian*. Syllabus, Bronx Community College of the City University of New York, New York, NY.

Chamcharatsri, B., & Iida, A. (2022). *International perspectives on creative writing in second language education: Supporting language learners' proficiency, identity, and creative expression*. London: Routledge.

Dixon, M. D. (2010). Creating effective student engagement in online courses: What do students find engaging? *Journal of the Scholarship of Teaching and Learning*, *10*(2), 1–13.

Green, W., Anderson, V., Tait, K., & Tran, L. T. (2020). Precarity, fear and hope: Reflecting and imagining in higher education during a global pandemic. *Higher Education Research & Development*, *39*(7), 1309–12. Accessed February 8, 2022. https://www.tandfonline.com/doi/full/10.1080/07294360.2020.1826029

Greenstein, G. (2013). Writing is thinking: Using writing to teach science. *Astronomy Education Review*, *12*(1). Accessed February 8, 2022. http://dx.doi.org/10.3847/AER2012037

Hass, M., & Osborn, J. (2007). An emic view of student writing and the writing process. *Across the Disciplines*, *4*. Accessed February 8, 2022. https://digitalcommons.chapman.edu/english_articles/48/

Kahu, E. R. (2013). Framing student engagement in higher education. *Studies in Higher Education*, *38*(5), 758–73.

Lee, J., Jeong, H. J., & Kim, S. (2021). Stress, anxiety, and depression among undergraduate students during the COVID-19 pandemic and their use of mental health services. *Innov High Educ*, 46, 519–38. Accessed February 28, 2022. https://doi.org/10.1007/s10755-021-09552-y

Manchón, R. (Ed.). (2009). *Writing in foreign language contexts: Learning, teaching, and research*. Bristol, Blue Ridge Summit: Multilingual Matters. https://doi.org/10.21832/9781847691859

Morgan, P. L., Farkas, G., Hillemeier, M. M., & Maczuga, S. (2009). Risk factors for learning-related behavior problems at 24 months of age: Population-based estimates. *J. Abnorm. Child Psychol*, *37*, 401–13. Accessed February 8, 2022. https://doi.org/10.1007/s10802-008-9279-8

Nguyen, K. H., Irvine, S., Epstein, R., Allen, J. D., & Corlin, L. (2021). Prior COVID-19 infection, mental health, food and financial insecurity, and association with COVID-19 vaccination coverage and intent among college-aged young adults, US, 2021. *Preventing Chronic Disease*, no. 18. Accessed February 8, 2022. http://dx.doi.org/10.5888/pcd18.210260

Nieto, S., & Bode, P. (2018). *Affirming diversity: The sociopolitical context of multicultural education*. New York: Pearson.

Norizan, A. R., Murad, S., & Zulkifli, A. (2013). Adopting social networking sites (SNSs) as interactive communities among English foreign language (EFL) learners in writing: Opportunities and challenges. *English Language Teaching*, 6(11), 187–98.

Núñez, A.-M. (2013). *Latinos in higher education and Hispanic-serving institutions creating conditions for success*. Hoboken, NJ: Wiley.

Picciano, A. G. (2002, July). Beyond student perceptions: Issues of interaction, presence, and performance in an online course. *Journal of Asynchronous Learning Networks*, 6(1), 21–40.

Richardson, J. C., & Swan, K. (2003, February). Examining social presence in online courses in relation to students' perceived learning and satisfaction. *Journal of Asynchronous Learning Networks*, 7(1), 68–88.

Rovai, A. P., & Barnum, K. T. (2003). On-line course effectiveness: An analysis of student interactions and perceptions of learning. *Journal of Distance Learning*, 18(1), 57–73.

Sun, Y.-C. (2010, August). Extensive writing in foreign-language classrooms: A blogging approach. *Innovations in Education and Teaching International*, 47(3), 327–39.

Supiano, B. (2020). Teaching: Why (some) professors are so worried about cheating. *Chronicle of Higher Education*. Accessed February 8, 2022. https://www.chronicle.com/newsletter/teaching/2020-10-29.

Valentine, J. C., DuBois, D. L., & Cooper, H. (2004). The relation between self-beliefs and academic achievement: A meta-analytic review. *Educational Psychologist*, 39, 111–33. Accessed February 8, 2022. https://doi.org/10.1207/s15326985ep3902_3

VanderStel, A. (2014). The impact of demographics in education. *Honors Projects*, 329. Grand Valley State University. Accessed February 8, 2022. https://scholarworks.gvsu.edu/cgi/viewcontent.cgi?article=1306&context=honorsprojects

Walton, G. M., & Cohen, G. L. (2011). A brief social-belonging intervention improves academic and health outcomes among minority students. *Science*, 331, 1447–51.

Willenborg, C. J. (2016). Demographic factors associated with student success in two upper-year agronomy courses. *NACTA Journal*, 60(1), 65–70.

Yeager, D. S., & Dweck, C. S. (2020). What can be learned from growth mindset controversies? *American Psychologist*, 75(9), 1269–84. Accessed February 8, 2022. https://doi.org/10.1037/amp0000794

Yukselturk, E., & Bulut, S. (2007). Predictors for student success in an online course. *Educational Technology & Society*, *10*(2), 71–83.

Zerbino, N. (2021). How the COVID-19 pandemic has impacted higher education. Accessed February 8, 2022. https://www.brookings.edu/events/how-higher-education-has-been-impacted-by-the-covid-19-pandemic/

Zhang, X. (2019). Exploring the relationship between college students' writing anxiety and the pedagogical use of online resources. *International Journal of Educational Technology in Higher Education*, *16*(18). Accessed February 8, 2022. https://doi.org/10.1186/s41239-019-0149-y

2

TALKING POINTS

Conversation Courses as Models for Multilevel and Multimodal Curricular Innovation

Julia Cozzarelli and Marella Feltrin-Morris

At Ithaca College, as at other small- to medium-sized liberal arts institutions, the struggle to keep the Italian program alive and thriving raises important ideological and practical considerations. In a climate where humanities programs must fight for a shrinking cohort of students, we are faced with the challenge of maintaining student-centered instruction with rigorous curricular standards, while at the same time adapting to pressing demands to raise enrollment caps. Courses must be reconfigured to become viable options for students in credit-intensive majors or professional programs with very limited elective opportunities, and faculty must continue to provide classes that fulfill the elementary- and intermediate-level language sequences in ways that avoid sacrificing upper-level conversation, culture, and literature courses. The emergence of a global pandemic only made these issues more pressing.

This essay will focus on how the Italian program at Ithaca College has addressed some of these challenges, using the example of the strategies adopted to redesign and successfully deliver the courses Parliamo! Italian Conversation and Conversazione e Cultura. In their original configuration, these were long-standing 300-level courses. The changes made at both the curricular and course-specific levels now allow them to accommodate intermediate-level students, who are enrolled in newly created 200-level courses taught concomitantly with the revised 300-level classes. The new courses fill a niche in that they allow intermediate-level students to enhance their conversational skills and confidence, while simultaneously reviewing intermediate-level grammar and vocabulary. Additionally, they provide a means for intermediate students to continue their Italian study even during semesters when the standard intermediate-level language courses cannot be offered. The reinvention of these conversation courses was initially sparked by the need to retain as many students as possible at all levels, but it has proved successful beyond that goal and has now become the model for other multilevel courses in language, literature, and culture. These innovative revisions allow our curriculum to serve both Italian majors or minors and students in other programs, and it has fostered a collaborative spirit among students at different levels.

BACKGROUND AND RATIONALE

A confluence of several factors inspired these curricular innovations in the Italian section of our department, now titled the Department of World Languages, Literatures, and Cultures (WLLC). Over the past decade, the department has been adversely affected by conditions both internal and external to the college. Our institution lacks a college-wide language requirement, leaving enrollments largely dependent on student exploration and favorable faculty advising. Student demographic trends in the Northeast have resulted in a smaller student body overall at the college, and, consistent with national trends that predate the pandemic, fewer students are opting for majors in language (Looney & Lusin, 2019). These reductions were compounded by changes to the college's general education program that further undermined support for language study. The college's efforts to reduce expenses in response to a smaller student body put additional pressures on the department: Course enrollments came under greater scrutiny, and credit hours generated were closely monitored. Hard-won victories by faculty to reduce language class sizes were erased, with caps raised once more as a means to cut the number of course sections offered. The most recent blow came as a result of the COVID-19 pandemic, when the college made drastic cuts to the faculty that greatly impacted language offerings in our department and included the elimination of adjunct positions in Italian. Despite these disheartening setbacks, a core group of students has remained passionate about studying Italian. Some wish to pursue a language major or minor; others have selected Italian as a language option for their degree program requirements; and of course, we also have students preparing for study abroad.

Clearly, all of these factors have compelled the Italian section to act in creative ways in order to meet the needs of our students despite a reduced faculty body and fewer course offerings. At the same time, the need to attract students from a dwindling pool has grown ever more pressing as the department is forced to defend its value, which is now determined primarily by numbers rather than by its contribution to student education. Our solution, as detailed in this essay, has been to create so-called "stacked" courses: These are courses with different numbers that serve different groups of students, but that have enough overlap in content to enable a faculty member to teach them at the same time, together in one room (or virtual space when classes needed to be held in a remote or hybrid format).

We recognize that the situation for language study at Ithaca College is far from unique and that countless institutions are suffering from similar pressures. The curricular changes we outline here could easily be adopted by language programs elsewhere, and within a range of languages and course content, just as the model we have established in Italian is now shaping the curricula of other languages we offer. It is important to emphasize, however, that the advantages of creating these courses are not limited to programs in crisis; they would be advantageous to even the most thriving program. The courses' benefits are pedagogical as well as curricular, resulting in more dynamic, actively engaged classrooms. In short, our goal in this essay is to demonstrate one way that any language program can add flexibility to its curriculum without sacrificing the quality or desirability of its offerings.

PEDAGOGICAL FOUNDATION

Naturally, the initial reaction to the idea of managing a classroom of students at different levels may be one of justifiable skepticism. After all, wouldn't the instructor who decides to embark on this quixotic feat be immediately faced with insurmountable difficulties in the very selection of the teaching materials? And what about assignments and Student Learning Outcomes (SLOs)? Surely they cannot be expected to be the same across the levels, but how to differentiate them? Even assuming that such hurdles can be overcome, wouldn't students feel alienated from one another—those at a lower level being intimidated by their more fluent peers, and those at a higher level demotivated when, inevitably, the presence of lower-level students results in a slower pace, less sophisticated reasoning, and frequent interruptions to go over basic grammar rules?

And yet, even despite rigorous placement tests and formal separations between levels, multiple degrees of proficiency have always coexisted informally in the same classroom. How many times have individual students pleaded successfully to remain at a lower level than the one indicated by their placement test score, citing as their (sincere or fabricated) motivation a certain apprehension with regard to the skills they were supposed to have already mastered? Given the different proficiency in aural, oral, reading, and writing skills even within the same student, how often is an instructor forced to devise strategies aimed at balancing out discrepancies so as to attain, for example, American Council on the Teaching of Foreign Languages (ACTFL) Intermediate-Mid-level proficiency across all four skills? Every foreign language instructor can recall conversations with colleagues centered around the frustrated recognition of having students at disparate levels in the same classroom and the shared challenge of adjusting one's teaching materials, expectations, and assignments so as to provide a meaningful and productive learning experience for all.

As an inexplicitly acknowledged and generally unwelcome reality, the multilevel foreign language classroom is further penalized by a lack of substantial scholarship focused not merely on examining its dynamics and proposing ways to minimize what are perceived as its detrimental aspects but on exploring its potential as an actually desirable learning format. Some valuable insight comes from the experiences of high school teachers and from studies conducted outside the United States (e.g., Russia, New Zealand). Within the US context, the scholarship applicable to teaching multilevel foreign language classes stems from two main realities: (1) that of rural schools, where the limited number of students requires the simultaneous delivery of instruction to groups of varying degrees of language proficiency; (2) that of English for Speakers of Other Languages (ESOL) courses, where, because of the vastly different settings and conditions under which the students enrolled may have been exposed to the English language, and the unique relationship between English and their native language(s), multilevel instruction represents the norm.

The general consensus appears to be that, while not ideal, a multilevel classroom can function effectively even without—indeed, *especially* without—creating separate lesson plans for each level. In part, this reassurance aims at easing every instructor's anxiety at the thought of having to double their workload for the same paygrade. However, feasible planning is only one incentive to consider multileveling the curriculum. Another, more appealing one is that, when the idea of individual growth through collaborative learning is emphasized consistently throughout a multilevel course, unhealthy competitiveness and the sense of inadequacy that leads too many language students to retreat behind a monolingual shield are minimized. The result is a positive experience that encourages lower-level students to continue their language study and that further motivates upper-level students. A particularly hopeful outlook comes from Gerry Wass, a retired high school teacher who taught multilevel Spanish in a rural K–12 school district in southern Missouri. Wass champions multilevel language classes, which he finds "superior to grouping students by either year or level of proficiency," and argues that the ultimate reason might be that "the endpoint of all passionate language study is social" (Hedstrom, 2016). Furthermore, in the article "Multilevel Courses and Blended Learning—Tools for Pedagogical Differentiation and Promoting Student Autonomy" (2022), Paul Pouzergues observes that multilevel language courses are becoming more common at the university level and acknowledges the potential for student growth:

> Despite the heterogeneities present within a class, studies on differentiated pedagogy have shown that it is possible to build a group where each student can evolve at his or her own pace—according to his or her level, profile, or needs. Furthermore, hybrid courses that are based on an authentic project pedagogy make it possible to offer differentiated courses, stimulate motivation, maintain group cohesion, and encourage the development of learning autonomy. (Pouzergues, 2022, p. 272)

COURSE DESIGN AND PLANNING

Bolstered by these favorable arguments, faculty can feel more confident in proposing a multileveled curriculum and ready to tackle the logistics of course development. There are several steps involved in configuring courses to serve multiple levels of students simultaneously. Current courses can be adapted to the new structure and/or new courses can be created using the same model. At Ithaca College, we developed our first multilevel course in Italian experimentally to meet the needs of students beginning the intermediate level together with more advanced students wishing to strengthen their conversational skills with a grammar refresher.[1] Prior to this, the Italian section had engaged with these student cohorts separately through two long-standing courses: a traditionally structured intermediate class (ITAL 20100 Intermediate Italian I, the first of a two-semester sequence) and an upper-level conversation class (ITAL 32300 Parliamo! Italian Conversation, typically the first of two conversation courses). Because both groups of students review similar grammatical structures, the courses aligned in a way that enabled us to pair them together. We were able to retain the catalog title and description for ITAL 32300, which remained largely the same in content, but because we intended to synchronize topics and emphasize conversational skills at both levels, we needed to create a new course to take the place of ITAL 20100. The new intermediate-level course was designed to review the same grammatical content as ITAL 20100 and to be used as a substitute for ITAL 20100 by students whose degree programs required intermediate Italian. For this reason, we elected to give it a similar number, ITAL 20101, but with conversational skills emphasized in the new course description and title (Intermediate Italian Conversation I). Intermediate Conversation I was introduced as "experimental," a curricular classification at the college that allows new courses to be taught on a limited basis without formally adding them to the course catalog. After teaching the course successfully throughout the pandemic in Zoom, hybrid, and in-person formats, we determined that the course should be integrated into our regular offerings. Moreover, with ITAL 20101 and ITAL 32300 as a model, we developed and taught a similarly "stacked" conversation course for the subsequent semester (ITAL 20024/ITAL 32400).

The stacked course model is not limited to language-skills classes. We also have adapted it successfully to literature and culture courses, enabling students with little or no Italian to enroll together with advanced students seeking to deepen their skills in the language through engagement with course content. Indeed, the combined 200- and 300-level conversation courses are, in many ways, more challenging to configure than courses focused primarily on literary and/or cultural content. The stacked conversation courses must, by necessity, have some overlap in content (course topics, for example), while also maintaining some differences in student learning outcomes and assignments for the two levels. While it is possible to create a single syllabus that encompasses both levels, the course requirements diverge in ways that can add visual complexity to the syllabus. Separate syllabi appear more streamlined and may more clearly communicate specific course expectations to the students in each cohort. Regardless of the direction taken, however, it is key that the syllabi be transparent to students so they are aware that they are sharing the classroom with another level. Moreover, since many course activities encourage or require interactions between the two groups as a way to enhance learning, it is a point that should be emphasized in the syllabus (or syllabi).

There are additional factors to consider when creating syllabi for multileveled language-skills courses that might not pertain to content-based courses. The combined 20101 and 32300 courses, for example, feature the review of specific grammar and vocabulary content from the present indicative through past, future, and conditional tenses. Although instructors can personalize some course content to fit their pedagogical approach, it is important that the grammar reviewed remain consistent each time the courses are offered, regardless of the instructor. This provides a stable framework for students' progression in the language and avoids disruptions to the sequencing of the curriculum. Most of the student learning outcomes, which ordinarily are required in the paperwork for new and revised course proposals, are also shared by both levels.[2]

INTEGRATION OF GRAMMAR AT MULTIPLE LEVELS

With regard to grammar, it is useful and reassuring to remember that all students, regardless of level, can benefit from periodical reviews of even basic structures, such as the difference between imperfetto and passato prossimo; direct, indirect, and combined pronouns; reflexive verbs; comparatives and superlatives; and relative pronouns. Indeed, many students enrolled in 300-level classes often spontaneously ask the instructor for such reviews and are grateful when the needs of less advanced students offer the opportunity for a brush-up. Advanced students who display no interest in grammar reviews are typically the ones who would need them the most, therefore the instructor should not be overly concerned when, in the midst of a class discussion, repeated mistakes make it necessary to devote some time to an impromptu refresher.

Integrating grammar reviews into conversation, culture, or literature courses is useful not only as a reminder of the structures needed to handle specific topics; the grammar review itself can be made part of the conversation effortlessly. For instance, while reflecting on the ways in which different cultures express praise or criticism, an overview of irregular comparatives and superlatives may lead to an interesting debate on the hyperbolic use of language and on the progressive loss of significance that originally "positive" adjectives such as buono [good] have suffered, to the point of actually suggesting a negative opinion and requiring increasingly frequent superlatives (buonissimo, ottimo) to counterbalance it. Students at both the intermediate and advanced levels can easily contribute to the conversation, each according to their specific proficiency, and practice exercises can be assigned to both groups.

Instructors who, during a grammar review, opt to assign the same exercises to both groups can, if they wish, differentiate them in terms of quantity (e.g., by requiring upper-level students to create a larger number of sentences with a specific grammatical structure, or a longer response to a question) and/or in terms of quality (by expecting a higher level of complexity in the use of the structure being reviewed). Differences in requirements and grading should, of course, be made clear both on the syllabus and on each assignment or assignment category.

A strategy for grammar review that promises to bring together both levels and at the same time relieves the instructor of the burden of creating separate explanations and assignments for the two groups is that of entrusting the upper-level students with the explanation of the structures and/or with the creation of exercises and activities for the whole class to complete. Conceptually, it is an excellent idea, but in reality it is quite challenging to carry out effectively and, more often than not, results in confusion and in more work for the instructor to prevent or correct mistakes. Still, if the cohort of upper-level students is particularly strong and motivated, this technique can translate into a valuable opportunity for creative, student-centered learning.

ASSIGNMENTS AND CLASSROOM ACTIVITIES

Aside from the expectation of possessing (and displaying) a greater mastery of grammar and vocabulary, upper-level students should be required to distinguish themselves from their lower-level peers in other aspects of the course as well. As with the grammar component, such distinction may be quantitative and/or qualitative. For example, upper-level students may be scheduled to deliver a greater number of oral reports, or the same number but longer, or the same number and length but more sophisticated. It is also possible to create one or more additional assignments exclusively designed for upper-level students, such as a research project. However, it is important to consider that any ad hoc components designed for a specific level of the course inevitably result in more prep work for the instructor, more time devoted to grading, and—potentially the most negative outcome—less cohesiveness between the levels, which may have a negative effect on the collaborative aspect of the course and on the overall classroom atmosphere.

Discussion questions based on readings and/or videos provide an ideal platform to create different expectations between levels without impeding an exchange that will involve all students. As an example, students in ITAL 20024/ITAL 32400 (Intermediate Conversation II / Conversazione e Cultura) were assigned an article on "Il divorzio breve" to read at home. They were also given a series of questions and instructed to prepare answers to be delivered orally in class. The questions included:

Domande per tutti:

Dopo quanto tempo dalla separazione ritieni che una coppia dovrebbe poter essere libera di divorziare?
Perché, secondo te, moltissimi matrimoni si concludono con un divorzio?
Naturalmente, la situazione è più difficile per una coppia con figli che decide di divorziare. Come possono i genitori rendere questo passo meno doloroso per i figli?

Solo per ITAL 32400:

Fai una breve ricerca per scoprire le statistiche sul divorzio negli Stati Uniti e preparati a condividere le informazioni che hai trovato con il resto della classe.

Once in class, the instructor could, for example, start the conversation by having the upper-level students share their findings on divorce statistics in the United States (or elsewhere, depending on the student body) and use the information as a springboard for the other questions, which would then require participation from the rest of the class. Reversing the order (i.e., starting with the questions designed for all students) has the advantage of involving everyone right away, but if the conversation turns out especially lively and takes up a substantial portion of the lesson—a very positive outcome, in theory—running out of time is not uncommon, and the question or activity designed specifically for the upper-level students often ends up being sacrificed. A way to ensure that no discussion material assigned exclusively to the upper-level students falls by the wayside is to require them to address it, for example, in a VoiceThread or in another recording activity to be carried out outside of class.

Alternatively, some instructors may envision the distinction between levels not so much in terms of homework or projects to be completed as in terms of greater or lesser responsibility and choose to put, on assigned dates, one or more upper-level students in charge of preparing a lesson plan and leading the class discussion. The success or failure of this strategy depends largely on the composition of the classroom: Small class sizes and/or groups where, as at Ithaca College, the disparity in fluency between the intermediate and the upper level is not especially marked might benefit less from this solution, which instead could be ideal for classes with a significant majority of intermediate-level students and a small group of particularly fluent upper-level students. Finally, a way to dedicate some undivided attention to assessing the separate and/or extra work carried out by each of the two groups is to conduct midterm and final exams in pairs (or in groups of three) by level. By assessing the intermediate and the advanced levels separately, the instructor can easily use the same format for both (e.g., four sections: vocabulary, grammar, the cultural material illustrated during the oral reports, and a conversation on the issues explored in the course of the semester), but adjusting it in order to reflect the higher expectations for the upper-level course—by requiring, for instance, knowledge of a broader vocabulary, a greater mastery of grammar, and a more elaborate, in-depth conversation. At the same time, evaluating students by level gives more structure and rigor to the exams and allows the students themselves to assess their own proficiency alongside comparable peers.

BEYOND CONVERSATION: OTHER COURSES SUITABLE FOR MULTILEVEL STRUCTURING

Literature classes are, perhaps, the least complex models for multilevel courses. The courses share a title, but the course assigned a 300-level number serves advanced students of Italian, and the course at the 200-level draws students with no or limited Italian language background. At Ithaca College, we have been informally mimicking the multilevel structure by allowing students who wished (or needed) to deepen their language skills to enroll in literature courses designed for students new to Italian. More recently, we have been adding a 200-level option to 300-level courses already in the catalog. Although the lessons are conducted in English, 300-level students focus on reading in the target language and complete their assignments in Italian instead of English. The language of instruction might be seen as the primary drawback when pairing a 300-level course previously taught in Italian with a 200-level course that must be taught in English. However, this shift can be offset in other ways. For example, an instructor with several advanced students, regardless of the level in which they are enrolled, can integrate conversation practice by grouping those students together periodically for in-class discussion, compensating in part for the lessons being conducted in English. Homework assignments requiring oral presentations (e.g., VoiceThreads) are also incorporated. Additionally, at Ithaca College a long-standing practice of the Italian program has been to pair up each student with a peer at an Italian high school for regular conversation practice to be held outside of class through Skype. Reports on these conversations can be required or counted for extra credit.

Multilevel literature courses can be proposed using courses that already exist in the curriculum, adapting the original assignments and course SLOs for the new level. Moreover, entirely new courses can be developed with the multilevel structure specifically in mind. For our first semester back to an in-person classroom after over a year of remote teaching, we taught a new multidisciplinary stacked course titled Experiencing Italy: Remarkable Cities. The levels share a course title but are distinguished by their numbers, ITAL 21000 and ITAL 31000, and by differing prerequisites. ITAL 310 requires the completion of intermediate Italian; ITAL 210 requires no Italian but does require coursework to ensure that students have some experience in the liberal arts. The course descriptions are very similar, although the expectations for language usage and practice are clearly distinguished. Because some majors have a language proficiency requirement, it is also specified in the catalog course description that the 200-level class cannot be counted toward such requirements.

Remarkable Cities is a course focused on the study of several Italian metropolitan areas from a multidisciplinary perspective. Students explore the history of each city and the art, architecture, and literature that characterize it. The class also examines the cultural differences of each area, including variations in traditions, language, cuisine, and music. The multidisciplinary nature of the course makes it, in many ways, a natural fit for the multilevel classroom. It draws students from a range of majors and with varying levels of personal experience with Italy, which adds to the richness of the class dynamics. The course structure involves in-class discussions of assignments that encompass readings, art, music, video clips, and films, supplemented by brief lectures on people and historical or cultural events related to the day's topic. Lessons regularly include brief presentations from one or two students on topics assigned for research, and near the end of the semester the class is broken into groups to conduct an exploration of one city in greater depth.

Students at both levels of Remarkable Cities are given the same core set of student learning outcomes pertaining to the content of the course.[3] The students enrolled in 310 are given an additional set of SLOs pertaining to language study.[4] Although students in both levels of Remarkable Cities are expected to complete the same assignments, the assignments are tailored in a way to allow the 300-level students to meet their language goals. The advanced students, for example, are selected to give minipresentations on language basics for their classmates, or on regional differences of dialect and pronunciation. All students in the course must complete a "weekly research journal" for which they find, then analyze, a website that deepens their knowledge of a subject that interested them from that week's classes (monument, person, work of art, dish, etc.). The 300-level students, however, are required to find Italian websites, to write their entries in Italian, and to identify the primary grammar point they wish to practice in that week's entry. Both groups of students are given the option of presenting their research journals in an oral format. In addition to supporting speaking practice in Italian, this option has the added benefit of broadening accessibility for all students. Similarly, the course's midterm and final projects may be submitted in a number of formats and media.

The appeal of this course to a range of majors and to students with varying levels of experience in Italian is an integral factor in its success. By using student-centered activities, such as class discussion and minipresentations, the students gain a sense of community and connection with one another. Discussions are enriched by the diversity of the participants, especially when students are required to work with different classmates on a regular basis. In student evaluations for the course, which were overwhelmingly positive, students were particularly enthusiastic in their praise for the discussion-based approach. They stated that it ensured all in the class were "actively engaging with every topic," and that learning about others' views while also pursuing their individual interests allowed them to "feel very connected to the class."[5]

Two other courses that have been adapted quite successfully to a multilevel format are ITAL 24500/ITAL 34500 (Italian Culture: A Culinary Journey) and ITAL 28000/ITAL 35000 (Italian Culture through Cinema). Both, like Remarkable Cities, require no knowledge of Italian for students enrolling at the 200-level, while students enrolling at the 300-level are typically majors or minors eager to improve their fluency in Italian while learning about culture and film. A Culinary Journey introduces students to Italian culture through the lens of its rich gastronomic tradition. Students explore a wide range of culinary-related materials, such as films, recipes, restaurant reviews, cooking shows, websites, and songs, as well as literary texts. Cultural topics considered include territory, regional differences, influences of recent immigration patterns, etiquette, and changing lifestyles. While the language of instruction is English, students enrolled at the 300-level are required to complete their written assignments in Italian and participate in VoiceThreads for oral practice.

As for Italian Culture through Cinema, its first experimentation as a stacked course happened in concomitance with the option, offered to faculty in the spring of 2021—when the pandemic became less severe but still a major concern—to continue teaching either remotely or in hybrid mode. Given the course's visual emphasis, the remote model would certainly have worked effectively, but along with the desire to return to the classroom and interact with students in person, there was also a certain curiosity to test the potential of the hybrid model. This choice proved particularly felicitous, if somewhat complex to organize, at least initially. Alternating between remote and in-person made it possible to create a tailored experience for both groups. The class met on a Monday-Wednesday-Friday schedule, and each week was dedicated to a different movie that students were required to watch in advance. Monday's class was held remotely in English and included student presentations on the director and main actors, as well as an overview of the film's historical and cultural background. On Wednesday, class was held in person in English for students in ITAL 280, who were required to read or watch some assigned material on the film in English and take part in the class discussion. Students in ITAL 350 were instead required, for that day, to participate asynchronously by recording themselves in a VoiceThread entitled "La battuta memorabile," for which they would select a particularly meaningful line from a movie, recite it with the appropriate intonation and sentiment, contextualize it and comment on it in Italian, as well as respond to at least one of their peers' comments. On Friday, the groups would switch: Class was held in person in Italian for students in ITAL 350, who were required to read or watch some assigned criticism on the film in Italian and take part in the class discussion. Students in ITAL 280 were instead required, for that day, to participate asynchronously in a written discussion thread entitled "Frame of the Week," for which they would select a memorable shot from the movie, contextualize it and comment on it in English, as well as interact with their peers' postings. As a closing activity after each movie, students in both groups would write a film review—ITAL 280 in English and ITAL 350 in Italian. While preparing separate materials for both groups was undoubtedly time-consuming, the level of engagement that all students were able to achieve through this format made it worth the effort and revealed the impressive versatility of the hybrid model. In their evaluations of the course, students remarked that this format "helped me analyze films beyond just liking or disliking something. I was thinking critically constantly," and that "personalized comments especially on voice thread and with reviews [helped] me improve the quality of my work."

CONCLUDING REMARKS

Multilevel courses, with careful planning and design, are one tool in the arsenal to support language study today, especially at institutions where language program resources and staffing are limited. The flexibility of such courses can be appealing to administrators and makes them an attractive option for departments wishing to protect their language curriculum from further erosion. Yet it is the dynamic, vivacious nature of the interactions within the multilevel classroom, along with their enhanced pedagogical effectiveness, that comprises the greatest strength of these courses, and that makes them valuable to any program of Italian, regardless of size or strength. At Ithaca College, we have been pleased by the way in which these Italian courses have been embraced by students and faculty alike, and in seeing the connections that are being forged within the classroom. In the most recent evaluations for ITAL 20024/ITAL 32400 (Intermediate Conversation II / Conversazione e Cultura), taught in spring 2022, students in both levels observed that "the homework and in-class discussion were very helpful in reinforcing my understanding of the Italian language"; "every assignment, discussion and homework integrated with each other"; grammar mistakes provided opportunities for the instructor to "teach something that benefited the whole class"; and the conversational structure of the course "helped fight off some of the nerves or anxieties that some people had."[6] Our model in Italian has now begun to be used for other languages at the college, and we continue to develop new courses along these lines. It is our hope that our experience can be of use to other institutions undergoing similar curricular self-examination.

NOTES

1. We would not recommend trying to combine more than two levels, due to the challenges inherent in the creation and attainment of course SLOs over such a range. Nor would we advise including 100-level language in multilevel courses. Students in multilevel language-skills courses should already have had at least one year of Italian in order to avoid too great a discrepancy in ability among students.
2. For example, the SLOs for ITAL 20101/32300 are the following:

    speak and express opinions competently (ITAL 323: competently and with confidence) on a wide range of topics (cultural, social, political, ethical, etc.);
    comprehend main ideas (ITAL 323: main ideas and the majority of details) communicated through written discourse (fiction, nonfiction, press, authentic sources) on a variety of topics;

express an intermediate (ITAL 323: Intermediate-Advanced) understanding of authentic conversational Italian at a variety of registers (formal, less formal, and idiomatic) when listening to conversations of native speakers, films, songs, and newscasts. demonstrate cultural awareness of the Italian-speaking world.

3. Specifically: (1) Demonstrate an understanding of Italy's regional differences as exemplified by each city, and of the key historical events and/or people that shaped them; (2) recognize and identify each area's characteristic architecture and art; analyze literary works within the context of their area of origin; and (3) articulate the ways in which popular culture and traditions differ within Italy, and how they compare to students' own experiences.
4. Specifically: (1) Recognize regional linguistic differences characterized by dialect, expressions, and/or pronunciation; demonstrate the ability for sustained discussion of the topics of the course in clear Italian, using appropriate vocabulary; and (2) clearly express, in grammatically correct written Italian, reflections and research on the course topics.
5. The course received a 100% response rate for both levels. Numeric feedback was 100% positive. All written commentary was similarly positive. Particularly encouraging was the following quote in relation to drawing students to the program: "[Taking this course] has made me look into classes that I would not normally look into. I normally wouldn't have taken this class since I have no Italian experience, but it went very well."
6. This course also received a 100% response rate for both levels, and numeric feedback was 100% positive. In terms of success in delivering a course across different levels that simultaneously emphasizes language, content, and the values at the core of the humanities, one of the students' comments summarizes it best: "This course is a wonderful way to improve Italian but also learn more about being a human and being empathetic and understanding different cultures."

BIBLIOGRAPHY

Ashton, K. (2019). Approaches to teaching in the multi-level language classroom. *Innovation in Language Learning and Teaching*, *13*(2), 162–77.

Balliro, L. (1997). Multiple levels, multiple responsibilities. *Focus on Basics*, *1*. https://www.ncsall.net/index.html@id=444.html

Bell, J. S. (2002). *Teaching multilevel classes in ESL* (2nd ed.). Don Mills, ON: Pippin Publishing.

Bowler, B., & Parminter, S. (2002). Mixed-level teaching: Tiered tasks and biased tasks. In J. Richard & W. Renandys (Eds.), *Methodology in language teaching: An anthology of current practice* (pp. 59–64). Cambridge: Cambridge University Press.

Hedstrom, B. (2016). *Gerry Wass on multi-level classes*. Bryce Hedstrom. https://www.brycehedstrom.com/2016/gerry-wass-on-multi-level-classes/

Hipwell, L. F., & Melucci, D. (Eds.). (2020). *Italian language and culture conference: Challenges in the 21st century Italian classroom*. Department of Italian, Georgetown University. https://repository.library.georgetown.edu/bitstream/handle/10822/1060512/ILCC%20Volume%201%20Final.pdf?sequence=1&isAllowed=y

Kadakin, V., Shukshina, T., Piskunova, S., Babushkina, L., & Falileev, A. (2016). Pedagogical conditions of multilevel foreign languages teaching in pedagogical higher education. *International Journal of Environmental & Science Education*, *11*(14), 6603–15. https://files.eric.ed.gov/fulltext/EJ1116065.pdf

Looney, D., & Lusin, N. (2019, June). Enrollments in languages other than English in United States institutions of higher education, summer 2016 and fall 2016: Final report. *Modern Language Association*. https://www.mla.org/content/download/110154/2406932/2016-Enrollments-Final-Report.pdf

Mockensturm, L. (2021). Teaching strategies for multi-level ESL classes. *EFL Magazine*. https://eflmagazine.com/teaching-strategies-for-multi-level-esl-classes/

Pouzergues, P. (2022). Multilevel courses and blended learning-tools for pedagogical differentiation and promoting student autonomy. *European Journal of Applied Linguistics*, *10*(2), 272–83.

3

DISCOVERING ITALIAN AMERICAN CULTURE THROUGH DIGITAL HUMANITIES

Building Language Competencies and
Community Engagement in the Italian Curriculum

Domenica Diraviam and Viviana Pezzullo

Modern languages and digital humanities (DH) are two fields that, despite sharing so many characteristics in terms of learning outcomes and teaching methodologies, tend to be considered separately—rather than adopting a comparative approach that emphasizes their overlapping traits. Notable attempts to integrate second language (L2) instruction with DH, namely by Thea Pitman and Claire Taylor, and Melinda A. Cro, underscore how the L2 class can thrive from DH and vice versa, fostering a learning environment where students develop communicative skills through a hands-on teaching approach. Because of the United States' linguistic and cultural background, DH have the potential to fully capture the diversity of the student population in American higher education, leaving room for growth for non-Anglophone projects. This connection between modern languages and DH in terms of interdisciplinary and pragmatic approaches to learning can encourage the implementation of DH projects in the L2 classroom. Indeed, according to Pitman and Taylor: "This should encourage us all in both ML and DH to strive to develop common languages between us, to keep the doors open to dialogue even if we all also need to strive to articulate coherent disciplinary identities for more pragmatic, institutional purposes" (Pitman & Taylor, 2017, p. 18). Such a pragmatic focus stems from the "inherently collaborative and cooperative nature of the L2 classroom, where meaning is built and evaluated in a community setting, [and] parallels the skills and methods valued in the DH classroom" (Cro & Kearns, 2020, p. 1). Collaboration does not simply create a sense of community in the classroom but also enhances students' learning experience by providing a safe environment for them to share their knowledge and interact with peers tackling a given task.

In this sense, DH lends itself as a pragmatic component to the language curriculum by relying on a task-based approach that fosters applicability of theoretical concepts while promoting the acquisition of soft skills. Such a pedagogical strategy combines the project work, which is student-centered and finalized to an end-product, with practice in the target language.[1] Task-based language learning is the ideal approach to engage students in the use of language outside the classroom while generating high-quality learning "with a sense of authenticity and relevance" (González-Lloret, 2017, p. ix). Such an approach enables students to feel comfortable in academic and professional communicative situations, demonstrate the ability to explain complex concepts and present and support opinions by developing cogent arguments and hypotheses (following the American Council on the Teaching of Foreign Languages [ACTFL] framework).

This chapter outlines a collaborative, task-based approach focused on DH and the study of Italian American culture. More specifically, it focuses on two case studies: workshops centered around the collections *Vivo-Fruttauro Letters* and *The Art of Tom DiSalvo*. Both projects belong to the website Italian American Memories (ITAMM), which collects Italian American cultural artifacts. We created and manage this website along with graduate students from the Italian Program at Florida Atlantic University. The collections themselves are the result of the work accomplished by the participants during DH extracurricular workshops. These events were promoted through an open invitation to undergraduate and graduate students, as well as the local community. The main learning objectives for undergraduate students consisted of practicing linguistic skills by describing events in the major time frames (past, present, and future), structuring arguments to support their opinions, and negotiating meaning to promote intercultural understanding, while performing archival research. Graduate students, in addition to becoming familiar with cross-disciplinary research, assisted undergraduate students with understanding cultural and linguistic nuances and gained experience in interpersonal, interpretive, and presentational modes of communication. Because each of the projects involved a different object of inquiry—textual and visual resources, respectively—students strengthened competencies with textual analysis, production, and comprehension, as well as with art appreciation and interpretation.

The collections *Vivo-Fruttauro Letters* and *The Art of Tom DiSalvo* are examples of public digital humanities (PDH) as they originate from and for the Italian American community, including, but not exclusively, the one in the Boca Raton (Florida) area. We made the material available not only to the students but also to the community members, who had access to the artifacts stored at the Department of Languages, Linguistics, and Comparative Literature (in the case of the Vivo-Fruttauro letters) or online (in the case of the artwork of Tom DiSalvo). Therefore, the community members participated in the workshops and worked alongside the students by providing their contribution, deciphering and interpreting the artifacts. Because of the dynamic of such a unique cohort, during the projects, students did not simply learn how to engage with peers on a given task but also how to interact with a diverse network of participants and develop a service-learning partnership.

ITALIAN STUDIES AND DH

As scholar Carol Chiodo convincingly argues specifically in the context of Italian studies, greater attention needs to be afforded to the development of a pedagogy that engages with DH, instead of focusing merely on the acquisition of exclusive skills: "Digital pedagogy is not simply the use of these technologies for teaching, but approaching these technologies with both the critical awareness that they demand and a heightened attention on their impact on learning" (Chiodo, 2017, p. 178). However, despite their mutually beneficial relationship, there is a relative scarcity of DH scholarship in Italian studies major journals and sessions organized for conferences in the discipline, proving that the field lacks a theoretical and methodological framework in terms of pedagogy.[2] In addition, when it comes to the diversity of projects, the panorama of DH Italian studies is mainly dominated by the preponderant presence of Dante, as Crystal Hall points out (Hall, 2019, p. 98). However, projects like those included in the 2017 NeMLA Italian Studies series "The Italian Digital Classroom" demonstrates how DH succeeds in exploring Italian studies in a transversal manner, providing both students and educators various ways of engaging with Italian culture.[3]

Integrating the study of the Italian American diaspora in the Italian language classroom would allow students to explore concepts of national, cultural, and ethnic identity, learn more about the history of Italian migration to America, and finally, look at current migratory events in the Mediterranean area from a different perspective. Although in the arch of the last twenty years Italian American studies have experienced an incremental growth in terms of coursework and programs across the United States, scholars have still granted very little attention to pedagogical methodologies about teaching Italian American culture specifically in the language classroom, much less in combination with the use of computational methodologies.

A focus on Italian American history and culture in the L2 class can present several benefits. Scholar Christina Tortora, discussing the reasons that lead students to enroll in Italian language courses, argues that "the teaching and learning of Standard Italian is often promoted as a way for members of the diaspora to connect with their heritage and/or their living parents or grandparents" (Tortora, 2014, p. 277). Despite dialect being such an essential part of Italian linguistic identity—especially in the context of Italian American heritage—it tends to be excluded from the Italian language classroom. Therefore, if the appeal to heritage becomes one of the ways to promote student retention in Italian programs, dialect can become an emotional incentive.[4]

THE VIVO-FRUTTAURO LETTERS WORKSHOP

In 2017, Patricia Badia donated the correspondence between her aunt and uncle, Leona and Danny Badia, to the Department of Languages, Linguistics, and Comparative Literature at Florida Atlantic University. These letters, dating from 1942 to 1945, formed the basis for a series of DH workshops designed to foster community outreach and unite undergraduate and graduate students from various levels of Italian language proficiency to engage in interpreting these artifacts. The project led to the creation of a website on Omeka, ITAMM, which stores and organizes this material into curated collections.[5] Following a presentation about ITAMM at the 2019 Italy in Transit Symposium, Joseph Sciorra, director for Academic and Cultural Programs of the John D. Calandra Italian American Institute, proposed to partner with us to transcribe, translate, and digitize correspondence from another Italian American family (the Vivo-Fruttauros). He had received the bundle of letters from a woman who salvaged them from the curbside in her neighborhood in Brooklyn, New York.[6]

Like the Badia family, the Vivo-Fruttauros were an ordinary Italian American family who maintained correspondence with their relatives in Italy via detailed letters during the late 1940s. Similar to the workshops centered around the Badia letters, we organized a series of events inviting undergraduate and graduate students and the local community. The presence of the community was essential for the vitality of the project as they played an important role both as donors and participants. Due to their generational proximity, and in many cases their direct experience with Italian American hybrid culture, the community members were able not only to interpret the content of the letters but also to provide contextual information to students, who did not live through these historical events. Therefore, it is the community's active involvement, and not merely the fact that the website is open access, that makes this an example of PDH, as it "identifies, invites in, and addresses audience needs in the design, as well as the approach and content, long before the outreach for a finished project begins" (Brennan, 2016, p. 384).

We ran two workshops focusing on the Vivo-Fruttauro letters during the fall 2019 and spring 2020 semesters. The Italian Program advertised both two-and-a-half-hour sessions (with an hour lunch break) through course announcements and email blasts from the Italian student association. The original letters were available to the students to peruse during the meetings. The group of twenty participants (including students and community members) worked on a body of fifty-three letters dated 1947, all handwritten in Italian and addressed to Giuseppina Vivo. The physical letters were divided into two main categories, those from Giuseppina's husband, Vincenzo, from Brooklyn, New York, and those from her daughter, Rosina, her son-in-law, and her grandchildren, from La Spezia. The workshop aligns with two learning objectives for the students: first, to interpret language and enhance reading comprehension and speaking competencies, and second, to produce Dublin Core metadata, tagging objects with keywords and writing short descriptions for the website, ITAMM.

READING COMPREHENSION

The first step of the workshop was to familiarize our students with Italian American culture, metadata, and, of course, with the texts. The original handwritten letters were a novelty to many students. Isabela Ribeiro-Ochoa, an undergraduate student, explains how a project like this can help bridge the gap between different generations, inviting students to connect historical artifacts with their personal experiences: "It's hard sometimes to feel the connection with past generations and these letters were not simply a perfect snapshot of that time period but also shows how similar we are in many ways to people even though so much has happened" (Isabela Ribeiro-Ochoa).

Because of the range of levels of language proficiency, we paired beginner students with more advanced ones for the reading activities. The goal was for the beginners to receive assistance and for the advanced students to practice their communication and translation abilities and feel empowered by their current competence. After reading and understanding the meaning, students worked individually on the letter, selecting excerpts and keywords, mapping relevant themes, and annotating the letter. Considering the fact that these letters were abandoned on the street and therefore did not contain references to the familial relationship between the protagonists, nor any timeline, students found themselves acting like detectives assembling clues: "It was a little bit of a challenge at the beginning to find out who all these family members were but at the same time, that mystery was even more engaging for us students because we were trying to piece everything together . . . and form our own theories and try to confirm that based on what everyone around the room was reading" (Isabela Ribeiro-Ochoa). Family tree diagrams were sketched on the board and modified throughout the course of the workshop. Each of the participants contributed to confirming the relationship among the family members.

Another difficulty—which was simultaneously an element of great interest to students—was the material nature of the text. Students handled letters from the 1940s, deciphering cursive calligraphy and interpreting stylistic differences in addition to the historically and culturally specific content. Hristo Joseph, an advanced undergraduate student, explains how he was surprised to discover how much the use of the language in the letters, a sort of transcription of spoken Italian (often with grammatical mistakes) mixed with dialect and slang, differed from the Standard Italian he was familiar with: "When I first did it [the workshop] I was in my third year [of Italian] already and I was more or less comfortable with it, but reading these letters was quite different. I saw a lot of things that I had never encountered before" (Hristo Joseph). For many of our students, this was the first time that they reflected on the use of dialect in Italians' everyday life. In this regard, Tortora points out how incorporating the dialect into the Italian curriculum can be beneficial for students as it represents a cultural marker, especially for those who relate to the language through their ancestral connection to spoken dialect and vernacular Italian.

While they did not perform complete translations of the texts, students practiced reading comprehension in both linguistic and cultural terms. For instance, one of the themes that students identified as noteworthy was food. Gastronomic memory is so central in Italian American literature and media, becoming an immediate point of contact with students, who hold their own memories associated with food and family. Students compiled a list of all the items recurring in the letters, reflecting on the role that food played in the dynamic of the family: una bella bottiglia di ciliegie, spaghetti, tagliatelle,

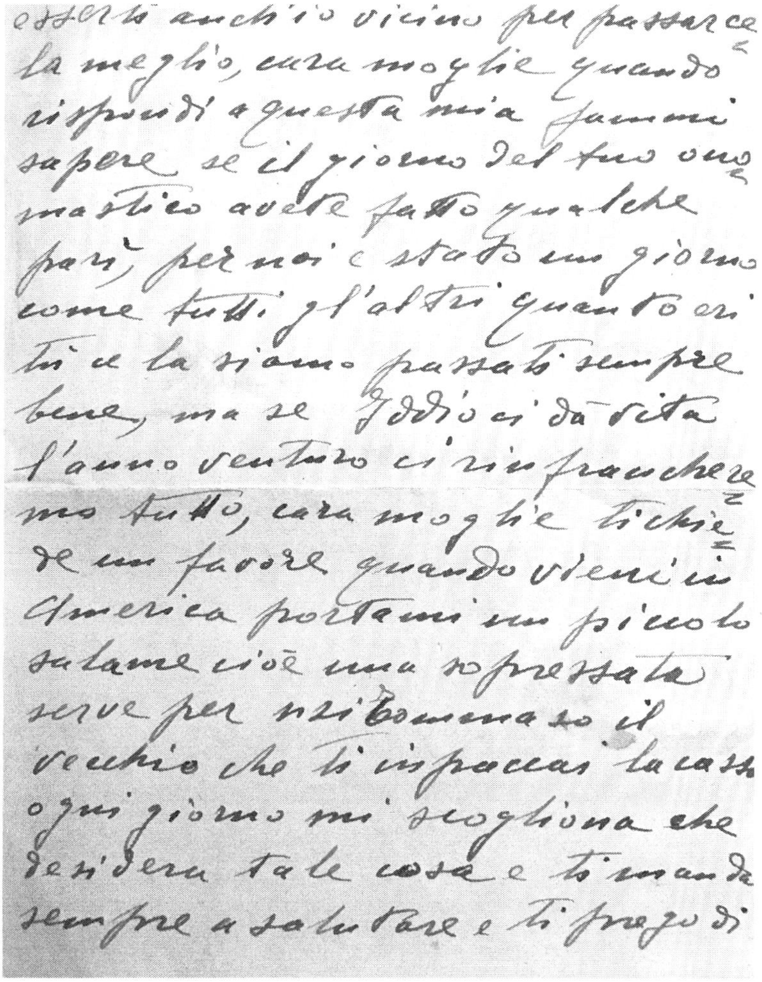

Discovering Italian American Culture through Digital Humanities

FIGURE 3.1. Excerpt of the letter from Vincenzo Vivo to his wife Giuseppina Vivo, dated March 18, 1947. It is a request for Italian food items to be brought to the United States.

salame, soppressata, and so on. The topic of food not only allowed us to explore the historical context of the Dopoguerra from the perspective of everyday life but also invited students to reflect on their personal family recipes, making the material at hand relevant to them. For instance, in a letter from Vincenzo Vivo to his wife dated March 18, 1947, one can read: "Cara moglie ti chiedo un favore quando vieni in America portami un piccolo salame cioè una soppressata" (Vivo, n.d.).[7] The same theme is also relevant in the letter that Rosa sends to her mother on February 21, 1947, in which she says: "I spaghetti l'abbiamo ricevuti e l'abbiamo gia fatti asciutti; sono speciali" (Fruttauro, n.d.).[8]

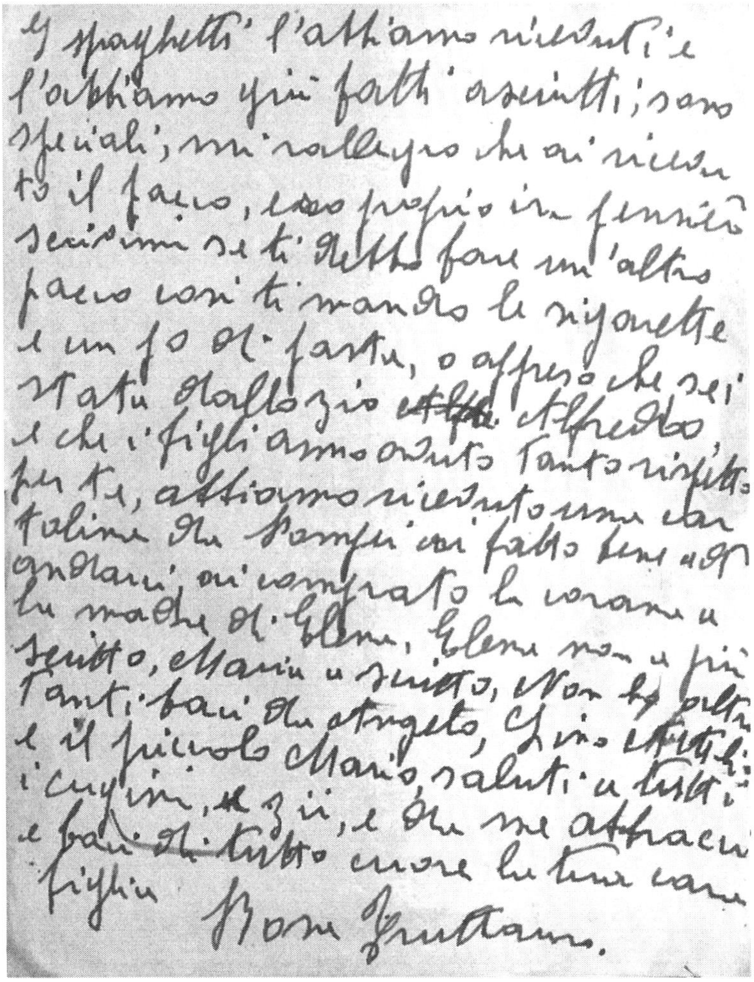

FIGURE 3.2. Excerpt of the letter from Rosa Fruttauro to her mother Giuseppina Vivo, dated February 21, 1947. It discusses a recipe for spaghetti.

CREATION OF METADATA

The second step of the workshop involved the preparation of the content for the digital archive. The students' task was to review and proofread the data, which was subsequently uploaded to the platform as metadata (through Omeka's plug-in, which supports csv files). The students compiled a data set with the information they collected in a Google Sheet. As McFall emphasizes, "Metadata is a crucial part of digital humanities because it provides a way of accessing and organizing data. . . . Therefore, metadata is the foundation of the work that is done by scholars" (McFall, 2020, p. 48). In other words, working with metadata provides students the necessary skills to embark on a future DH project by encouraging them to follow instructions and, most importantly, directing them in compiling intuitive descriptive data. While metadata may seem quite abstract to students, we emphasized their importance and practical function for the operation of the website, making sure that students could "see" and understand the reasoning behind their entries. As one student remarked, "When you are in the room working on the letters, it simply says 'put the tags here' and while you do it you may not be thinking that far ahead especially if you have never done something like this . . . but seeing the final product makes you appreciate the work that goes into it and that was another great experience" (Isabela Ribeiro-Ochoa).

THE ART OF TOM DI SALVO WORKSHOP

Following the positive outcome of the work on the Vivo-Fruttauro letters and the growing public interest in ITAMM, we organized a subsequent workshop, shifting the focus from textual to visual analysis and bringing attention to the paintings of Italian American artist Tom DiSalvo (1947–2011). For the workshop, students, faculty, and the community were invited to interpret his unique works combining adaptations of familiar icons. Participants with backgrounds in the arts were encouraged to share their personal knowledge and expertise. Closely examining digital representations of his massive canvases, the community teased out underlying symbols and text. Through thoughtful and iterative interpretation, the participants decoded poetic verses, word play, and innuendos that distinguished different facets of the artist's identity. Participants employed problem-solving skills as well as prior knowledge of language, art, and literature. In addition to strengthening these skills, the workshop design emphasized soft skills such as intergenerational and interdisciplinary communication, negotiating the use of resources, and respecting diverse opinions.

This workshop was scheduled in the height of the pandemic; thus, we were able to reimagine the Tom DiSalvo workshop as a three-hours virtual event on Zoom. We arranged participants in breakout rooms, providing each group with an image of a DiSalvo painting and having them decipher the enigmatic underlying textual component. While cooperating on this task, they could also compile reflections and emotional responses to the painting based on their personal experiences and familiarity with art and literature. We believed that the data extrapolated would formulate a more complete image of very abstract and complicated works that have been relatively obscured from public view. The workshop encouraged introspection and collaboration among a diverse group of contributors as demonstrated by the community's involvement. Tom DiSalvo himself was a member of this community, and therefore the DiSalvo estate donated to Florida Atlantic University an entire collection of his paintings that adorns the interior of the Arts and Humanities Building on the Boca Raton campus, which students see daily.

We included both asynchronous and synchronous components in the workshop. The planning began with an invitation to undergraduate students and community members via course announcements and email blasts wherein we attached links to online resources, including the virtual exhibit *Beyond the Nets* curated by Domenica Diraviam. Within the digital exhibit viewers could familiarize themselves with DiSalvo's visual art (zooming in for details and reading accompanying background information) and learn his history and motivations through video clips presented by art and Italian faculty, the artist's brother, and the exhibit's curator. This exposure lowered the participants' affective filter, prioritizing creative and interdisciplinary awareness over language proficiency or artistic expertise.

On the day of the workshop, we shifted to online synchronous engagement. We created a shared Google folder containing a selection of high-resolution images of DiSalvo's art, representing a range of his collections, themes, and styles. A shared Google Sheet served for participants and facilitators to create metadata and copy and paste textual translations, tags, and observations as they collaborated in Zoom breakout sessions. As in the *Vivo-Fruttauro Letters* workshop, the results of this activity populated the collection *The Art of Tom DiSalvo* on ITAMM. To further assist students in becoming familiar with creating metadata, we also created an auto-captioned video tutorial of the intended workshop outcomes and our suggested methodology for examining the works and cataloging the data.

Breakout rooms allowed small groups (of undergraduate and graduate students, faculty, and community members) to complete an in-depth analysis of individual DiSalvo paintings. The artist is noted for his semiotic translation of iconic pieces of music, art, and literature. Thanks to the prior availability of visual examples, participants were familiar with DiSalvo's artistic style and therefore able to distinguish a layer of meaningful base text that is not immediately apparent to the first-time viewer. Subsequently, participants discussed visible or hypothetical cultural and ethnic motifs, listed tags, and suggested references and correlations to existing art and literary works.

Based on previous experiences, we recommended the photo editing tools and the app Snag-It for enlarging and filtering the works, but undergraduates were innovative and resourceful in discerning alternative applications such as Concepts for the iPad. By zooming into the image in search of clues and questioning the purpose and placement of overlapping text and images, each student gained a deeper appreciation of the artist's intentions and distinguished the detailed brushstrokes and techniques. In the small group context, participants generated and discussed ideas. For instance, community member Sandra Curtis collaborated with an Italian faculty to decipher the painting *Machu Picchu (Silence)*.[9]

Being professionally skilled in graphic design, Curtis enlarged the image of the original painting and viewed it using different filters on her iPad. Once she was able to interpret the word "silence" in a quadrant, she ran it through Google Translate in various languages and discovered that the other text and symbols represented translations of the word in German, French, and Japanese. She also revealed other symbols and imagery by using the app Google Lens.

This is a tenable demonstration of the advantage of combining technology and prior knowledge in an interdisciplinary environment. By the conclusion of the workshop, the participants had analyzed nine works of art using a similar process as the one outlined while providing novel techniques on approaching the remaining works. In combination with oral history interviews also collected during the pandemic, the compiled data enhanced our ongoing digital archive, where we created a collection of DiSalvo's art with the students' interpretations, which served to introduce DiSalvo to the Italian, Italian American, and global community of scholars and enthusiasts.

The content and outcome of both the *Vivo-Fruttauro Letters* and *The Art of Tom DiSalvo* workshops can be adapted to curricular modules in beginning/novice and advanced Italian courses as well as in cross-disciplinary learning communities and virtual exchanges. The assessments in the appendix to this chapter have been implemented in both levels of Beginning Italian. They are structured as peer discussions for the classroom environment wherein the discussion may take place in the face-to-face environment (for traditional and web-enhanced modalities) or within the online discussion forum in the learning management system (for hybrid, synchronous, and asynchronous modalities). These sample discussion-based assessments are intended to increase student awareness of, and engagement with, the PDH collections on the ITAMM website and promote a sociocultural view of second language acquisition (SLA), inviting reflection, selection, and evaluation (Cro, 2020, p. 18). Beyond the stated language outcomes of the discussions, students reveal their unique cultural nuances and experiences with oral history, world cuisine, and appreciation for visual art styles and genres (Chiodo, 2020).[10]

The DiSalvo Art Discussion was incorporated into the course curriculum for the first level of Beginning Italian and demonstrated that students were intrigued by this style of art and DiSalvo's ethnic heritage. Students engage with the target language at their level of mastery, compiling lists of familiar nouns and adjectives ("la stella bianca," "un uomo grande"), but they are also encouraged to apply their grammatical knowledge to new terms and grow their vocabulary list ("l'astronauta volante," "la conchiglia grigia"), exemplifying real-world application of the grammatical concepts. The Letters Discussion, aimed at students enrolled in the subsequent level of Beginning Italian, requires the learners to compose a narrative related to personal memories of food. This represents an opportunity to revisit core vocabulary and learning outcomes such as family and food, while focusing on the past tense grammatical structures imperfetto and passato prossimo ("Mia nonna cucinava . . . non abbiamo mai mangiato . . ."). In both discussions students are effectively communicating in the target language. By leveraging English for the peer responses, all students are equipped to engage in critical thinking either through an analysis of DiSalvo's painting, or by comparing culinary experiences across cultures.

CONCLUSION

At the end of the workshops, participants shared thoughts and reflections on the overall experience. Some indicated that this was their first interaction with faculty members outside of a classroom setting and their first opportunity to engage in a scholarly project without formal assessment.[11] Informal conversations with the participants revealed that they were proud that their work on the metadata would enrich the ITAMM website and enhance users' experience. They also appreciated acquiring research and scaffolding skills to be used in both professional and academic environments. Students see themselves as part of the Italian American local community, practicing their speaking skills while discovering what it means to be Italian across different generations. However, this community is not limited to the Boca Raton area; it becomes global as our students interact with scholars of Italian studies around the world. For instance, two of our undergraduate students participated in a formal interview with the John D. Calandra Italian American Institute where they talked about their textual analysis and general impressions of their work with DH, and several others presented aspects of their engagement with the *Vivo-Fruttauro Letters* at international conferences in the discipline.[12]

In terms of meeting the learning objectives set for both the *Vivo-Fruttauro Letters* and the *Art of Tom DiSalvo*, this pragmatic task-based work allowed students to familiarize themselves with datasets; most importantly, it also encouraged them to develop their own understanding of Italy and its diaspora, constantly negotiating their previous knowledge of both its language and culture. For instance, having firsthand experience with both dialect and grammatical errors led them to prioritize active reading over passive reading, strengthening their comprehension skills. Similarly, the study of a figure like DiSalvo helps students investigate Italian transnational culture and hybrid identity, dispelling eradicated stereotypes about Italian Americans.[13] Once again, referring back to Carol Chiodo, the goal was not simply to put the emphasis on the acquisition of single technical competencies but also to provide students with a methodological and pedagogical apparatus. This will allow them to apply their knowledge to their own projects in the future, paving the road for educators who want to incorporate aspects of DH into the Italian classroom. Consequently, DH allows students to reflect on their own place as learners of Italian, because, as Robert Voss points out, "getting students to explore difficult topics using digital tools is interesting but getting students to ask new questions and incorporate new digital tools is exciting" (Voss, 2020, p. 22).

APPENDIX A

DiSalvo Art

Introduction

In this discussion, you will view and discuss some Italian art as well as practice your vocabulary.

Get Ready!

To Prepare for this Discussion:
- Visit The Art of Tom DiSalvo collection. You will enjoy viewing a variety of works by the Italian American artist, Tom DiSalvo. A curated selection is also available at the virtual art exhibit, Beyond the Nets.
- Examine the paintings as well as the links to details on the works and the videos about the artist.
- Review definite articles and the number and gender of nouns in Italian.

Share Your Thoughts

IN ITALIANO

Take a screenshot of one or more of DiSalvo's works in the exhibit and label each one with as many words as you can in ITALIAN.

- You should have at least thirty unique labels.
- They may be nouns, verbs, adjectives, numbers, and familiar expressions.
- Consult the vocabulary lists in your textbook first. If you cannot find thirty, then resort to an online dictionary such as wordreference.com.
- Any words that are NEW (not from the textbook to this point) should be labeled in a different color from the rest.

IN INGLESE

Look at the images your classmates selected. Discuss the unique traits of Tom DiSalvo's art that you see in them. Share your opinions of his style. Art is very subjective! Lastly, compare DiSalvo's art to your favorite style of art. Share images or links so that we can appreciate it too. Your response is in ENGLISH. It should be well formulated and display proper grammar and syntax. Continue the conversation with your classmates, justifying your choice.

Letters

Introduction

In this discussion, you explore correspondences that demonstrate the importance of food in Italian American culture and reflect on its place as a part of your own ethnic identity.

Get Ready!

To Prepare for this Discussion:

- Explore the Vivo-Fruttauro Collection. There are a variety of letters, postcards and artifacts that preserve the experiences of this Italian immigrant family and their extended relations. Focus on the recurring theme of food.
- Review present indicative, 'passato prossimo' and 'imperfetto' verb tenses in Italian.

Share Your Thoughts

IN INGLESE

Based on what you interpreted in the archives about the Italian American relationship with food, write (or record) a well-constructed discussion comparing the role of food in your life and cultural experience. Include concrete examples from these resources to support your argument.

IN ITALIANO

Recall a food or culinary experience from your childhood. Write a paragraph describing this food and how it impacted you. Here are some suggested prompts:

- When did you eat it?
- Who prepared it?
- What were the ingredients?
- How did it make you feel?
- Do you still eat it today?

[For the instructor: Include a personal example]

Respond to Your Colleagues

IN INGLESE

Read your classmates' submissions about their cultural response to food and their memories of a particular food. Share your reactions including similarities and differences in your experiences. Your response is in ENGLISH. You may write or record it. It should be well formulated and display proper grammar and syntax. Continue the conversation with your classmates, justifying your choice and your perspective.

NOTES

1. For additional reference see Fried-Booth (2013).
2. For a thorough list of panels about Italian studies and DH see Hall (2019).
3. Within the realm of medieval literature, one can also remember the *Decameron Web* (Brown University), *Oregon Petrarch Open Book* (University of Oregon), and *Petrarchive Project* (Indiana University). DH projects embracing modern and contemporary Italian authors include but are not limited to: *Galileo's Library* (Bowdoin College), *Garibaldi & the Risorgimento Archive* (Brown University), and *The Italian Women Writers* (University of Chicago Library).
4. It is worth mentioning that heritage is not the only factor that leads students to enroll in Italian classes. They may come as well from other fields and backgrounds, such as performing arts (opera singers), art history, and classical studies.
5. George Mason University's Roy Rosenzweig Center for History and New Media (CHNM) developed Omeka explicitly for non-IT specialists to facilitate the work of museums and library professionals interested in creating archives and exhibitions without programming. For this reason, this software is particularly helpful also in the context of a classroom that does not directly engage with computer sciences. Another pedagogical example of the use of Omeka is: Marsch, A. C. (2013). Omeka in the classroom: The challenges of teaching material culture in a digital world. *Literary and Linguistic Computing, 28* (2), 279–82.
6. Additional information about the story of the discovery of these letters can be found in: Scarinci, J. Love has no borders. A family's discarded letters find a new home thanks to the Calandra Italian American Institute, a Florida Atlantic University archive, and a fateful discovery. *Queens, 24*(1), 18–19.
7. A digitized version of this letter is available on ITAMM. See: Vivo, V. March 18, 1947. Letter from Vincenzo Vivo to Giuseppina Vivo. *Italian American Memories: Documentary Archive.* https://itamm.omeka.net/items/show/319
8. A digitized version of this letter is available on ITAMM. See: Fruttauro, R. February 21, 1947. Letter from Rosa Fruttauro to Giuseppina Vivo. *Italian American Memories: Documentary Archive.* https://itamm.omeka.net/items/show/302
9. A digitized version of DiSalvo's painting *Machu Picchu (Silence)* is available on ITAMM. DiSalvo, T. *Machu Picchu (silence), Italian American Memories: Documentary Archive.* https://itamm.omeka.net/items/show/363
10. For an additional example of a discussion board engaging with DH and Italian studies, see Chiodo (2020).
11. Further research about rethinking assessment in project-based assignments is very much needed. We as educators are gradually starting to replace traditional

formative assessments with group and individual projects, which, while being engaging for students, also present a gray area of how to evaluate students' output.
12. Furthermore, the Vivo-Fruttauro family was able to reach out from Italy via ITAMM and subsequently rediscover their legacy.
13. Several scholars have approached this topic, an example for all: Cavallero, J. J., & Plasketes, G. (2004). Gangsters, fessos, tricksters, and Sopranos: The historical roots of Italian American stereotype anxiety. *Journal of Popular Film and Television*, *32*(2), 50–73.

BIBLIOGRAPHY

Al di là delle reti/Beyond the nets: The art of Tom DiSalvo. Accessed February 26, 2022. https://theexhibit.io/exhibition/al-di-la-delle-retibeyond-the-nets-the-art-of-tom-disalvo

The art of Tom DiSalvo. Italian American Memories. Accessed February 26, 2022. https://itamm.omeka.net/collections/show/6

Brennan, S. A. (2016). Public, first. In M. K. Gold & L. F. Klein (Eds.), *Debates in the digital humanities* (pp. 384–89). Minneapolis: University of Minnesota Press.

Chiodo, C. (2017). De nostri temporis studiorum ratione and the digital humanities. *NeMLA Italian Studies*, *39*, 177–79.

Chiodo, C. (2020). Beatrice in the tag cloud. In C. Kleinhenz & K. Olson (Eds.), *Approaches to teaching Dante* (pp. 257–261). New York: Modern Language Association.

Cro, M. A. (2020). *Integrating the digital humanities into the second language classroom: A practical guide.* Washington, DC: Georgetown University Press.

Cro, M. A., & Kearns, S. K. (2020, January). Developing a process-oriented, inclusive pedagogy: At the intersection of digital humanities, second language acquisition, and new literacies. *DHQ: Digital Humanities Quarterly*, *14*(1). digitalhumanities.org/dhq/vol/14/1/000443/000443.html

Fried-Booth, D. L. (2013). *Project work second edition—Resource books for teachers.* Oxford: Oxford University Press.

Fruttauro, R. February 21, 1947. Letter from Rosa Fruttauro to Giuseppina Vivo. Italian American Memories: Documentary Archive. Accessed November 21, 2022. https://itamm.omeka.net/items/show/302

González-Lloret, M.. *A practical guide to integrating technology into task-based language teaching. Digital shorts.* Washington, DC: Georgetown University Press.

Hall, C. (2019, September). Digital humanities and Italian studies: Intersections and oppositions. *Italian Culture*, *37*(2), 97–115.

McFall, L. M. (2020). Metadata in the classroom: Fostering an understanding of the value of metadata in digital humanities." In C. J. Young et al. (Eds.), *Quick hits for teaching with digital humanities: Successful strategies from award-winning teachers* (pp. 48–53). Bloomington: Indiana University Press.

Pitman, T., & Taylor, C. (2017). Where's the ML in DH? And where's the DH in ML? The relationship between modern languages and digital humanities, and an argument for a critical DHML. *DHQ: Digital Humanities Quarterly*, *11*(1). http://www.digitalhumanities.org/dhq/vol/11/1/000287/000287.html

Tortora, C. (2014). Heritage nation vs. heritage language: Towards a more nuanced rhetoric of "heritage" in Italian language pedagogy. *Forum Italicum*, *48*(2), 268–91.

Vivo-Fruttauro letters. Italian American Memories. Accessed February 26, 2022. https://itamm.omeka.net/collections/show/4

Vivo, V. March 18, 1947. Letter from Vincenzo Vivo to Giuseppina Vivo. Italian American Memories: Documentary Archive. Accessed November 21, 2022. https://itamm.omeka.net/items/show/319

Voss, R. (2020). Teaching with digital humanities: Engaging your audience. In C. J. Young et al. (Eds.), *Quick hits for teaching with digital humanities: Successful strategies from award-winning teachers* (pp. 18–24). Bloomington: Indiana University Press.

4

THE CAPITALS OF ITALIAN CULTURE

Teaching, Learning, and New Technologies

Patrizia Palumbo and Alessandra Saggin

While the use of technology, including that of digital platforms, is by now quite common, the choice of cities as the content of an online platform for language teaching and learning requires some sustaining arguments and clarifications.

Many language programs encourage students to spend time in the country whose language they learn. This is the case, for instance, in many of the language departments of Columbia University. For New York University's Program of Global Liberal Studies, studying in a foreign city is a requirement. Students respond positively to this exhortation or obligation, and this is one of the main reasons why we chose cities as the matter of our platform. With this platform we intend to offer students a means to familiarize themselves with the country in which they are going to spend a summer, a semester, or an entire year. Nevertheless, this online platform will be equally if not more important for the students who will not have the opportunity or the privilege to participate in any study abroad programs.

In general, through the use of our platform on the capitals of Italian culture, students will not only develop their listening, writing, and speaking skills, design projects, and cooperate with their peers, but they will also gain a good knowledge of the distinctive traits of Italian cities, as well an appreciation of Italy as a whole, acquiring therefore a solid cultural competence.[1]

In order to recognize the pedagogical value of this platform, it is important to consider the significance of cities in the production of national languages, which have been generated and changed not only by capitals, but by all the most prominent cities of a country. The same is true at the cultural level, although language and culture cannot be separated but give life to and transform each other. Our updatable platform is therefore the ideal means to offer a view of Italian language and culture as nonmonolithic and atemporal but as composite and ever-changing entities. Others have opted for an online platform as the pedagogical means for their language courses. At the University of Arizona, Giuseppe Cavatorta, associate professor of Italian, created an online platform, Italian in Wonderland, which provides a good teaching and learning tool, taking advantage of several new technologies and responding to the technological orientation of a new generation of learners. Cavatorta's well designed platform, which he presented at the annual conference of the American Council on the Teaching of Foreign Languages (ACTFL), held in November 2021, relies on a number of traditional modules, such as Environment, Work, Immigration, Fashion, Cuisine, and so on, that commonly constituted the topics of the textbooks for Italian classes. Certainly, unlike a textbook, Cavatorta's platform can be continuously updated and its topics are unquestionably essential when talking about a country's culture. However, we believe that the same topics would be more incisive and articulated if dealt with within the frame of the Italian cities that together have marked deeply Italian culture over the centuries. The environmental concerns and initiatives of a big industrialized city like Milan, for instance, are very different from those of the smaller Florence, and different is these two cities' contribution to Italian fashion, respectively prevalently industrial and artisanal.

Dealing with Italian cities, our platform showcases their distinctive and ever-evolving culture. It illustrates, that is, how the ten cities selected for the project have transformed over the years in all their components, including their topography. In the course of time, these cities have expanded or entire sections have been demolished and redesigned. Rome is the best example of an Italian city with a plan adapting to political goals. It is well known that the fascist regime, for instance, destroyed and rebuilt large sections of the capital in order to create a monumentality mirroring its imperial ambitions. In very recent years, the continuous emergence of ruins has in some cases even required the diversion of subway lines. Conversely, in the last decades Milan has been shrinking (Fabris et al., 2019). Acknowledging that urban spaces are subject to continuous changes corroborates the validity of an online platform whose content may be updated and modified.

The platform on Italian cities deals with their past and contemporary changes as well as their historical ties and/or rivalries and exchanges. It is meant, in sum, to prepare students on the complexity of Italian culture and to fill in the blanks in the students' image of Italy that is often, and understandably so, fragmentary and crystallized.

In addition, the input on each of the ten capitals of Italian culture on the platform aims to delineate the multifaceted nature of their identity: the traditional layer made of, for instance, celebrations of patrons, processions, festivities, and so on; the subculture, the marginal component, like that of graffiti artists and skateboarders; and the dominant culture whose values and patterns of behavior are imposed through economic, mediatic, or political power. An exhaustive representation of Italian cities must also take into account the potent American influence on their culture, giving the students the opportunity to expand their intercultural literacy. The changing cultural and linguistic multiplicity of Italian cities doesn't privilege the capital or the greatest industrial centers of the Italian peninsula but each of the ten cities included in our platform.

Lastly, it is important to underline that the choice of ten cities of big and medium size does not mean disregarding the smaller ones or the towns of the Italian peninsula. The existence of any city cannot be prescinded from its surroundings, particularly in a country as small and as densely populated as Italy. There is first of all a geographical continuum as well as historical, political, and commercial interdependence. Art too recalls this tie between Italian cities and towns. Neapolitan painting, for instance, owes to the regional landscape much of its inspiration and beauty. The selection of ten cities, therefore, may not imply dismissing the rest of the country; it rather represents the frame of an ample cultural panorama.

ITALIAN CITIES IN THE FOREGROUND

As mentioned in the previous section, ten cities are to be presented on the platform of the Italian cultural capitals: Turin, Milan, Genoa, Bologna, Venice, Trieste, Florence, Rome, Naples, and Palermo. This means, first of all, that all the three areas of the Italian peninsula, the northern, the central, and the southern, are included. Nevertheless, these ten cities do not only figure as representative of parts of the peninsula; they were chosen for the forefront position they have enjoyed in the history of Italian culture. Although it is not possible to condense, within the space of a chapter, the entire history of ten Italian cities, we will limit ourselves to recalling salient moments, casting light on some of the significant contributions that each city gave to Italian culture, hoping to clarify the criteria on which our selection was based.

Turin, the first capital of Italy (1861–1865), was the city where the Savoy dynasty and its parliament conceived the unification of the country, previously divided into small independent states. After unification was achieved, the Savoy, from their sumptuous Turinese palaces, ruled over the entire nation. Turin's closeness to France, moreover, gave this city a particular cultural and linguistic French imprint (Oliva, 2014). More importantly, at the end of the nineteenth century, Turin was where a big industrial sector developed, a sector that grew rapidly until a labor force from the impoverished regions of southern Italy became necessary. This created a sort of bridge between North and South that resulted in a—not always welcomed—cultural hybridization (Fofi, 2009).

Since the sixteenth, seventeenth, and eighteenth centuries, Milan has been an important cultural and commercial pole with a great international exposure (Tonelli, 2020). During Austro-Hungarian domination, this city was the most advanced in the peninsula (Cantarella & Cardini, 2010), and later, like Turin, developed so greatly industrially that it became one of the most coveted destinations of southern emigrants (Panichella, 2014). Currently, Milan is the capital of Italian fashion and design, admired and reproduced all over the world.

Genoa, ancient flourishing thalassocracy and colonial power, has always been an important cultural center, due to its vast commercial activities and its great expansionist ambitions, leading the Genoese to the neighboring countries of Spain and France as well as the more distant shores of the Aegean and the Black Sea (Salonia, 2017). Since the nineteenth century, Genoa, with Turin and Milan, formed the so-called Italian industrial triangle and gave life to a vibrant literary and musical scene. Today, this port city maintains its important industrial profile and, in addition, has become a prominent center of the hybridization of Italian culture, because of the continuous flux and transiting of migrants from all corners of the world.

Venice, with its past as a great power with an enormous mercantile economy and overseen colonies, has connected other Italian cities with the rest of the world and innovated the commercial strategies and operations of other countries (Crowley, 2013). Today, its Biennale exposes Italy to contemporary global arts and the endless flow of foreign visitors crowns it the capital of tourism, reaffirming the international vocation of the city.

Under the Habsburg monarchy for centuries, Trieste, now bordering Eastern Europe, has been the fertile terrain for a distinct hybrid culture that has attracted the likes of James Joyce and Sigmund Freud, to mention only names of great international fame. Because of its large port and the richness of its culture, Trieste has been called the "Vienna by the sea" (Hametz, 2005). It is indeed the fascinating meeting point of Latin, Slavic, and Germanic cultures, a frontier city greatly important over the centuries for its commercial activities and the originality of its cultural productions (Ara & Magris, 2014).

Home to the oldest university in the Western world, Bologna has always had a diversified young population comprising both students coming from other Italian cities and foreigners. Since the Middle Ages, when the university was founded, the presence of this prestigious institution has provided the city with a progressive ethos and an alternative and engaged youth culture. It has also educated those who would become prestigious names in many different fields, namely cinema, music, literature, and the arts. In addition, after World War II, Bologna, situated within an important agricultural region, developed into a large industrial hub (Ferri & Roversi, 2005). Lastly, talking about Italian gastronomy and food industry means talking particularly about Bologna.

Florence has been perennially recalled as the cradle of the Renaissance and the birthplace of the Italian language (Najemy, 2006), a role that cannot be denied and that is obviously highlighted on the platform. Nevertheless, Florence is also the city where the idea of an exclusive prestigious past is challenged, for instance, by contemporary artists dedicated to more accessible and collaborative artistic creations. The veneration for Florence's past splendor and wealth also has been defied by the monumental costs of the preservation of its vast artistic patrimony, the counterfeiting of what was traditional and valuable artisanal work, and the difficult integration of foreign immigrants. The platform's aim is, consequently, to provide an image of Florence that is not museal but dynamic, comprising the challenges that its glorious artistic traditions keep entailing.

Capital of Italy and of an ancient empire, seat of the Italian government, Rome has obviously always been in the foreground of Italian culture (Beard, 2016). Because of its imperial past and its being the seat of the Roman Catholic Church, Rome has always been the city where different civilizations met. Rome is also a place where the past continues to reemerge in the form of ruins, complicating the city's temporal stratification. As the capital of the Italian nation, with the greatest presence of embassies in the world (greater than New York, which is the seat of the United Nations) and the important studios of Cinecittà, moreover, Rome may be defined as a global city, particularly in its historical center, while the autochthonous cultures are often confined to the margin where dissent ferments. Our platform intends to display this fascinating cultural puzzle for students to explore.

Naples, capital of the Bourbons' kingdom, has always been in the limelight in Italy and abroad for the extraordinary beauty of its gulf and its surroundings, and its closeness to Capri and Ischia. Both the city and the nearby islands have for centuries inspired and provided comfort to foreigners coming from colder countries (Moe, 2004). Besides these geographical merits, Naples has to be recognized for the vibrancy of its culture, its collection of antiquities, and its baroque art and architecture (Hughes & Buongiovanni, 2015). Just as charming is its colorful street life, its musical and artistic traditions, and its greatly popular cuisine. Because of its history and its contemporary cultural vitality, Naples has offered an enormous wealth of materials, which students have found very engaging. Lately, thanks to the novels Elena Ferrante set in Naples, this city has aroused the curiosity and interest of a huge number of readers in Europe and in the United States as well. We were happy to take advantage of this incredible notoriety and included the series "My Brilliant Friend" based on Ferrante's novels in our platform.

Palermo, the capital of Sicily, conquered by the Greeks, the Byzantines, the Arabs, the Normans, the Spanish—when it competed with Naples for the title of capital of the Kingdom of the Two Sicilies—and the French, has a very well-nourished cultural history (Dummett, 2015). Traces of all these foreign dominations can be found, indeed, in its architecture, its language, its music, and its cuisine. Thanks to its port, one of the major ones in the Mediterranean, Palermo, like Genoa, has always been open to other cultures since ancient times when the city was founded by the Phoenicians. The materials collected in the section of our platform dedicated to this city are meant to help students see this city as a point where many different cultures have converged.

Notwithstanding the value of cities as a pedagogical tool, the digital material based on them is often in English or has superficial and touristic overtones that are not conducive to learning at a college level. Equally important is the fact that none of the sites currently available is endowed with the array of teaching and learning tools that, on the contrary, our platform is going to provide.

THE PLATFORM'S EMBRYONIC PHASE

The idea for this platform originated in the roundtable "The Visible Cities: Teaching Language and Culture through the City," co-chaired by the authors of this article in March 2019 at the NeMLA annual conference. At this conference, we presented some pedagogical activities focused on the idea that the city and its representation in film, literature, and popular culture is a privileged window through which students have the opportunity to explore many tangible and intangible cultural products as well as historical, political, artistic, and social issues. Through this window, students may also become familiar with all the dynamic practices through which individuals structure and understand the world around them (Cutshall, 2012).[2] Moreover, the focus on urban spaces, an essential element of Italian heritage, is also a response to the global fascination aroused by Florence, Venice, Rome, Milan, and Naples, in particular. This focus enriches the lessons of language instructors and stimulates the students' interest in cultural contents.

After the NeMLA conference, the positive feedback received from other participants was quite encouraging; consequently, the original ideas were developed and refined to merge in the planning of an online platform dedicated to the most prominent Italian cities, a single space in which we could incorporate and organize authentic materials, various types of input (aural, visual, and textual), and activities already partially tested in the Italian language courses, intermediate and advanced, taught at Columbia University.[3]

In addition, one of the motivations for the design of the platform was the need to address various problems that college-level foreign language education faces today. Intermediate textbooks published in the last decade are organized around written texts whose topics could be of interest to learners but tend to become obsolete in a short time. In these textbooks, the primary focus is language (vocabulary, grammar, and syntax), and the potential for intellectual engagement with the content tends to be secondary. Furthermore, in these textbooks, cities are reduced to fragments, separated from one another, fragments that are too often overlooked by instructors who would rather concentrate on the topics dealt with in each chapter (fashion, immigration, cuisine, etc.). While textbooks by nature can only present culture as static, the authentic materials delivered through digital media create a more dynamic environment with direct access to most current practices, perspectives, and urban cultural life in general. This online platform, indeed, casts light on each city as a whole, with all its interdependent components, and highlights the changes and hybridity (in music, literature, cuisine, cinema, etc.) of language and culture, to which immigrants have greatly contributed in the last three decades. In addition, the design of this platform gave us the opportunity to reflect, even more, how teaching culture and its multifaceted and dynamic aspects is enhanced by internet technologies. Indeed, besides a well-planned choice of technological resources, it is essential to design activities and tasks that can lead students to achieve intercultural understanding and to develop critical awareness and those skills that will help them in other fields of knowledge and in becoming citizens of the world (Guth & Helm, 2019; Youngs, 2019).

TECHNICAL CHOICES

For the creation of the platform, the choice fell on WordPress (https://wordpress.com/), the content management system (CMS) most adopted internationally. WordPress is suitable for the creation of any type of site, and its functions are increasingly being expanded. It is very simple to both install and set up, and it has a very easy to use intuitive interface. Furthermore, thanks to a highly manageable text editor, WordPress allows users to plan, publish, and update content quickly and easily. WordPress offers at the same time a large number of plug-ins to adapt the website to one's needs. Thanks to this last feature, the use of H5P (https://h5p.org/), an open-source interactive tool that helps produce and run interactive content, was made possible. Also, all the quizzes, comprehension questions, games, and other assessment activities are carried out with this tool, allowing students to have immediate feedback. On the other hand, the teacher can see students' progress and can monitor their engagement.

Besides H5P, other applications, originally developed for different purposes, have been integrated to facilitate other kinds of tasks and help students become more active, create their own content, work independently outside the classroom, and support "their lifelong language learning" (Arnold & Ducate, 2019). Indeed, the multimodality of these applications, entailing different channels of communication (images, sound, and text) and high levels of collaboration, enables students to interact and participate in activities that model authentic use of technology (Bustamante et al., 2012; Blake, 2016; Elola & Oskoz, 2019; Kress, 2000). Among these applications is izi.TRAVEL *(*https://izi.travel/*)*, an open platform for storytelling that gives the opportunity to create one's own audio guides (audio stories), tie them into the locations or sites of one's choice, and add as many photos, texts, and videos as one desires. Then, visitors from all over the world can enjoy and share the audio guides via the free izi.TRAVEL app downloaded on their smartphones. Originally created for travelers and tourists, this app's features are perfectly suited to language learners and for their city-related storytelling (Compagnoni, 2022), especially for tasks carried out collaboratively for midterm or final projects, as you can see in the tasks illustrated in the next paragraphs (see activities with the maps illustrating the places from where the painters of the Scuola di Posillipo painted their landscapes and the map with all of Caravaggio's paintings that can be seen in Rome). For other real tasks, Google Arts and Culture provides very helpful tools, such as the gallery offering the opportunity to explore collections of art and museums, and design and create one's own permanent or temporary exhibit. Another app used in the platform is Thinglink (https://www.thinglink.com/), which is very useful for creating interactive images by embedding text, other images, videos, audio, and/or links, thus creating an additional layer of information about the visual content (Pacansky-Brock, 2017). Through this app, learners can explore areas relevant to their studies in a dynamic way and also create their own projects.

BUILDING THE WEBSITE

In conclusion, after deciding to use WordPress for its simplicity, manageability, and the increasing variety of its functions, we selected the applications that would most stimulate students' creativity and independence, two goals essential to our pedagogical approach.

Cultural Puzzle

We divided each of the ten selected cities into eight content sections (History and Geography, Art and Architecture, Industry and Craftsmanship, Music, Literature, Cinema, Popular Culture, and Culinary Culture) containing different activities based on authentic materials meant to present the cultural variety characterizing Italian cities. These activities are organized in intermediate and advanced level, but in this initial stage of the project we devoted greater attention to the intermediate level.

The activities designed for the platform, which can be frequently updated and used in online, hybrid, and face-to-face courses, are based on different inputs (newspaper articles, poetry, novels, movie clips, songs, works of art, documentaries, etc.). The various information these inputs convey is aimed to stimulate students' interest and, through specifically designed activities, to test their comprehension and analytical skills, encouraging them to be active and independent protagonists of their learning process. In addition, in designing and creating materials, the students' involvement in collaborative activities, especially writing (Eiola & Oskoz, 2017) and interdisciplinary cross-cultural learning, have always been guiding criteria. These materials are meant to foster higher-order thinking and lead the students to uncover and examine the hidden meanings and significances embedded in L2 (second

FIGURE 4.1. Homepage of the platform.

language) culture. Indeed, one of the ultimate goals of this platform, together with the fostering of a deeper knowledge of Italian cities and their interconnections, is to encourage and enable learners to work independently outside of the classroom. In the context of an American institution like Columbia University, language learning happens in the classroom for about four hours per week spread over two, three, or four days, therefore it is important to give students the opportunity and the technological tools to explore the language through meaningful activities and projects outside of the classroom. With this purpose in mind, at the end of each section of our platform we inserted inputs, apps, and tools students can use to create original presentations and projects based on the interests sparked by the material provided by the instructors and studied during class. These activities are meant to reinforce their learning experience inside and outside of the classroom, engaging them in tasks aimed at creating with the language in real-life situations.

Throughout the platform, the instructions are in Italian. Starting from the homepage (see Figure 4.1) and clicking on the different cities, the various sections open up (Figure 4.2). This platform makes it easier to organize different materials and search them using a "search" button, and allows students and instructors to create connections among the cities that may even be surprising.

All the activities start from authentic and different inputs on one Italian city and are organized with specific objectives:

⋄ Stimulate students' interest;
⋄ Reinforce old and introduce new vocabulary;
⋄ Reinforce and review grammar structures in context;

FIGURE 4.2. Sections in the platform's homepage.

⋄ Test students' reading and listening comprehension with specific activities that have immediate feedback; and
⋄ Suggest ideas for final projects that may be individual or collective. These ideas may be used for periodic assignments or, on a larger scale, as an assessment tool for midterm or final exams.

Selected Examples from the Platform

As said before, some activities are suitable for the classroom, others are more appropriate for specific independent study and projects aimed to assess students' progress during midterm or final exams. All the exercises aimed to promote and test lexical knowledge and comprehension are created with H5P. Each unit starts with a focus on vocabulary in order to get students ready to read a text and understand a video. The exercises are aimed at retrieving words already familiar to the students and creating a set of new words. We find that crosswords, "find the words," or matching activities that can be done at the beginning of class or as preparatory homework are particularly useful exercises. The second part of the unit is usually based on a visual input like a video (a movie clip, an interview, a documentary, etc.), whose comprehension is tested with interactive questions, or on the reading of an authentic text (a literary text, a newspaper article, a brochure, etc.) followed by comprehension activities. Special attention is given to projects whose main purpose is to stimulate and assess students' analytical skills, to kindle their creativity, and to encourage their use of the language in real situations.

Unit 1, Scuola di Posillipo Painters, is included in the section "Art and Architecture" of Naples, and the activities we designed are based on the 2019 exhibit *La luce di Napoli che conquistò il mondo*, about a group of painters active in Naples in the second half of the nineteenth century and devoted to painting landscapes with an innovative use of light. The unit is so organized:

- ◇ Vocabulary activity with the goal of retrieving already known words and introducing new ones, organized with some features of H5P (crosswords and grid word search game);
- ◇ Reading of a section of the guidebook issued during the exhibition, followed by reading comprehension questions with H5P interactive true or false quizzes; and
- ◇ Interactive vision of the official video with the interview with the exhibit's curator, featured on the national TV news, with questions embedded in the video to facilitate comprehension.

Tasks to be carried out collaboratively outside of the classroom

Some activities and tasks used in the platform were designed with the idea that they would not be completed individually online but would instead be completed in groups.

- ◇ "Reading the painting": Each student has to choose a painting and make it interactive through the Thinglink app. Linking together different media (images, videos, texts), with the image as the center of the content, the learners can create a narrative with different layers of information about the place and the monuments represented, the landscape, and the painting techniques (Figure 4.3).
- ◇ "Become a curator": This is an example of a real task. With this activity, the students become curators and design a virtual exhibit using the gallery of Google Arts & Culture, which has powerful search capabilities that can help learners find artwork easily and intuitively. It filters the searches according to artist, museum, medium, date, country, art movement, historic events, or even colors, so that for the students it is quite easy to browse the images. The main purpose of this task is to organize an exhibit with a few works of art to show the innovative ideas of the artists and then write a brief report on the concept of the exhibit and the curatorial choices, using Google docs.

FIGURE 4.3. Image from Thinglink app with interactive points on a painting.

⋄ "Create an audio guide": Another example of user-created content is the audio guide (audio story) created with the app izi.TRAVEL. The students work collaboratively to create and illustrate a map of the places from where the painters of the School of Posillipo painted or the map of Rome with the churches and places where Caravaggio's paintings are found (Figures 4.4 and 4.5). They can create an itinerary with many stops where they can upload images, text, and an audio story about the painters.

The tasks "Become a curator" and "Create an audio guide" are carried out in pairs or small groups with collaborative writing and peer feedback (Elola & Oskoz, 2017). The students need to negotiate in the target language the choice of the paintings for their exhibit, define the rationality behind their choice, or decide which itinerary to design and in which city.

The structure of each of the above projects is the following:

⋄ Goal of the project,
⋄ Create a permanent or a temporary exhibit of an artist of their choice or create an audio guide for the city or the museum of their choice,
⋄ General description, and

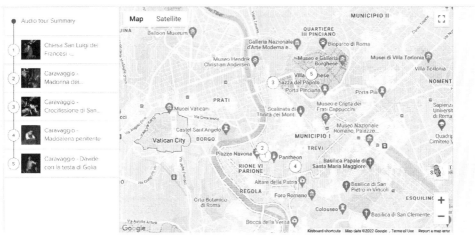

FIGURE 4.4. Map from the audio guide showing locations of Caravaggio's paintings in Rome.

FIGURE 4.5. Map from the audio guide showing some of the vantage points of the Posillipo paintings.

- Through Google Arts & Culture, students select paintings or sculptures to create an exhibit with a specific title and concept; students choose a city where they want to create an audio guide through the app izi.TRAVEL.

TASKS

This list illustrates the sequence of steps to complete the project.

- Choosing topics—In class and guided by the teachers, the students decide which project they want to work on (audio guide or exhibit), which artist, which city they prefer.
- Work plan—Once the students define their project, it is important to assign roles and parts of the task to each pair or group. It is important to choose a group leader who reports back to the instructor and is responsible for monitoring the project's progress.
- Research—The students start their own research on the web and on websites selected by the teacher, choose the images, decide which resources to use, and decide how to organize their ideas. It is important that students, at this stage of the project, take into account the type of audience for the exhibition or audio guide in order to be able to communicate effectively.
- Writing, editing, and peer feedback—Each student writes their part (using Google docs) and peers give their feedback. The edits and comments must be explained and always traceable.
- Presentation—Each pair or group presents its work in front of the class.
- Survey—All the students fill out a brief anonymous survey in order to provide feedback about their own and their partners' contribution to the project.

ASSESSMENT

As in all L2 teaching contexts, the evaluation of students' outputs is essential, because it gives students important feedback about the content and the form of their contribution. For these tasks we chose in part a quantitative evaluation for subcategories like grammar and vocabulary, then we concentrated on a global score that matched the criteria of the "authentic" objectives. Indeed, we considered central to the tasks' assessment categories like "effective use of visual/auditory content," "amount of contribution," "task completion," "use of good sources," "creativity," "style," and "register" (Abrams, 2006, 2019).

FINAL THOUGHTS AND FUTURE GOALS

The platform is still a work in progress, but we have already been able to evaluate the students' response to some of the tasks (the creation of the audio guide and the organization of an exhibit) assigned for midterm or final projects in two classes of Intermediate II with a total of twenty-one students. The students provided their anonymous feedback through Google forms (see Table 4.1).

Most of them found the activities interesting, and they particularly appreciated the opportunity to work in collaboration with their classmates in creating a "real" guide and exhibit. Indeed, one of the positive aspects underlined by many of the students is that they took advantage of the time outside of the classroom to meet classmates and work together. Moreover, they liked the organization and the variety of the materials (collected with the teacher's help, but also independently), which allowed them to have a real Italian experience, even if they had never traveled to Italy. We think that through materials we selected, we have been able to activate multiple sensory and communicative modes that can encourage students to immerse themselves more deeply in an Italian reality, increasing their metacognitive awareness, self-esteem, and individual accountability. Furthermore, through the first students' comments, we have seen how the use of the apps may boost their creativity and imagination. Apps constitute a means of communication that perfectly works for students, who are digital natives. Indeed, in the digital age, multimodality has become even more central to communication and this is especially true for language learners, who depend on the multiplicity of channels available on a screen to help them pick up meaning in a target language. After reading the students' comments, we believe that we are realizing our main original objectives. One was helping the students orient themselves at the geographic, linguistic, and cultural level in their journey, real or virtual, on the Italian peninsula and through its major cities. The other was doing so in Italian and using tools that play such an important role in the students' daily lives and that are, we could say, their own language.

In the next phase of our project, we plan to integrate material for all ten cities and for all eight sections, both for the intermediate and the advanced

TABLE 4.1. Students' Views of Creating Audio Guides and Designing an Exhibit

Survey statements	% of agree and strongly agree
1. I had a positive experience in creating an audio guide and/or designing an exhibit	84.3%
2. I found topics interesting and stimulating	86.0%
3. I found the apps user-friendly	85.2%
4. I enjoyed using instructor-assigned materials	84.2%
5. I enjoyed doing my own research	85.9%
6. I enjoyed working with classmates outside of the classroom	86.3%
7. I found peer comments informative and engaging	86.1%

levels. This will be done by consistently working to highlight all the connections between cities while underlining their cultural specificities in order to present students with all the richness and complexity of Italian culture that they will have to navigate.

We believe that our platform will become a useful tool for all our colleagues working in the Department of Italian and that it will also help graduate students to find materials ready to use and ideas for developing their own activities. Furthermore, thanks to our students' initial response, we are confident that this platform is going to increase and consolidate their interest in Italian culture for years to come.

Hopefully, online platforms similar to Capitals of Italian Culture. Language and Culture in the Urban Context will be adopted by instructors of languages other than Italian so that a greater community of instructors and students will be able to exchange innovative ideas to improve the efficiency of this pedagogical tool.

NOTES

1. The platform, Capitals of Italian Culture, is hosted on Columbia University's server. Its web address is https://capitalitaliane.lrc.columbia.edu/.
2. This shift toward a more dynamic understanding of culture is reflected in the ACTFL World Readiness Standards for Culture, which assume that learners need to engage with cultural products (tangible or intangible creations), cultural practices (behaviors and patterns of interactions), and cultural perspectives (beliefs, attitudes, and worldviews).

3. The professional development grant that we received in 2021 from the Language Resource Center of Columbia University and the technological assistance of Andrew Wyatt, graduate student at Columbia's Department of Italian, made it possible for us to proceed toward our goal. In addition to providing us with technological assistance, moreover, Andrew Wyatt has also given us a great contribution in creating content regarding the city of Trieste, a city whose culture is the topic of his doctoral dissertation.

BIBLIOGRAPHY

Abrams, Z. (2006). From theory to practice: Intracultural CMC in the L2 classroom. In L. Ducate & N. Arnold (Eds.), *Calling on CALL: From theory and research to new directions in foreign language teaching* (pp. 181–209). CALICO Monograph Series 5. San Marco, TX: Computer Assisted Language Consortium.

Abrams, Z. (2019). Interpersonal communication in intracultural CMC. In N. Arnold & L. Ducate (Eds.), *Engaging language learners through CALL* (pp. 267–308). Sheffield, UK: Equinox.

Ara, A., & Magris, C. (2014). *Trieste. Un'Identità di frontiera*. Bologna: Einaudi.

Arnold, N. & Ducate, L. (Eds.). (2019). *Engaging language learners through CALL* (pp. 267–308). Sheffield, UK: Equinox.

Beard, M. (2016). *SPQR. A history of ancient Rome*. New York: Liveright.

Blake, R. (2016). Technology and the four skills. *Language Learning & Technology*, *20*(2), 129–42.

Bustamante, C., et al. (2012). Web 2.0 and language learners: Moving from consumers to creators." In T. Sildus (Ed.), *Touch the world, 2012 report of the Central States Conference on the teaching of foreign languages* (pp. 109–31). Richmond, VA.

Cantarella, E., & Cardini, F. (2010). *I giorni di Milano*. Roma: Laterza.

Compagnoni, I. (2022). Designing digital audio guides for language learning with izi.TRAVEL. *The FLTMAG (online magazine)*. Accessed November 27, 2022. https://fltmag.com/digital-audio-guides-izitravel/

Crowley, R. (2013). *City of fortune. How Venice ruled the sea*. New York: Random House.

Cutshall, S. (2012, April). More than a decade of standards: Integrating "cultures" in your language instruction. *The Language Educator*, 32–37.

Dummett, J. (2015). *Palermo, city of kings*. London: Tauris.

Elola, I., & Oskoz, A. (2017). Writing with 21st century social tools in the L2 classroom: New literacies, genres, and writing practices. *Journal of Second Language Writing, 36*, 52–60.

Elola, I., & Oskoz, A. (2019). Writing between the lines: Acquiring writing skills and digital literacies through social tools. In N. Arnold & L. Ducate (Eds.), *Engaging language learners through CALL* (pp. 240–66). Sheffield, UK: Equinox.

Fabris, L. M. F., Semprebon, G., & Fu, F. (2019). Greenways as a new potential for shrinking cities. The case of Milan (Italy). *Proceedings of the Fábos Conference on Landscape and Greenway Planning, 6*, Article 54, 1–8.

Ferri, A., & Roversi, G. (2005). *Storia di Bologna*. Bologna: Bologna University Press.

Fofi, G. (2009). *Immigrazione meridionale a Torino*. Torino: Aragno.

Guth, S., & Helm, F. (2019). Culture and CALL. In N. Arnold & L. Ducate (Eds.), *Engaging language learners through CALL* (pp. 93–140). Sheffield, UK: Equinox.

Hametz, M. (2005). *Making Trieste Italian 1918–1954*. Rochester, NY: Royal Historical Society.

Hughes, J., & Buongiovanni, C. (2015). *Remembering Parthenope: The reception of classical Naples from antiquity to the present*. Oxford: Oxford University Press.

Kress, G. (2000). Multimodality. In B. Cope & M. Kalantzis (Eds.), *Multiliteracies: Literacy learning and the design of social futures* (pp. 182–202). London: Routledge.

Moe, N. (2004). *Un paradiso abitato da diavoli. Identità nazionale e immagini del Mezzogiorno*. Napoli: L'ancora del Mediterraneo.

Najemy, J. M. (2006). *History of Florence 1200–1575*. London: Wiley-Blackwell.

Oliva, G. (2014). *Storia di Torino*. Torino: Biblioteca dell'immagine.

Pacansky-Brock, M. (2017). *Best practices for teaching with emerging technologies*, New York: Routledge.

Panichella, N. (2014). *Meridionali al Nord: Migrazioni interne e società italiana dal dopoguerra ad oggi*. Bologna: Il Mulino.

Salonia, M. (2017). *Genoa's freedom: Entrepreneurship, republicanism, and the Spanish Atlantic* (pp. 3–27). Lanham: Lexington Books.

Tonelli, G. (2020). La Milano degli Asburgo: "città emporio" sovrana nel commercio internazionale. In R. Cancila (Ed.), *Capitali senza re nella Monarchia spagnola: Identità, relazioni immagini* (pp. 187–204). Palermo: Mediterranea.

Youngs, B. L. (2019). SLA theories and practices in CALL. In N. Arnold & L. Ducate (Eds.), *Engaging language learners through CALL* (pp. 7–50). Sheffield, UK: Equinox.

5

EXPERIENTIAL LEARNING OPPORTUNITIES AND HIGH-IMPACT PRACTICES IN INTERMEDIATE AND ADVANCED ITALIAN LANGUAGE COURSES

Paola Bernardini and Tatiana Selepiuc

In 2020 the sudden switch from in-person to online instruction made promoting the acquisition of language skills as well as the understanding of social and cultural norms more challenging. To avoid merely accommodating the move from in-person to remote instruction, redesigning courses and updating learning outcomes were essential to further bridge the gap between an in-person versus a behind-the-screen classroom experience. As the quick shift to remote delivery of curriculum presented challenges, it simultaneously presented opportunities to include and validate virtual experiential learning (EL) that would otherwise not have been accessible to learners. EL and high-impact practices (HIPs) promote an overall well-rounded and meaningful university experience in person and online and inspire students to "explore cultures, life experiences, and worldviews different from their own" (Kuh, 2008). To inspire high-level exchanges, intermediate and advanced Italian language courses at the University of Toronto Mississauga (UTM) were reframed to focus on high-impact educational practices that were diversity-oriented and globally focused in a virtual environment. This article presents innovative and resourceful EL opportunities inspired by several HIPs and digital humanities (DH) tools, which have elevated the Italian studies (IS) classroom in ways that can continue to be employed, regardless of lecture-delivery mode. It also addresses several outcomes, implications, and possible future directions for blended learning (BL) in upper-level foreign language

(FL) courses in a world where information and communication technologies (ICT) increasingly communicate with each other, and interactivity and interculturality are crucial for the continuity and stability of the ever-changing learning environment.

The disjuncture between Italian beginner classes and the design of intermediate and advanced courses may be measured and understood by the shift from experiential to traditional methodologies, causing a weakening of intercultural focus typically only found in language classes open to the general undergraduate audience. Traditional grammar-based instruction and textbooks—although useful for the development of the four language skills (listening, speaking, reading, and writing)—do not effectively encourage students to become aware of the communicative functions of texts and the cultural practices of reading and writing and, most of all, the power of culturally appropriate communication and intercultural awareness. Moreover, crosslinguistic and cross-cultural comparisons are key for intermediate and advanced learners, strengthen their interlinguistic and intercultural awareness, and nurture their language-learning strategies (Meissner, 2011). To guide programs in the process of transitioning to blended instruction (from traditional or online instruction), documenting the successes and challenges encountered in our teaching and learning experiences at UTM is necessary. This article is divided into three distinct sections: first, a description and breakdown of the intermediate Italian language course, including best practices of teaching FLs with technology and meaningful EL opportunities; second, a description and breakdown of the advanced Italian language course, including impactful models of HIPs and community-based engagement; lastly, a reflection on incorporating a blended approach with an intercultural focus in online and face-to-face (F2F) settings.

THE INTERMEDIATE ITALIAN LANGUAGE EXPERIENCE

Student learning can be influenced by many factors including the technology and media used for delivery and the type of classroom interaction, as documented in much of the learning styles literature that has evolved in cognitive and educational psychology.[1] Academic program and course goals and objectives should drive the pedagogical approaches and technologies used. The intermediate Italian language course at UTM is a mandatory part of the three Italian studies' program paths (Minor, Major, Specialist). The course acts as a sampler of Italian studies, introducing language learning via Italian culture, literature, music, cinema, and so on, and promoting upper-year courses and interdisciplinary and collaborative approaches to learning and research.

In summer 2021, the UTM Global Classroom Initiative ("Building Glocal Learning Communities in Italian Studies") increased EL opportunities for all students of the course. This initiative granted access to strategic professional partnerships that would provide virtual live walking tours in select Italian cities. These virtual experiences were consistent with course material and objectives, proved to be highly impactful for students' intercultural awareness, and presented minimal barriers to access. They meaningfully enhanced content by allowing it to be referenced in lecture material and assessments, which created a more active online learning environment and provided students with authentic input while simultaneously giving them opportunities to produce language (Payne & Ross, 2005; Payne & Whitney, 2002). Technology was effectively used to allow students to interact with native speakers of Italian to better understand facets of the FL culture and develop and strengthen intercultural competences (Darhower, 2006).

Good preparation on the part of the instructors was essential to designing effective connections between courses and (virtual) on-site activities, including being directly involved in the creation of these tours (months before they were scheduled) and selecting impactful and current topics that would not only interest students but also further enhance course learning objectives. Our cross-institutional partnerships, supplementing our language and culture curricula, helped inspire students to synthesize, analyze, and reflect on course material as they experienced it firsthand and enabled students to strengthen their global fluency skills. Two examples of topics covered in the virtual live walking tours are described below.

Italy of the Past

Through the exploration of select medieval and Renaissance cities, such as Florence, Siena, and Bologna, students practiced speaking, writing, and reading about the past while observing and reflecting on the Italian cities in real time. Student agency was respected as students were encouraged to ask questions; request different views of the city or additional information about its architecture, history, culture, and so on; and freely communicate with the on-site virtual tour guides. Students completed a range of directed activities, including content-related questions, research-based projects, and readings of literary excerpts, and engaged in weekly reflective practices, satisfying students' desire to graduate with more diversified portfolios.

North vs. South

Through the exploration of select northern and southern Italian cities, such as Milan and Naples, students investigated and debunked cultural stereotypes and read about the target Italian cities and their regional differences. Students listened to songs in northern and southern dialects, watched movie clips that emphasized various stereotypes between the North and South of Italy, and critically analyzed their virtual live tour observations while engaging in reflective practices to improve their own understanding and make key personal connections. Online discussion forums were also used to build a sense of belonging and class community, facilitate collaboration, and support peer learning by allowing students to see and respond to one another's submissions. For example, students were asked to describe what differences they expected to notice before the Milan and Naples virtual tours, and then confirm or reject their assumptions after the tours. This experience also created space for the review of intermediate aspects of the subjunctive mood.

Outcomes of EL

Following each EL opportunity, students were asked to perform self-assessments and reflect on the virtual experiences in the context of specific learning outcomes (e.g., What did you observe? What were your initial expectations? Has the virtual walking tour affected your perception of Italy? How did the virtual tour relate to coursework?). The following student comments confirm that when students can deliberately identify the purpose, impact, and relevance of any given activity, they more easily take on a reflective mindset and make learning their own:

> Student 1: "The virtual tours offered a candid experience of the sights and sounds characteristic of each Italian city—highlighting regional differences in culture and history. The opportunity of being able to interact with a live tour guide and share our experiences with one another afterwards enriched my learning experience tremendously. As the closest alternative to being there physically, the virtual tours allowed for a more personal experience where I observed subtle details that I wouldn't have fully grasped from simply reading about it. I hope the virtual tours will continue to run for years to come! Overall, the course was well-adapted to a virtual setting, and it inspired in me a lifelong passion for the Italian language and culture."

Student 2: "The virtual tours allowed me to learn about different monuments and Italian culture in greater depth, more than one would reading about it in a textbook. I gained so much knowledge from the tours about diverse Italian traditions, making me become more open to embrace new things. That element of isolation that sometimes comes with online learning was completely removed by having this unique experience. Moreover, touring different Italian cities inspired me to seek more information about the country and motivated me to study and engage with the course's material in order to improve my language skills to hopefully one day become close to fluent."

Thanks to the numerous successful outcomes of the virtual live walking tours, including high student engagement, improved recall of course material, increased critical thinking, a rediscovered sense of class community, and more, this initiative was also implemented in UTM's advanced Italian language course, allowing upper-level students to also reflect on complex cultural differences and analyze nuances of the Italian language by explicitly connecting course material to authentic observations and discoveries of Italian cities.

THE ADVANCED ITALIAN LANGUAGE EXPERIENCE

A variety of online projects were implemented in UTM's advanced Italian language course with real-world experiences and applications. Incorporating authentic EL activities such as book translations, film subtitles, portfolios of language games, and writing original short stories enhanced communicative abilities and writing skills, bridging the gap between theory and practice. These projects derived from real-world sources and were incorporated in advanced-level synchronous and asynchronous Italian courses. In a collaborative setting, these "cultural capsules" promoted the inclusion of the target culture and constituted an amplification of course materials that boosted learners' creativity and critical thinking skills. The sudden switch from in-person to online instruction prompted the reframing of learning outcomes to encourage students to take the lead on experiential approaches and help develop their intercultural awareness.

Through real-world authentic educational experiences, students were exposed to complex grammar concepts and enhanced language skills by exploring different aspects of Italian culture, reading and analyzing Italian texts and films, and conducting interviews through workshops with authors, renowned filmmakers, actors, singers, and other Italian celebrities (such as

Paolo Cognetti, Takohua Ben Mohammed, Francesca Inaudi, Luca Ragazzi, Gustav Hofer, Marina Spada, and Elisa Toffoli). These workshops offered unique opportunities for hands-on learning, and the goal of these tasks was to engage students in critical thinking and application. The interviews, for example, were used as a learning tool of communication as it allowed students to learn new vocabulary and build confidence as they spoke to native speakers in a journalistic setting within the academic environment. Students had the opportunity to explore narration, editing, creative writing, film language, and visual literacy and learn from international best-selling authors and acclaimed filmmakers. Learners engage in intercultural communication in the target language by interacting with native speakers (Darhower, 2006). Students worked on questions for Q&As and completed reflections based on their conversations with guest speakers. Through guidance and mentorship, some students were able to successfully publish their work and interviews in a magazine, experiencing firsthand application of their learning. As Groeger and Schweitzer (2020) state, "Students are motivated and inspired to learn by experiencing the practical relevance of knowledge" (p. 44).

An abundance of research exists on the transition from in-person to online or blended instruction. Despite the initial challenges of implementing new teaching models and methodologies and preparing new course materials with online content and assignments, using interdisciplinary and collaborative approaches benefited both blended and online courses. Bridging the gap between experimental methods and traditional teaching increased students' engagement and collaboration. Providing resources like self-assessments, weekly reflections, class discussions, directed activities, discussion posts, and also course content–related boards, through which students answered each other's questions, increased interlinguistic and intercultural awareness and nurtured authentic language learning strategies. Let's look at some examples of these assessments and cooperative projects.

Writers' Workshops

Students attended several writing workshops delivered by prominent novelists. In their interaction with authors, students were introduced to literary techniques and received frequent feedback that increased their willingness to engage with Italian and explore current events related to the country of study. Formative assessments such as laboratory sessions, in which groups of students explored and analyzed readings in a range of contexts and genres, were also impactful; moreover, through action-based projects, students actively acquired knowledge through experience and were able to identify and reflect on how theories and contexts in the classroom mirror real-world situations. Digital tools in online or blended courses can empower students' acquisition of language skills as well as the understanding of social and cultural norms, as noted in the following student comment:

> Student 3: "What I liked the most about this guest lecture was Paolo Cognetti's advice on exploring writing though short stories rather than trying to take on writing a novel right away. I found that very encouraging and also liberating because it opens many doors. I agree with him that novels are very constricting, and for young writers who want to be successful, it can feel like an insurmountable mountain. I like the flexibility short stories have, there's so much more possibilities when it comes to experimenting and exploring one's own writing. Another thing that I found liberating is his advice to imitate and even copy our favourite authors to practice writing. There is a lot of pressure on trying to be as creative and unique as possible, but that can't be done without experience, which comes from learning from others. It was also encouraging to hear that with more life experience comes more and better writing and writing material."

Book Translations

This project provided training in areas such as terminology, morphosyntactic ability, interpretative translations, learning slang, and idiomatic expressions. Students translated a book from Italian to English—thanks to professional partnerships established with Italian authors. Pre/post translation tests were designed to assess students' skills and increase self-confidence and interaction. In groups, students presented and reported on their work, focusing on key points of their translated chapter and highlighting any problems they encountered in their process of translation. In collaboration with the authors, students analyzed concepts and translation strategies and were able to ask questions on core elements of meaning and textual and historiographical interpretation. At the end of the course, students submitted their final translation that would then be published with their names included.

Film Subtitles

This creative experience inspired students to create attractive and contextually appropriate film subtitles and understand subtitling approaches. Students worked on the semester-long project to create English subtitles for an Italian film on YouTube. Translation is frequently used as a method for assessing students' command of second language capabilities, for the study of grammar rules, "lexical translation rather than contextualization" (Richards & Rodgers, 2001, p. 101). Students were required to analyze film subtitles, paying careful attention to their linguistic and contextual meaning and recognizing code messages, intercultural interpretations, intersemiotic translations, and adaptation to real-life contexts. Through "Group Reports" students provided self-assessments of their learning objectives, sharing original reflections and their own observations on translations of audiovisual materials, major cultural and linguistic issues, linguistic choices, English subtitling in handling culturally specific issues and in conveying messages across cultures, linguistic features, and differences based on different cultures. This project expanded students' research capabilities in different fields of translations, allowing them to learn by applying theory to practice and empowering student agency.

Portfolio of Italian Language Games

This project was an effective method to motivate active learning and let students play a key role in their own experience of FL acquisition. Students created a portfolio of activities with lexical combinations of puzzles, word searches, and riddles that will be used by students of nonlinguistic background through an Italian Grammar Open Textbook. As Marcel Danesi and Anthony Mollica—the creator of *ludolinguistica* (Recreational Linguistics), a pedagogical approach applied to foreign language teaching—outlined: "In the area of second-language teaching, *puzzleological* techniques such as crosswords, word searches, scrambled words, simulations, interactive games, board games, etc. have now become intrinsic components of many approaches, and the choice of many teachers, as formats for students to review and reinforce grammar, vocabulary, and communication skills" (1994, p. 14). In groups students learned to work toward the same goals together, encouraging each other and discussing concepts and strategies needed to complete tasks and solve problems. Within a cooperative learning environment students strengthened leadership and decision-making skills.

Using capstone projects and implementing an inclusive cooperative learning environment allow for hands-on experiences that promote student agency and encourage reflective practices.

BL AND COMMUNITY COLLABORATION IN THE DEPARTMENT OF LS AT UTM

The intermediate and advanced Italian language courses at UTM both actively continue to nurture global perspectives and intercultural awareness. After overcoming initial perplexities related to online teaching and a complicated transition period in our intermediate and advanced Italian language courses at UTM, it is evident that BL has become a popular (and necessary) model of instruction. It must nonetheless encourage students to take the lead on experiential approaches and investigate Italian through a variety of blended activities even in upper-level language courses. BL can shape the combination of in-class and online discussions, directed activities, interactive simulations, and a variety of assessments that engage, instruct, and assess student learning. Online and blended instruction improved learning outcomes in our experiences and unveiled future opportunities as a framework for developing projects to promote collaborative learning environments and opportunities for virtual EL. Our classroom experiences have undoubtedly unveiled significant advantages of BL. We continue to support BL at the Department of Language Studies (LS) at UTM as it has proven to be effective for the continuity and stability of the ever-changing learning environment and an impactful way for students to approach FL acquisition with minimal barriers to access.

Providing students with opportunities to examine issues of different cultures, strengthen their interdisciplinary global lens, and interpret our interconnected world is a key part of UTM's academic plan to better prepare students to live, work, and succeed in a culturally diverse and global-minded society. The Department of LS at UTM offers a Certificate in Global Perspectives that (a) encourages the examination of issues from different cultural, economic, and socio-political perspectives, and (b) provides an interdisciplinary or disciplinary lens through which to interpret and evaluate our interconnected world.[2] Moreover, UTM's Summer Abroad program (Woodsworth College) and the Explore program have both enjoyed strong appeal from UTM LS students in the last few years. Our curriculum currently offers in-person, online, and blended language courses that cover all periods of literature, major aspects of the Italian language, recent research in teaching and learning Italian as a second language, and significant expressions of Italian culture such as its theater, cinema, and lively contemporary civilization. The ethnic and cultural diversity of the students enrolled in our LS department is contemplated in the Italian Minor, Major, Specialist programs.

Over the years, Italian studies at UTM has been engaged in many community initiatives designed to foster a better understanding and appreciation of Italian language and culture. Italian theater, first introduced as an extracurricular activity at UTM in collaboration with the Maschere Duemondi theater troupe in 1986–87, became a student-centered as opposed to teacher-centered tri-dimensional (literary, linguistic, and performative) course in 1992–93 (Bancheri, 2008). Students take charge of their own learning by analyzing literary artifacts and texts, translating and communicating their message, collaborating with professionals and artists of the Italian community, and performing the plays in front of real audiences. In March 2022, the Italian theater course was offered as a blended course for the first time, combining F2F and online instruction. The online setting, which replaced a portion of F2F time, allowed students to develop intercultural competence by interacting with native speakers of the Italian community, enhanced motivation, and supported different learning styles. Before rehearsals and the recording of the final performance of *Le vedove scaltre* (an adaptation of Carlo Goldoni's *La vedova scaltra* [1748]), students were able to conduct interviews and attend workshops with actors and theater scholars during their theatrical production experience. For example, in October 2021 students participated in a workshop with Michela Mocchiutti[3] (Accademia Carlo Goldoni and La Biennale Educational in Venice) and actor Giorgio Bertan,[4] focusing on the importance of masks in the theater, theatrical language (i.e., rhythm, intonation, repetition), set design, costumes, and character interpretation. This impactful experience was described by one of the students:

> Student 4: "The virtual lecture with industry professional Michela Mocchiutti was a truly engaging and impactful experience. Right from the beginning of the talk, the exhibition of the masks of Pantalone and Arlecchino was of particular interest given their essentiality for their respective characters. Her description of these masks as tools and representations of the character was quite interesting. Furthermore, when Giorgio Bertan described the mask as an extension of a person following many years of acting in a particular role was a noteworthy sentiment. Her description of the strength of the female characters, particularly Rosaura and Marionette within this drama, along with the use of varied speech assisted in further contextualizing the drama's main themes. Michela's personal experience within this field was of immeasurable contribution as it provided practical knowledge that can be utilized for the 'Maschere Duemondi' adaptation. She noted that it was not always easy to act in these roles as they require plenty in order to

successfully interpret them. Moreover, she described how it is often necessary to use the language of the people, dialects, or even other languages (in the case of this drama) to deliver a true performance. Her advice in the areas of stage presence (i.e., rhythm, intonation, repetition), set design, costumes, and characterization were also impactful. They assisted in detailing the acting conventions and on a personal level it assisted in the early formulation of ideas surrounding production techniques along with theatrical innovations that can be incorporated into this version of 'La vedova scaltra.'"

Moreover, in November 2021 students interviewed Italian actress (and protagonist of Goldoni's play) Francesca Inaudi, who shared experiences and expertise on how to better connect with theatrical characters in a performance setting. Knowledge application (performance) and self-evaluation go beyond knowledge acquisition, and assessments that focus on FL exposure in a multitude of real-life and authentic tasks (from translations to community business letters to experiential interactions with actors and scholars of theater) have evidently produced positive student feedback.

Embedding community collaboration into an FL course creates space for spontaneous and exploratory work outside of the educational setting, emphasizing the valuable learning that arises from experiences beyond the four walls of a classroom or the screen. The four components of Kolb's (1984) EL—experiencing, reflecting, thinking, and acting—strengthen with each experience.[5]

NOTES

1. Anthony G. Picciano's multimodal model "recognizes that because learners represent different generations, different personality types, and different learning styles, teachers and instructional designers should seek to use multiple approaches including face-to-face methods and online technologies that meet the needs of a wide spectrum of students" (2009, p. 7).
2. This proposal is part of a tri-campus initiative (University of Toronto [UofT] Global U Framework) aimed at developing globally minded citizens across disciplines to create a series of new academic certificates that aligns with their expertise and academic priorities. See https://utm.calendar.utoronto.ca/program/ercer2019. In addition, the University of Toronto Scarborough (UTSC) recently added a new academic unit called the Department of Global Development Studies (DGDS). Thanks to increased enrollment in the Certificate in Global

Development, Environment, and Health, the development of an undergraduate Tri-Campus (St. George, Mississauga, Scarborough) Minor program in Global Leadership at UTSC was approved.
3. Michela Mocchiutti is an actress, speaker, professor of theatrical techniques at the Accademia Carlo Goldoni—Teatro Stabile del Veneto, and acting coach at La Biennale Educational in Venice. She trained at the Civica Accademia d'Arte Drammatica "Nico Pepe" in Udine, the Teatro Stabile del Veneto, and in physical theaters in Italy and abroad. Since 1993 she has been equally well accomplished in theater, movie, and television acting.
4. Giorgio Bertan is an Italian actor and theater director. He has specialized in Commedia dell'Arte techniques for decades, working with important teachers like Giovanni Poli (director and founder of the Ca' Foscari University theater in Venice), Pavel Rouba (pantomime), Bob Roboth, and Nelly Quette. Bertan reinvented the character of Capitan Spaventa, staging shows throughout Europe. He teaches theatre and performance and hosts workshops on Commedia dell'Arte masks.
5. "Place-based learning is one of several experiential approaches to learning that is guided by certain principles including: promoting hands-on learning, using a problem-solving process, addressing real world problems, encouraging student interaction with each other and the content, engaging in direct experiences, and using multiple subjects to enhance interdisciplinary learning" (Wurdinger, 2017, p. 38).

BIBLIOGRAPHY

Bancheri, S. (2008). The theatrical workshop in the Italian curriculum. In N. Marini-Maio & C. Ryan-Scheutz (Eds.), *Set the stage! Teaching Italian through theater* (pp. 83–113). New Haven: Yale University Press.

Danesi, M., & Mollica, A. (1994, Winter). Games and puzzles in the second-language classroom: A second look. *Mosaic*, *2*(2), 14–22.

Darhower, M. (2006). Where's the community?: Bilingual internet chat and the "fifth C" of the national standards. *Hispania*, 84–98.

Groeger, L., & Schweitzer, J. (2020). Developing a design thinking mindset: Encouraging designerly ways in postgraduate business education. *Design Thinking in Higher Education*, 41–72.

Kolb, D. A. (1984). *Experiential learning: Experience as a source of learning and development*. Upper Saddle River, NJ: Prentice-Hall.

Kuh, G. D. (2008). *High-impact educational practices: What they are, who has access to them, and why they matter*. Washington, DC: Association of American Colleges and Universities.

Meissner, F. J. (2011). Teaching and learning intercomprehension: A way to plurilingualism and learner autonomy. In I. De Florio-Hansen (Ed.), *Towards multilingualism and the inclusion of cultural diversity* (pp. 38–58). Kassel, Germany: Kassel University Press.

Payne, J. S., & Ross, B. M. (2005). Synchronous CMC, working memory, and L2 oral proficiency development. *Language Learning & Technology*, *9*(3), 35–54.

Payne, J. S., & Whitney, P. J. (2002). Developing L2 oral proficiency through synchronous CMC: Output, working memory, and interlanguage development. *CALICO Journal*, *20*(1), 7–32.

Picciano, A. (2009). Blending with purpose: The multimodal model. *Journal of Asynchronous Learning Networks*, *13*(1), 7–18.

Richards, J. C., & Rodgers, T. S. (2001). *Approaches and methods in language teaching* (2nd ed.). Cambridge: Cambridge University Press.

Wurdinger, S. D. (2017). Turning your place into projects. In D. Shannon & J. Galle (Eds.), *Interdisciplinary approaches to pedagogy and place-based education* (pp. 37–53). Cham, Switzerland: Palgrave Macmillan.

6

RE-VISIONING THE LINGUISTICS LANDSCAPE THROUGH A MULTILITERACIES FRAMEWORK

Authorizing Learners' Personal Semiotics in a Glocal Space

Barbara Spinelli

The mobility processes enabled by globalization have intensified the interconnectedness of communication, information, ideas, and human relationships at the international, national, and local level. In such a complex environment, individuals become members of diverse, adaptive, and accessible communities that may be crucial for their identity formation and life goals. Despite globalization, local settings embed unique and diverse ideologies, practices, and events, although their "local uniqueness" is, in turn, already a product of wider contacts (Mannion, 2015). Consequently, there may be tension between people's participation in these global, local, and overlapping communities.

Globalization invites language educators and teachers to be concerned about and to reflect upon these changes that affect our ways of thinking, learning, and knowing, as "language and language education are at the forefront of those concerns" (Kramsch, 2014, p. 297).

Language education, therefore, needs to take into consideration the effects of such global and local processes on language learners' motivation, investment, and sense of identity (Kanno & Norton, 2003; Norton & Toohey, 2011; Pavlenko & Norton, 2007) and to empower their literacy skills by integrating social interaction, multiple forms of knowledge, and strategies in order to deal with this challenging world (Cope & Gollings, 2001; Kress, 2003; New London Group [NLG], 1996, 2000).

This chapter discusses how these global and local interrelations can be explored by second language (L2)/third language (L3)/any additional language (Ln) Italian language learners through the ways in which they imagine, perceive, and live their multicultural urban space and how these personal interpretations involve learners' unique social, intellectual, and affective capital.

GLOCAL AND MULTILITERACIES APPROACH TO LANGUAGE EDUCATION

In higher education, there has been a growing interest in how global concerns and concepts, such as global citizenship, impact educational policy and programs (Rizvi & Lingar, 2009). As Mannion (2015) points out, researchers are also drawing their attention to the implementation of glocalization theory in teaching and learning, including language and online learning (Coupland, 2010; Joseph & Ramani, 2012; Lusianov, 2020).

The term *glocalization* was first coined by Robertson (1994) with the aim of indicating the tension between global and local forces, previously mentioned. Glocalization, therefore, "helps us capture the idea that the local is always with, through and within the global" (Mannion, 2015, p. 4). Glocal approaches to teaching and learning are, therefore, concerned with ways in which local and global issues are connected and how relevant their interrelation is to learners' identity and life. These approaches focus on the "local" as a meaningful place in which global forces take shape and where learners can encounter and deal with difference. Hence, learners' educational experience is based on situated places that afford their response, negotiation, and meaning making. This symbolic process of meaning-making can be seen as a "third culture space" (Kramsch, 2011) in which learners can reconcile their multiple sense of belonging and diverse cultural worldviews, avoiding "either/or" solutions. Learners' engagement with the environment and the creative act of construction of meaning are also values of a pedagogy of Multiliteracies (Cope & Kalantzis, 2008, 2009; Menke & Paesani, 2021; NLG, 1996, 2000; Menke & Paesani, 2021), which shares the following keywords for educational objectives with glocally oriented pedagogies: variability, agency, subjectivity, creativity, and hybridity. Multiliteracies is a way to focus on and deal with the complex world that learners need to read critically and diversely. While interacting with local diversity and global connectedness, linguistic and cultural differences, multiple communication patterns, and diverse communities, learners need to become "active designer(s) of meaning" (Cope & Kalantzis, 2009, p. 177). Designing is an act that allows learners to use multiple resources and modes of meaning-making (Available Designs)—linguistic mode, visual mode, audio mode, gestural mode, spatial mode—they can find in their contexts and cultures and to creatively combine them (the Redesigned) in order to express their own voice and their own understanding of the world. This dynamic process of representation and play of subjectivities and meanings underpins the pedagogical project described in this chapter.

IMAGINED COMMUNITIES AND L2/L3/LN IDENTITIES

In lifelong learning experiences, individuals become members of diverse communities that may affect their identity. According to Wenger (2000), the sense of belonging to a community can take different forms of participation from the local to the global level. This participation occurs through three modes: (1) "engagement" or direct involvement with the community; (2) "imagination," namely through affective and emotional connections; and (3) "alignment," which represents the way in which individuals organize their interpretations and actions to develop their sense of belonging to a community. In the global world, the imagination mode of participation is particularly relevant because the mobility of images, ideas, and information transcends national borders, reaching a larger number of people (Appadurai, 1997). This imaginary connection is even more meaningful for language learners who may have limited opportunities for immediate engagement with the L2/L3/Ln culture. They may access the L2/L3/Ln imagined communities,[1] which consist of "groups of people not immediately tangible" (Kanno & Norton, 2003, p. 241), through the power of their imagination. The affective and emotional involvement with these communities may affect the way in which language learners invest their symbolic, cultural, and linguistic capital in their learning process (Norton & Toohey, 2011; Pavlenko & Norton, 2007). In this respect, imagination "can become the fuel for actions" (Appadurai, 1996, p. 7), instead of an escape from a complex living context. It allows individuals to expand upon their views of the world and their selves because their "identity is not only locally defined" (Wenger, 2000, p. 240). In multicultural settings, the interplay between the imaginative connection and the global/imagined community as well as the direct engagement with cultural localities may provide significant opportunities for language learners' identity construction.

LINGUISTIC/SEMIOTIC LANDSCAPE AND PERSONAL NARRATIONS OF PLACE

Global mobility, as stated previously, is a pivotal factor in defining the multiple lives of multilingual, multicultural, multiracial local places (Hall, 2009). These places are themselves "mobile" (Stroud & Jegels, 2014, p. 180), that is, they change shape and architectural configuration through time. Furthermore, fluxes of people (e.g., migration flows) affect the cultural and linguistic setting of the site and its situated social interrelations. This dynamic and transitory nature of place affects the postmodern concept of space. In fact, the latter is no longer viewed as static and passive background, but rather an arena of struggling human actions that shapes individuals' beliefs, values, and principles (Knott, 2005: Lefebvre, 1974; Soja, 1989). In this respect, referring to Lefebvre's spatial theory (1974), Malinowski (2015) points out how spatial understanding is crucial to language learning, as the latter is "not just a social practice, but a spatial practice" (p. 100); in other words language learning entails a holistic—physical, social, and mental—interpretation of space. Spatial understanding becomes a relevant component for glocally oriented approaches to language teaching and its focus on how global forces shape locality.

The complex cultural narrative of a local place is de facto observable in the complexity and multilayered meanings of its linguistic and semiotic landscape. Therefore, location and territory are not only where everyday actions occur, but they are also "sites of engagement" (Jones, 2010, p. 152) and "settings" for investigation (Hall, 2009, p. 572). Urban public signage, shops, restaurants, street names (Gorter, 2013; Malinowski, 2008; Shohamy et al., 2010), as well as buildings, statues, towers, and gardens (Jaworski & Thurlow, 2010; Lawson, 2001) become semiotic objects for individuals' spatial narration. As mentioned, this narration involves different systems of discourse: (1) the way in which individuals interact with their environment, which is affected by their unique memories, experiences, and subjectivities; (2) the analysis of how the located visual, verbal, aural, gestural communication modalities interplay; (3) the observation of the relationship between the semiotic objects (e.g., statues) and their placing in the urban environment (Scollon & Scollon, 2003). In light of the above considerations, exploring different modalities and practices through which these semiotic artifacts are embodied and creatively incorporated in personal narratives may become a crucial experience for language learners.

THE PEDAGOGICAL PROJECT

The main goal of the classroom project was to enable university students to explore interlinkages between their participation in a larger and global community called "Italicity" (Bassetti, 2003) as L2/L3/Ln learners of Italian, and in the local urban communities of New York as people living in the city. New York historically represents a trans-local space of flows and a dynamic and mobile multilingual urban environment; therefore, it offers a pivotal setting for students' engagement and investigation. Based on their understanding of the relationship between the above global and local communities, students were asked to develop their unique cultural script[2] (Goddard & Wierzbicka, 2004) and to represent it through a multimodal approach using multimedia software (e.g., PowerPoint, Prezi, Story Maps, Emaze).

Participants and Settings

The total number of students involved in the project was 29. All were third-year students of an Italian Intermediate Conversation II course offered in a university in New York. Students were undergraduate and graduate students between the ages of 18 and 27. Although the majority of them were American (20)—among whom 6 were Italian heritage language students—there were also 6 international students (4 from France, 1 from China, and 1 from Albania) and 3 Latin American students. The Italian Intermediate Conversation II class is particularly focused on the development of oral and pluricultural skills. It meets two days a week for fourteen weeks and lasts one hour and fifteen minutes. Topics and learning objectives of the course have been identified respectively using the Common European Framework of Reference[3] (CEFR) (Council of Europe, 2001, 2020) and the Framework of Reference for Pluralistic Approaches (FREPA)[4] (Candelier et al., 2012). The student-led project was developed as the major oral exam for the course and was presented during the eleventh week of class.

Instructional Design Model and Sequencing

The discursive and symbolic nature of the interaction between learners' personal life experiences and the multilingual and multicultural urban communities calls for a dynamic pedagogical model, such as the Multiliteracies framework proposed by the NLG (1996) and revised by Cope and Kalantzis (2005, 2009). This model is "characteristically transformative" because it is based "on [the]

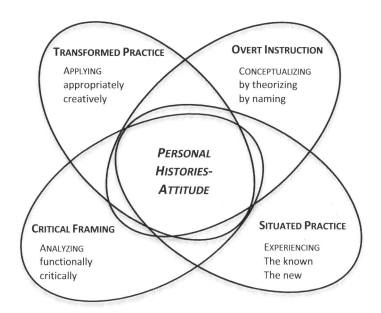

FIGURE 6.1. Pedagogical sequences of the project.

notion of design and meaning-as-transformation" (Cope & Kalantzis, 2009, p. 184), described previously in this chapter. As stated earlier, this dynamic process focuses on learners' agency in meaning-making construction and embodies cultural context-specific analysis. Through "Learning by Design," learners can develop strategies to critically read and re-read the new and unfamiliar through their own experiences and, consequently, add something of themselves to the new meanings. This design-based framework promotes a holistic approach to learning. It engages individuals as "whole persons" in their learning process, and thus integrates rather than compartmentalizes the multidimensional aspects of their existence (Spinelli, 2018, 2020). The Multiliteracies model (Cope & Kalantzis, 2009; NLG, 1996), de facto, involves four modes of learning: (1) Overt Instruction (conceptualizing); (2) Situated Practice (experiencing); (3) Critical Framing (analyzing); and (4) Transformed Practice (applying). These four components of the learning process are dynamically interconnected, and although these sequences represent the underlying pedagogical cycle of this project, learners were able to find their own alternative learning pathways (e.g., moving backward and forward between modes) according to their analytical perspective and modalities of meaning making. Figure 6.1 summarizes the pedagogical sequences of the project.

Overt Instruction involves explicit learning and the process of "conceptualizing." During this phase, by means of multimedia materials in English and in Italian (e.g., excerpts from scientific papers, books, Wikipedia, and video such as online tutorials and interviews), the teacher engaged students in a discussion to move them progressively toward a stronger understanding of the theoretical and conceptual framework that underpinned the project. Students were able to familiarize themselves with concepts and theories (i.e., "Imagined Community," "Italicity," "Cultural Script," "Linguistic/Semiotic Landscape," "Glocal Theory"), seeking links between them in order to understand the Design and "naming" and putting these key terms together into interpretative frameworks needed to develop their project.

Situated Practice involves experiential learning. According to Cope and Kalantzis (2005, p. 75), "experiencing" enables students to connect theory/knowledge and practice/action through immersion in the real and everyday world that is, in this case, their surrounding multicultural setting. Scaffolding outlines were provided to help students reflect on their own experiences and interests (the known) in order to find their subjective reading key to explore how specific global values of Italicity are shaped, negotiated, and contrasted in their local living space (the new), as well as identify which component of the urbanscape would be their unit of observation (e.g., street signs, graffiti, images, statues, buildings, gardens, etc.). Students were able to access multiple resources (available Designs) to collect their data. This collection took place in both the physical (e.g., walking tour, on-site pictures, fieldwork interviews, local government policies, and real estate ads) and virtual (e.g., Google Maps, YouTube, websites, online libraries, etc.) space, taking into consideration that the internet and mobile technology change spatiality and the ways in which the physical world can be interpreted (Liang & Huang, 2009) or experienced (Jones, 2010). The use of these multiple resources also allowed students to avoid the restricted one-sidedness of text interpretation (Jarowski & Thurlow, 2010; Malinowski, 2008; Shohamy & Gorter, 2008).

Critical Framing entails learning to enhance critical thinking skills and involves the process of "analyzing." In this phase, students explored intersemiotic interrelations between their data (images, interviews, leaflets, graffiti, funeral notices, online information, etc.)—what Cope and Kalantzis (2005) define as "analyzing functionally." This process of Designing involved the organization and categorization of collected materials through the conceptual framework identified during the first phase of the project. At this stage, students also critically analyzed the relationship between their known and new experiences and recontextualized the collected materials according to their unique individual perspective and new emerging meanings—analyzing critically.

Transformed Practice involves transformative learning and includes two processes that represent the outcome of the previous designing: "applying appropriately" and "applying creatively." The former entails students' capacity to apply the new learning to the real world, and the latter allows learners to creatively establish connections and represent the world in a new way according to their personal histories, memories, and interests. During this phase, students developed their own cultural script by innovatively combining their data in their own narration and creating unique semiotic artifacts through a multimodal pattern of representation (linguistic, visual, audio, etc.), using multimedia software (PowerPoint, Prezi, Emaze, etc.). In other words, they transformed the Available Designs of meaning in their Redesigned distinctive product. In this sense, transformative learning is crucial for identity construction and brings about changes in understanding the self, system of beliefs, and behaviors. It is, therefore, of the utmost importance to encourage students to develop a meta-reflection on this transformative process and experience. To this end, students were asked to complete a self-awareness questionnaire after the presentation of their project. This questionnaire was divided into two sections: the first consisted of open-ended questions to encourage students to reflect and collect qualitative feedback on the general effectiveness and outcomes of the project, and the second includes a self-evaluation based on a selection of the FREPA transcultural descriptors to gather quantitative data. These descriptors—divided into the three main categories of competence, skills, and attitude—enabled students to focus on the impact that the learning experience had on their knowledge system, mediation and negotiation abilities, and identity formation.

The Conceptual Framework: Italicity and Italic Community

The earlier discussion of glocalization and language learning highlighted the role of imagination in learners' sense of belonging and aspiration to be members of larger communities, and how that may challenge them to reconcile the values associated with the global culture and local values. This is the reason why Bassetti's transnational theory (2003), known as "Italicity," was adopted as the basic analytical and exploratory tool of the conceptual framework of this project to develop learners' individual investigation.

Bassetti defines the concept of "Italic people," which he distinguishes from "Italian people," not as an ethnic, linguistic, legal, or institutional sense of belonging as Italian citizens, but rather as a sense of membership in a more global and "widest cultural sense" (Bassetti, 2003, p. 13). Italicity, therefore, involves an extensive group of peoples who "feel Italic" as they share values and interests most commonly connected to Italian culture, which they came in contact with due to the global mobility of goods (e.g., "Made in Italy" products), information (e.g., through communications technology and cinematic and visual arts), and people. De facto, behind the concept of Italicity as an Imagined Community, there are many centuries of transnational mobility of Italian migrants, particularly in America, a group that has developed interconnections across the world. As stated earlier, this mobility has been intensified through global communications networks and processes and multiplied the potential encounters between people and "Italic" values. In this respect, Italicity "differs from and goes beyond the sense of being Italian in the more traditional national terms" (Bassetti, 2003, p. 19).

Consequently, Italicity membership includes not only third- or fourth-generation Italian migrants but also a larger number of people who belong to the same "community of feeling" (Bassetti, 2003, p. 19), who can imagine and extend their life models to those practiced by "others," such as L2/L3/Ln Italian language learners. These models and practices entail values such as: (1) the acceptance of difference due to the long Italian history of coexisting local identities and the short experience as a nation state; (2) the central role of family and social relationships in everyday life originating in Roman Catholic values; (3) the sense of aesthetics and beauty (from food to fashion, design, and art); and (4) the creative work that is grounded in centuries-long artisan traditions. Bassetti (2003) states that he is perfectly aware that all these positive values may have or have had a negative side (e.g., creativity at work may also imply a lack of organization), but he adds that this positive emphasis was necessary to reconcile them with negative stereotypes that have been associated with Italian migration throughout the world for a long time.

This theory, even though mainly related to business and marketing principles, is particularly interesting for educational purposes. As a matter of fact, Italicity focuses on the "multiplicity of belonging," a concept that views identity as a fluctuating process rather than as a product by emphasizing the central role that these values play on the construction of people's identity. Consequently, this conceptual framework may enable students to reflect on this multiple level of interpretation of glocal spaces, providing opportunities to develop their "third cultural space."

Additionally, since the Italic Imagined Community is by nature dynamic, it fits with the design and goals of the project described in this chapter. Bassetti (2003) himself suggests that Italicity "is a great resource to be used to tackle the challenges of the global world" (p. 21). Therefore, within the adaptive multiscapes of New York City, it provided the departure point for students' narrative trajectories to describe compatibilities or conflicts between such "community of feeling" main values and everyday local life.

DISCUSSION

In this section, students' individual itineraries will be discussed,[5] drawing on a selection of their personal semiotic artifacts and considering their unit of observation and subjective conceptual framework. In this analysis, the focus is also on practices and mechanisms behind the meaning-making of place and how personal histories are incorporated into students' narrations.

Then, in order to explore students' understanding and perceptions of the project, additional data collected through the students' self-awareness questionnaire (i.e., post-project survey) mentioned previously will be analyzed.

Illustration and Analysis of Students' Cultural Scripts

The project of an international student of economics coming from a university in Lyon, France, focused on the nature of commercial solicitation and sales practices adopted by waiters standing outside Italian restaurants along Mulberry Street in Little Italy. His attention to this particular aspect was linked to the memory of his first visit in this neighborhood during which he was particularly struck by the waiters' commercial practices in the street. These practices reminded him of the presentation of an Italian colleague in his economics class at his university in France. In this presentation, the Italian colleague provided the example of an Italian vendor's commercial practices in an Italian market as the best commercial procedures producing the most desirable results (see Figure 6.2).

The student linked this information to his general knowledge about the centuries-long Italian history of "mercantile experiences of travelling around the world," as also described by the Italicity theory (Bassetti, 2003, p. 21). The relationship between this global knowledge and its possible local implementation in Little Italy represented the rationale behind the student's Designing. Through Google Maps (Available Design), he identified the Italian restaurants on three blocks of Mulberry Street where he would focus his investigation. He analyzed his data collected by means of on-site pictures and individual field interviews with 18 waiters (Available Designs), finding that only 3 out of 18 waiters were Italian while the others were from Albania, Colombia, Russia, Turkey, Ukraine, and the United States. He also found

FIGURE 6.2. Student's view of commercial solicitation practices (Italian market and Little Italy).

that only 4 out of 18 spoke Italian (3 Italians and 1 Albanian). The other 14 waiters used the same memorized chunks of language without, in fact, having any knowledge of Italian language and culture.

The process of global and transnational mobility affects the distribution of human activities in space, and zones of social life may offer affordances, some of which are compatible, overlapping, or conflictual. These places may become highly "contested spaces" (Pavlenko, 2008, p. 1) like, for instance, Little Italy, where an increasing influx of Chinese migrants in the late seventies extended the boundaries of Chinatown and dramatically contracted the Italian American population living in the area. The student provided an example of this impact by using Google Maps to show the proliferation and compression of Italian restaurants in a reduced space (28 restaurants only on Mulberry Street). According to the student's view, the resulting competition affected and changed local commercial practices, ritual, and discourses. In these terms, this is an example of "urban regeneration and redevelopment" (Jaworski & Thurlow, 2010, p. 31) that brings about an acceleration of the consumption of services. The student noticed that these commercial rituals lose their original cultural value due to the circulation of tourist capital, increased by globalization. In other words, the answers of the interviewed waiters show that their commercial practices are tailored to the Italian Imagined community of consumers, giving them the impression that they are receiving an "authentic" experience, while waiters are only concerned with endorsing local ecological sustainability. Therefore, due to the overlapping and competing communities, the "local is performed for the mass audience" of tourists (Coupland, 2010, p. 3) and texts, as commercial discourses and practices "becomes commodified [. . .] and consumed by the gaze of the international tourists" (Jaworski & Thurlow, 2010, p. 32). In these terms, this place turns into a "non-place" (Augé, 1995), that is, a space of standard where the local historical identity is reduced to a stereotype for touristic attraction (the Redesigned).

A Latin American art history student at the university in New York decided to analyze how some Italic values are conveyed and take shape through street art in the multicultural neighborhood of Little Italy (Designing). In particular, this student was impressed by a project she found surfing on the web (Available Design), which had been developed through the collaboration of two organizations: the Little Italy Merchant Association (LIMA), whose mission is to preserve and promote the Italian culture in that area, and the Little Italy Street Art Association (LISA), a group of American artists who aim to create mural arts in order to encourage New Yorkers, tourists, and all people interested in art to visit, or rather "re-visit" Little Italy. The student explained that the main aim of this collaborative project was to endorse the sustainable development of the neighborhood, particularly on Mulberry Street, re-presenting Italian cultural values through new forms of visual representations. First, in order to deeply understand the multilayered cultural

FIGURE 6.3. Student's view of *Mona Lisa if painted by Leonardo's Kids*.

history of the place, the student gathered information through newspaper articles, essay excerpts, and written interviews of neighborhood residents (Available Designs). She explored the history of different migrations in Little Italy starting from the second half of the nineteenth century and studied the relationships between the Italian American community and other local communities. Second, through an on-site walking tour, she collected data (i.e., pictures); afterward, she read further information (Available Designs) online about the aforementioned collaborative project. She analyzed how this "space is now narrated" (Pennycook, 2010, p. 137) through these murals, as they are an integral part of Little Italy's urban landscape. The first mural she analyzed was titled *Mona Lisa if painted by Leonardo's Kids* and represented a modern re-visitation of the painting as seen through the eyes of a new generation with subtle references to Japanese cartoon figures (see Figure 6.3).

According to the student, this modern interpretation of the *Mona Lisa* in this specific collocation has a twofold meaning—it does not only recall the collective aesthetic imaginary of the inhabitants or visitors but it also represents an action of reappropriation of the space. Therefore, time, location, and authorship of visual representation (e.g., murals in this context) are of relevant importance for its interpretation because they give "a new meaning to the space where it occurs" (Jaworski & Thurlow, 2010, p. 32). In these terms, the

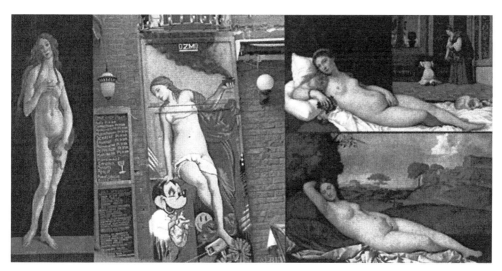

FIGURE 6.4. Student's view of *Lisa the Half Naked Princess*.

urban landscape is viewed as "a constructed space written" through a claiming semiotics rather than "an artist's blank canvas" (Pennycook, 2009, p. 308). Therefore, aside from producing standardized practices as mentioned above, global forces may also provide opportunities for communities to define who they are and endorse their identities through cultural aspects that the community believes worthy of reproduction—in this case, the "Italy of art" as defined by the Italicity theory (Bassetti, 2003, p. 21), a sort of "reconciliation" with the Italic value of sense of beauty. This aspect emerges from another mural on which the student focused her attention called *Lisa the Half Naked Princess*. The student noticed that this mural also clearly recalled the aesthetic beauty of Renaissance figurative art as shown in her personal semiotic narration (see Figure 6.4).

However, she also observed this "italic quotation" is embedded in a hybrid representation that symbolically includes iconic references of American culture (i.e., Minnie Mouse; emoticons; blue, red, and white background). Consequently, in both murals she saw a link between the past and the present (i.e., past and modern Little Italy), and between the use of a global language (i.e., cult images coming from different cultures such as Italian, Japanese, American references) and its local performance (i.e., to endorse the local voice). In particular, she realized how these visual representations mirror the "multiple sense of belonging" described by the Italicity theory, and how they can represent a hybrid and creative response to potential tension between overlapping communities (the Redesigned). On the one hand, Little Italy murals express and assert the local Italian population's voice. On the other hand, the latter is embedded in a global representation that visually depicts the interpermeability of a multilayered living space.

An American student decided to go back to the Italian neighborhood of Carroll Gardens Historic District in Brooklyn, New York, where he had lived for a period of time. His goal was to explore the borough through a different lens using the Italicity conceptual framework. The student was particularly interested in examining the impact that gentrification processes starting in the 1960s had on this neighborhood and how these processes affected local social practices and the urbanscape (Designing). In order to better understand the history of the neighborhood, he referred to the *New York City Encyclopedia* and read *New York Times* articles (Available Designs). He explained that Carroll Gardens was originally part of a working-class neighborhood that became a contested space between Italian and Irish immigrants in the late nineteenth century. In the 1960s, several middle-class professionals moved to this area because of the more affordable rents in comparison to Manhattan. The neighborhood was renamed Carroll Gardens Historic District to draw attention to the gardens in front of the brownstone houses of the area in order to emphasize the more attractive "profile" that the place was acquiring through gentrification. According to the student's observation, these gardens may reflect the multiple dimensions of the local community. As a matter of fact, gardens "act as texts that can be explored to gain insight into historical and current relationships with the land" (Trifonas, 2015, p. 11). They not only mirror individuals' interaction with the soil, flowers, and plants, but they also provide information on the communities and societies that created them (Jagger, 2015). According to the human uses, the garden can be interpreted differently such as a space for food or aesthetic experience, or for encouraging activity and nurturing the spirit (e.g., the use of monastic gardens for contemplative proposes) (Jagger, 2015). The student explained that the gardens he observed reflect this latter use, recalling Roman Catholic values through the use of religious figures such as the Virgin Mary. Devotional statues and law shrines have, in fact, become popular in New York through their use by Catholic immigrants and their descendants, surviving even after their owners die or move away (Sciorra, 2015). The student also noticed that this type of garden differs from others found alongside that are embellished with more laic ornaments used for entertainment purposes (see Figure 6.5), potentially reflecting different values in the local multilayered community.

The process of gentrification also attracted global companies that opened their stores in this area, including Dunkin' Donuts, where the student liked to

FIGURE 6.5. Student's view of gardens in the Carroll Gardens District.

FIGURE 6.6. Dunkin' Donuts in the Carroll Gardens District.

spend time. He realized that this coffeehouse may be considered an example of co-adaptive practices due to the old original architecture of the building where the shop was located (see Figure 6.6).

This building has a garden with a trellis and religious figures and ornaments—likely indicative of a previous Italian cafe or restaurant—where clients can consume their beverages and food at outdoor tables. The tendency of global chains is to offer homologated and standardized services, and consequently to produce highly predicable, routine, and repetitive practices (Ritzer, 2015) (e.g., staying in line, choosing the number of food, etc.) like most of the Dunkin' Donuts stores. In this case, therefore, the context-sensitive localization and the local culture work in opposition to the mechanisms of globalized systems and to the "one size fits all" homogenization experience (Skutnabb-Kangas & Phillipson, 2010, p. 91).

The student concluded that although he had known that the neighborhood had Italian origins, he had never considered it before so thoughtfully. As a result of this experience, he became aware of how social and economic reconfiguration of a place may impact spatial human practices and the reconceptualization of the space itself (the Redesigned).

As seen so far, students' cultural scripts mainly focused on tension patterns and adaptive processes that neighborhoods with diverse ethnoracial and socioeconomic compositions may display through their discursive signage and practices. This heterogeneity may, de facto, affect residents' local participation and compromise their accommodation within the neighborhood. However, the stability and sustainability of a community may also depend on different factors such as social interaction and networks that can be established between its members (Tran et al., 2013). The last project of this itinerary on students' personal narratives was focused on this aspect, namely on complementary and creative responses that communities may provide in a space hosting "micropublics living together in proximities of difference" (Stroud & Jegels, 2014, p. 180).

The international student coming from a university in Paris, France, was interested in analyzing the district of Arthur Avenue, Little Italy in the Bronx. Through an online search on several websites (Available Designs), she found that Arthur Avenue is considered nowadays the most "authentic" Italian borough in New York City; therefore, her goal was to investigate how and which "Italic values" take shape on the local site (Designing). Even though this is a plural community, which also hosts Latin American and most recently Albanian migrants, the presence of the Italian population that settled in this area from the first years of the twentieth century is still evident in many grocery stores, bakeries, churches, and an Italian school built in 1924 and still operative today. According to the student's interpretation and data (i.e., on-site pictures, leaflets collected during a walking tour, and residents' online interviews (Available Designs), the local community seems to provide compatible rather than conflictual answers to its plural membership. In her opinion, one of the reasons for the community's stability may be due to cultural proximity and the shared values of its members (Italians and Albanians, Italians and Latin Americans). As a matter of fact, mediation processes for the development of a plural community may be facilitated by its membership of the same "cultural area" (Zarate, 2003, p. 106) that is sharing the same values due to historic, geographic, and economic contacts and common experiences—even though many other variables come into play, as other narratives have shown here. The

Re-Visioning the Linguistics Landscape through a Multiliteracies Framework   109

FIGURE 6.7. Student's view of Our Lady of Mount Carmel Church.

student provided two examples of this compatible coexistence. She visited Our Lady of Mount Carmel, a Catholic church founded at the beginning of the twentieth century for Italian migrants who had brought with them strong faith and family values. She explained that this church continues to serve the Italian community (see Figure 6.7); yet it also welcomes new migrants coming from Latin America who share the same Catholic values with Italians.

This church, therefore, plays the role of an aggregating and collective point of religiosity for the plural community, as the student illustrated through a leaflet that she found at the site. This leaflet contains religious texts in three languages (i.e., Italian, English, and Spanish) and informs parishioners that some religious services and rituals are held in all three languages (see Figure 6.8).

The meetings that occur in this place reinforce social ties that play a moderating factor in the ethnically diverse neighborhood. As a matter of fact, according to the "intergroup contact" theory, these interactions can "reduce stereotypes and prejudices [. . .] while bringing collaboration [. . .] towards common goals" (Tran et al., 2013, p. 190).

Additionally, the student provided evidence of this sense of familial relationships through online interviews with Italian Americans living in the area and owning businesses such as grocery stores and restaurants. They pointed out that in this place there is, of course, competition but also collaboration

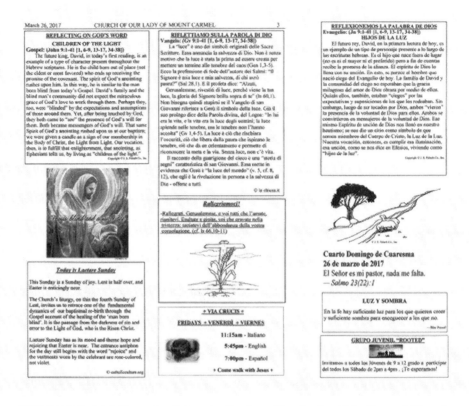

FIGURE 6.8. Multilingual religious leaflet from Our Lady of Mt. Carmel Church.

because the failure of a colleague is the failure of the entire neighborhood, and it would seem like "a death in the family." The student highlighted that this statement reminded her of the concept related to the economy described by Bassetti (2003) in his "Italicity" theory, namely the "non-economistic" conception of economy "which cannot be separated from an ethical view of life" (p. 20). The student was particularly struck by this feeling of attachment to the country that some of the interviewees had never visited before, and, at the same time, by the acceptance of differences. She has a pluricultural identity, having grown up in Paris with a Togolese mother and French father, and was spending a semester in New York and studying Italian. Therefore, this experience also allowed her "to re-think" about her own identity construction process (the Redesigned), as described in the following paragraphs.

Students' Perceptions and Responses to the Project

During the project students had opportunities to reflect on how the "interpenetration of global and local processes/geographies" (Mac Giolla Chríost, 2007,

p. 3) may determine cultural variations, tensions, dialectic forms of accommodation and resistance, and hybrid solutions. According to the postproject survey, students' unique micro-perspectives led to diverse transformative learning experiences and outcomes. The dynamic interplay between the imaginative connection with the Italic community and the participative observation of the local urban environment caused, in some cases, tension between students' "knowledge" and "action." In fact, the student who talked about commercial practices in Little Italy pointed out: "The concept of Italic community allowed me to reflect upon the concept of identity and how that can be manipulated by diverse actors for personal interests, which may be different and divergent." In other cases, the experience had the opposite impact and opened up space for "reconciliation" between the multiple levels of a plural identity. The French-Togolese student confirmed this feeling, stating:

> I have never heard about Italicity and I have always asked myself what link could relate Italian-Americans—who are very proud of their roots but without speaking the language and having visited, in most of the cases, their homeland—to Italian citizens [. . .] talking about Italicity allowed me to reconcile these identities. Personally, I ask myself to what extent I belong to the Togolese community without knowing the local languages and having little information about my mother's homeland. The concept of Italicity and seeing with my own eyes the Italian-American community made me realized about the existence of a plurality of signs and values.

In these terms, the student found her "alignment" (Wenger, 2000, p. 240) among her multicultural dimension, embracing the idea that multiplicity may imply partial/imperfect views and competences. For other students, this multimodal discursive analysis led to a "re-location of self" in the environment through a new conceptualization of the space (Jarowski & Thurlow, 2010, p. 7), as indicated by the student who went back to his old neighborhood: "I lived in this neighborhood for many years but have never seen it through this lens."

CONCLUSION

This chapter described the potentialities of a Multiliteracies-based project aimed at encouraging students to find their own voice to narrate the surrounding world and be active members of their global and local communities. Analysis of students' semiotic artifacts and postsurvey responses revealed that the project was effective in promoting their sensitivity to multimodal codes, critical thinking, and identity negotiation. The project, de facto, encouraged students to be intentional, agent, and purposeful in designing their unique narrative of place and its meanings. By engaging students' identity, individual stories, and imaginative and life experiences, the Multiliteracies approach enabled them to develop their own critical perspective instead of being stuck in a more standardized and accepted generalization about culture and its traditionally observed products (e.g., food, art, fashion, etc.). As a matter of fact, this dynamic "act of design" involved individuals' symbolic capital, developed alternative ways of viewing the world (Cope & Kalantzis, 2008, p. 208), and led them to "radical cultural creativity" (Kostogriz, 2004, quoted in Malinowski, 2015, p. 102). To achieve this goal, the Multiliteracies-based meaning-making process was endorsed by a holistic and multimodal learning experience.

This approach indeed afforded students the opportunity to become intensively engaged with local places as forums of critical viewing and thinking, as well as with a wide range of Available Designs (e.g., linguistic, visual, and behavioral codes). As students' cultural scripts showed, the transformative nature of their subjective interpretations triggered diverse learning orientations (e.g., "re-reading" familiar and unfamiliar places, "relocating" themselves in their space, "renegotiating" their identity). This student-led investigation involved different levels of "reading" and depths of interpretation as it depends strictly on individual variables such as a student's competences, knowledge, and experiences. Given the interdisciplinary nature of the project and its concepts originating from different disciplines (e.g., sociology, geography, sociolinguistics, etc.), it may be considered too demanding for both teachers and students. In their postproject survey, 20% of students pointed out that at the beginning of their project it was challenging to identify the rationale of their designing process even though it was worthwhile. In these terms, the adoption of Italicity as a conceptual framework showed a great potential to bridge theory and experimental practices (Pavlenko & Norton, 2007). It would probably be ideal to develop collaborative work with colleagues who are expert in different fields. However, it is worth noticing that the approach to be adopted depends significantly on the instructional context, goals, and expectations of the project's design. Additionally, since the meaning-making is a challenging long-term process that "involves a constant interplay between practices and identities" (Wenger, 2010, p. 187), it demands a range of experience and the accumulation of formative events, relationships, and competences that develop over time.

Both the students' semiotic artifacts and survey responses showed that significant educational objectives have been reached. Educating students to negotiate meanings created by others and by themselves and to explore the significance of multimodality and intertextuality in communicating these meanings can be effective in encouraging them to become active "designers" and "re-designers" of their future lifeworlds.

NOTES

1. The term was first coined by Benedict Anderson, *Imagined Communities: Reflections on the Origin and Spread of Nationalism* (New York: Verso, 1983), to define the processes by which a nation may exist largely in the imagination of its members. This concept has been expanded to groups that are established within different national societies (i.e., transnational communities) who act on the basis of shared interests (e.g., migrant populations) and to the target cultural communities of second language learners.
2. A "cultural script" is a script that forms an interpretive background against which individuals position their own acts and those of others.
3. The Common European Framework of Reference (CEFR) (Council of Europe, 2001) is an instrument of reference that was designed to provide a transparent, coherent, and comprehensive basis for the elaboration of language syllabi and curriculum guidelines, the creation of pedagogical materials, and the assessment of foreign language proficiency.
4. For FREPA descriptors, see http://carap.ecml.at/CARAP/tabid/2332/language/en-GB/Default.aspx.
5. Due to space issues, only a selection of students' cultural scripts will be described in this chapter. However, many topics have been involved in students' narratives. Examples of these topics include the analysis of the iconic and revisited representation of Italic values through Annie Leibovitz's photography for the Lavazza—an Italian manufacturer of coffee products—calendar for 2009; a comparative study of the links between Italicity and the world of Eataly—a large chain of Italian markets that opened many locations around the world, including in New York; and the deconstruction of Italian cultural stereotypes through an investigation of public gardens' signs.

BIBLIOGRAPHY

Appadurai, A. (1996). *Modernity at large*. Minneapolis: University of Minnesota.
Appadurai, A. (1997). Discussion: Fieldwork in the era of globalization. *Anthropology and Humanism, 22*(1), 115–18.

Augé, M. (1995). *Non-places. Introduction to an anthropology of supermodernity.* London: Verso.

Bassetti, P. (2003). Italicity: Global and local. In P. Janni & G. F. McLean (Eds.), *The essence of Italian culture and the challenge of a global age* (pp. 13–24). Washington, DC: The Council of Research in Values and Philosophy.

Candelier, M., Camilleri-Grima, A., Castellotti, V., de Pietro, J. F., Lőrincz, I., Meißner, F.-J., Noguerol, A., & Schröder-Sura, A. (2012). *FREPA. A framework of reference for pluralistic approaches to languages and cultures.* Strasbourg: Council of Europe.

Cope, B., & Gollings, G. (2001). *Multilingual book production, technology drivers across the book production supply chain, from the creator to the consumer.* Melbourne: Common Ground.

Cope, B., & Kalantzis, M. (2005). *Learning by design.* Melbourne, Australia: Common Ground.

Cope, B., & Kalantzis, M. (2008). Language education and multiliteracies. In S. May & N. Hornberger (Eds.), *Encyclopedia of language and education* (pp. 195–211). Boston, MA: Springer.

Cope, B., & Kalantzis, M. (2009). Multiliteracy: New literacies, new learning. *Pedagogies: An International Journal*, no. 4, 164–95.

Council of Europe. (2001). *The common European framework of reference for languages: Learning, teaching, assessment.* Cambridge: Cambridge University Press.

Council of Europe. (2020). *The common European framework of reference for languages: Learning, teaching, assessment—Companion volume.* Cambridge: Cambridge University Press.

Coupland, N. (2010). Introduction: Sociolinguistics in the global era. In N. Coupland (Ed.), *The handbook of language and globalization* (pp. 1–27). Chichester, UK: Blackwell.

Goddard, C., & Wierzbicka, A. (2004). Cultural scripts: What are they and what are they for?" *Intercultural Pragmatics*, *1*(2), 153–66.

Gorter, D. (2013). Linguistic landscape in multilingual world. *Annual Review of Applied Linguistics*, no. 33, 190–212.

Hall, T. (2009). Footwork: Moving and knowing in local space(s). *Qualitative Research*, *9*(5), 571–85.

Jagger, S. (2015). What does your garden show? Explorations of the semiotics of the garden. In P. P. Trifonas (Ed.), *International handbook of semiotics* (pp. 629–45). New York: Springer.

Jaworski, A., & Thurlow, C. (2010). Introducing semiotics landscapes. In A. Jaworski & C. Thurlow (Eds.), *Semiotic landscapes: Language, image, space* (pp. 1–40). London: Continuum International.

Jones, R. H. (2010). Cyberspace and physical space: Attention structures in computer mediated communication. In A. Jaworski & C. Thurlow (Eds.), *Semiotic landscapes* (pp. 151–67). London: Continuum International.

Joseph, M., & Ramani, E. (2012). Glocalization: Going beyond the dichotomy of global versus local through additive multilingualism. *International Multilingual Research Journal*, *6*, 22–34.

Kanno, Y., & Norton, B. (2003). Imagined communities and educational possibilities: Introduction. *Journal of Language, Identity, and Education*, *2*(4), 241–49.

Knott, K. (2005). *The location of religion. A spatial analysis*. London: Equinox.

Kostogriz, A. (2004). Rethinking the spatiality of literary practices in multicultural conditions. In *AARE 2004 International Educational Research: Doing the public good, positioning the Educational Research Conference proceedings* (pp. 1–11). Melbourne: AARE.

Kramsch, C. (2011). Third culture and language education. *Language Teaching*, *44*(3), 354–67.

Kramsch, C. (2014). Teaching foreign languages in an era of globalization: Introduction. *Modern Language Journal*, no. 98, 296–311.

Kress, G. (2003). *Literacy in the new media age*. London: Routledge.

Lawson, B. (2001). *The language of space*. Oxford: Architectural Press.

Lefebvre, H. (1974). *The production of space*. Oxford: Blackwell.

Liang, R.-H., & Huang, Y.-M. (2009). *Visualizing bits as urban semiotics*. International Conference on the Association for Computer-Aided Architectural Design Research in Asia, 33–42.

Lusianov, J. D. (2020). Post-method era and glocalization in language teaching and learning. *Advances in Social Sciences, Education, and Humanities Research*, *509*, 360–66.

Mac Giolla Chríost, D. (2007). *Language and the city*. New York: Palgrave Macmillan.

Malinowski, D. (2008). Authorship in the linguistic landscape: A multimodal performance view. In E. Shohamy & D. Gorter (Eds.), *Linguistic landscapes: Expanding the scenery* (pp. 107–25). New York: Routledge.

Malinowski, D. (2015). Opening spaces of learning in the linguistic landscape. *Linguistic Landscape*, *1*(1), 95–113.

Mannion, G. (2015). Towards glocal pedagogies: Some risks associated with education for global citizenship and how glocal pedagogies might avoid them. In J. Friedman, V. Haverkate, B. Oomen, E. Park, & M. Sklad (Eds.), *Going glocal in higher education: The theory, teaching and measurement of global citizenship* (pp. 19–34). Middleburg: University College Roosevelt.

Menke, M. R., & Paesani, K. (2021). Understanding teacher discourse around multiliteracies pedagogy. In B. Dupuy & K. Michelson (Eds.), *Pathways to paradigm change: Critical examinations of prevailing discourses and ideologies in second language education* (pp. 83–107). Boston: Cengage.

New London Group. (1996). A pedagogy of multiliteracies: Designing social futures. *Harvard Educational Review*, *66*(1), 60–92.

New London Group. (2000). A pedagogy of multiliteracies. Designing social futures. In B. Cope & M. Kalantzis (Eds.), *Multiliteracies literacy learning and the design of social futures* (pp. 9–38). London: Routledge.

Norton, B., & Toohey, K. (2011). Identity, language learning, and social change. *Language Teaching*, *44*(4), 412–46.

Pavlenko, A. (2008). Multilingualism in post-Sovietic countries. *International Journal of Bilingual Education and Bilingualism*, *11*(3/4), 275–314.

Pavlenko, A., & Norton, B. (2007). Imagined communities, identity, and English language learning. In J. Cummins & C. Davison (Eds.), *International handbook of English language teaching* (pp. 669–80). New York: Springer.

Pennycook, A. (2009). Linguistic landscapes and the transgressive semiotics of graffiti. In E. G. Shohamy & D. Gorter (Eds.), *Linguistic landscape: Expanding the scenery* (pp. 302–12). New York: Routledge.

Pennycook, A. (2010). Spatial narrations: Graffscapes and city souls. In A. Jaworski & C. Thurlow (Eds.), *Semiotic landscapes*, (pp. 137–50). London: Continuum International.

Ritzer, G. (2015). *The McDonaldization of society* (8th ed.). Los Angeles: Sage.

Rizvi, F., & Lingar, B. (2009). *Globalizing education policy*. London: Routledge.

Robertson, R. (1994). Globalization or glocalization? *Journal of International Communication*, *1*(1), 33–52.

Sciorra, J. (2015). *Built with faith: Italian American imagination and Catholic material culture in New York City*. Knoxville: University of Tennessee Press.

Scollon, R., & Scollon, S. W. (2003). *Discourses in place: Language in the material world*. New York: Routledge.

Shohamy, E., Ben-Rafael, E., & Barni, M. (2010). *Linguistic landscape in the city*. Bristol, UK: Multilingual Matters.

Shohamy, E., & Gorter, D. (2008). *Linguistic landscapes: Expanding the scenery*. New York: Routledge.

Skutnabb-Kangas, T., & Phillipson, R. (2010). World languages trends and futures. In N. Coupland (Ed.), *The handbook of language and globalization* (pp. 101–22). Chichester, UK: Blackwell.

Soja, E. (1989). *Postmodern geographies*. London: Verso.

Spinelli, B. (2018). Localizing the global: Exploring responsive forms of inclusive pedagogy in order to preserve linguistic biodiversity. In M. Hepp & M. N. Curcio

(Eds.), *Plurilingual education: Research, teaching and language policies* (pp. 105–22). Roma: Studi Germanici.

Spinelli, B. (2020). Nuovi Modelli di Multiliteracies in classi plurilingue: Riflessioni teoriche ed implicazioni didattiche nel sistema di istruzione superiore statunitense. *Italiano LinguaDue*, no. 1, 78–96.

Stroud, C., & Jegels, D. (2014). Semiotic landscapes and mobile narrations of place: Performing the local. *International Sociology of Language*, *228*, 179–99.

Tran, V., Graif, C., Jones, A. D., Small, M., & Winship, C. (2013). Participation in context: Neighborhood diversity and organizational involvement in Boston. *City and Community*, *12*(3), 187–209.

Trifonas, P. P. (2015). Apologia. In P. P. Trifonas (Ed.), *International book of semiotics* (pp. 1–25). New York: Springer.

Wenger, E. (2000). Communities of practice and social learning systems. *Organization*, *7*(2), 225–46.

Wenger, E. (2010). Communities of practice and social learning systems: The career of a concept. In C. Blackmore (Ed.), *Social learning systems and communities of practice* (pp. 179–98). London: Springer Verlag and the Open University.

Zarate, G. (2003). Identities and plurilingualism: Precondition for the recognition of intercultural competences. In M. Byram (Ed.), *Intercultural competence* (pp. 84–119). Strasbourg: Council of Europe.

7

AUDIOVISUAL TRANSLATION IN LANGUAGE LEARNING AND TEACHING

The "Learn Italian with Subtitles" Project at the University of Liverpool (UK)

Rosalba Biasini and Francesca Raffi

In the 1990s, audiovisual translation (AVT) became a recognized academic discipline, mainly concerned with "the transfer of multimodal and multimedia speech (dialogue, monologue, comments, etc.) into another language/culture" (Gambier, 2013, p. 45). Scholars have produced a wealth of material on AVT over the last decades, especially with regard to subtitling, the most widely used form of AVT. This fast and flexible technique for enabling the audience to access and enjoy audiovisual content is less expensive than other AVT modalities. Moreover, subtitling is able to meet the needs of a varied user typology.

Subtitles can be either interlingual or intralingual, depending on the linguistic transfer. Interlingual subtitling has been defined as "a rendition in writing of the translation into a TL [target language] of the original dialogue exchanges uttered by the different speakers, as well as of all other verbal information that is transmitted visually (letters, banners, inserts) or aurally (lyrics, voices off)" (Díaz Cintas, 2019, p. 212). Thus, subtitles in this context present a translation of the source language soundtrack into a different language, generally aimed at foreign language (FL) viewers but also, and most interestingly for the purposes of the present chapter, useful for language learners (Díaz Cintas, 2001, 2006). Intralingual subtitling is a practice that "consists of presenting on screen a written text accounting for the dialogue, music, sounds and noises contained in the soundtrack for the benefit of audiences with hearing impairments" (Díaz-Cintas, 2019, p. 212). This implies maintaining the language of the original soundtrack but adding relevant auditory details (i.e., linguistic and paralinguistic features) that are important for understanding the storyline.

A subtitled product is the result of the interplay of "the original spoken/written word, the original image and the added subtitles" (Díaz Cintas, 2010, p. 344). This calls for a variety of skills, which can be taught and improved through well-planned activities covering the different steps of the subtitling process. In the communicative context created by the audiovisual product, different signifying codes "operate simultaneously to produce meaning" (Chaume, 2012, p. 100), and a translator must understand the functioning of these codes to convey the equivalent message in the target language, taking into account the various components, which can be acoustic-verbal (dialogue), acoustic-nonverbal (score, sounds), visual-nonverbal (image), and visual-verbal (subtitles). The need for synchrony between these components, along with the change of mode from oral to written, imposes both temporal and spatial constraints, which make a literal, word-for-word translation impossible, necessitating the use of condensation and reformulation strategies (Díaz Cintas & Remael, 2021). The visual context is explicit and needs to be taken into consideration in the translation process, together with cultural and intercultural issues and pragmatic aspects of communication. Therefore, subtitling offers the opportunity to negotiate meaning and to work, simultaneously, on multiple aspects of a given language. The Common European Framework of Reference for Languages (CEFR) distinguishes between language activities in terms of production (oral and written), reception (aural, visual, and audiovisual), interaction (spoken and written), and mediation or translation (oral and written) "using new technologies" (Council of Europe, 2001, p. 71). Hence, subtitling can be considered an effective language learning tool that can be integrated into FL study to help students develop competence in these different areas.

With all this in mind, this chapter discusses a research-led learning and teaching experience at the University of Liverpool (UK) focused on the use of AVT, specifically interlingual subtitling (FL>L1), in a final year module of Italian as a FL. Although some scholars have evaluated the direct experience of using AVT techniques in the classroom (see the section "The Learn Italian with Subtitles Project"), further reflection is needed on the successful implementation of subtitling activities in FL learning and teaching and on how the use of subtitles should be employed more regularly and consistently in language education.

Through a collaboration between the Universities of Macerata (Italy) and Liverpool (UK), we initiated the Learn Italian with Subtitles project in Liverpool, aimed at the systematic use of interlingual subtitling activities in language education. The project, which merges AVT studies and FL pedagogy, aims at developing advanced language and language-related skills while exploring the deployment of digital technologies and AVT tools as well as their applications and social impact on language learning and teaching.

After this introductory section, the next section discusses a number of studies and projects that have demonstrated the benefits of interlingual subtitling in the FL classroom. Then, after a description of the Learn Italian with Subtitles project just outlined, initial results are discussed.[1] Finally, some conclusions are drawn.

INTERLINGUAL SUBTITLING IN THE FL CLASSROOM

The first studies of audiovisual materials and their applications in formal language-learning contexts were conducted in the late 1970s, at a time when only intralingual subtitles for deaf and hard-of-hearing learners were seen as effective pedagogical tools (see Davila, 1972), and this attitude remained prevalent in the 1980s (see Baker & Damper, 1986; Caldwell, 1973; among others). However, in the same decade, scholars also started to investigate the effectiveness of subtitling for hearing learners (see Lambert et al., 1981; among others), thanks to developments in cognitive psychology, which offered a more solid starting point for exploring new tools able to facilitate cognitive processes in the FL classroom. A key turning point was the publication of Paivio's (1986) dual coding theory (DCT), according to which multiple representations (i.e., both verbal and nonverbal) of the same information help to improve memory and learning.

In the 1990s, several scholars in the field of FL education further investigated the effectiveness of both intra- and interlingual subtitling. Danan (1992) conducted research on interlingual subtitling[2] using Paivio's (1986) DCT to demonstrate the usefulness of interlingual subtitling for FL acquisition among beginner and intermediate learners. He explained its success by the multiple memory paths created by the visual and bilingual input.

Moving from the 1990s to the 2000s, one of the most prolific scholars of this decade in the field of subtitling applied to language education was Caimi (2002, 2005; among others), who strongly advocated the use of subtitles to stimulate students in their learning development in terms of phonetics, vocabulary, grammar, and pragmatic competence by focusing on multiple channels of communication (both verbal and nonverbal) and behavior patterns, thus exposing students not only to the target language but also to the culture characteristic of another community.

In line with Caimi's (2005) study, Borghetti (2011) discussed the ways in which the active creation of interlingual subtitles can be used to better promote the development of students' intercultural awareness in the FL classroom, in particular helping learners to reflect on their own role as mediators between two cultures. For example, students can be asked to choose between strategies of foreignization or domestication (Venuti, 1995) when making translation choices to deal with cultural references, encouraging them to reflect on their responsibility to the target audience.

A few years later, Baños Piñero and Sokoli (2015) presented ClipFlair, a European-funded project aimed at providing an easily accessible online platform for FL learners, which included subtitling. According to the results of student surveys, subtitling activities created an interactive and entertaining learning environment, which increased student motivation and independence and provided exposure to nonverbal cultural elements, as well as authentic linguistic and cultural aspects of communication in context. Interestingly, the two authors also shed light on the potential of subtitling to promote "transferable skills" (2015, p. 204), which are indeed expected to grow exponentially in the coming years (see the section "The Learn Italian with Subtitles Project"), "thus demanding a set of add-on skills that higher education institutions will have to include in their existing curricula in order to boost graduates' employability" (Díaz Cintas & Remael, 2021, p. 62).

More recently, Lertola (2019) has offered a systematic review of the empirically based experimental studies conducted in the last 20 years that have foregrounded the positive links between subtitling tasks and FL education. Positive learning outcomes are reported on incidental vocabulary acquisition, idiomatic expression retention, development of pragmatic awareness, listening comprehension skills, and writing and translation skills.

As far as the teaching of Italian is concerned, few studies and projects have been carried out so far, despite the bulk of research conducted over the years and despite the growing interest related to the use of interlingual subtitling in FL classrooms. Among the few studies that have been published, Lertola (2013) described an experiment involving undergraduate students of Italian as a FL (A1–A2), mainly with English as their first language, at the National University of Ireland, Galway. It was demonstrated that subtitling promotes the incidental acquisition of new word meanings in terms of productive recall.

Moving from linguistic to cultural competence, Borghetti and Lertola (2014) further expanded Lertola's (2013) experiment by focusing on A2/B1 level students of Italian; findings confirmed that the use of subtitling tasks help students better develop intercultural skills. Incalcaterra McLoughlin and Lertola (2014) discussed the introduction of subtitling activities as a regular part of Italian language courses, in this case at B1–B2 level, and reported on students' feedback on their subtitling experience. According to students' responses, subtitling improved their motivation in learning Italian. Most interestingly, their opinions on subtitling and translation as language-learning tools were different and tended to be more positive in relation to subtitling (see the section "Preliminary Results").

More recently, Beltramello (2019) explored the combination of subtitling and other AVT tasks with Italian learners in their fourth and final years of their bachelor's degree (B2), also at the National University of Ireland, to help students develop awareness of pragmatic features of conversation and the dynamics of face-to-face interaction (i.e., pragmatic and sociolinguistic competence). The subtitling tasks proved to be effective in guiding students to question the meaning of certain utterances, the intention behind a speaker's utterance, and social relationships between interlocutors.

To the best of our knowledge, the only project based outside Ireland and related to English as L1 and Italian as FL is the one discussed in McKenzie (2018), conducted at Victoria University of Wellington, New Zealand. The project involved undergraduate students of Italian (A2–B1) who were asked to subtitle the comedy classic *Il secondo tragico Fantozzi* into English. The same sample of students also answered a survey to reflect on the effectiveness of the project, which was confirmed by positive results, both in terms of linguistic/cultural competence and motivation/enjoyment.

Therefore, as the aforementioned studies and projects have proven, interlingual subtitling is certainly beneficial in the FL classroom by virtue of its capacity to enhance both language and cultural skills, capitalizing on the richness (thanks to the multisemiotic reception of the stimuli presented) and authenticity (audiovisual language inputs) of audiovisual texts, as well as the enjoyment offered by learning tasks related to subtitling.

Such tasks enable students to practice listening, reading, and writing skills through entertainment and exercises using authentic materials. In a subtitling task, the communicative reason for performing the activity is immediately evident, giving a clear purpose, a sense of achievement, and a functional dimension to the new text and, consequently, to the students' exercise, easily transferred into real-life situations (see Talaván, 2006).

Subtitling, finally, offers the opportunity to develop learner-centered tasks based on interactive activities, which can be performed individually and in groups. This can be done under the guidance of the teacher or independently to promote autonomous and cooperative language learning, which enhances student motivation and proves to be fundamental in situations where teaching is carried out remotely, as further discussed in the following section.

THE LEARN ITALIAN WITH SUBTITLES PROJECT

To the best of our knowledge, the project is the first to center on Italian as a FL at the undergraduate level in a UK-based university. It is still running and was launched in the academic year 2019–20 at the University of Liverpool, within the Department of Languages, Cultures and Film (LCF), as a component of a final year Italian language module (B2+-C1). The "subtitling class" takes place in a fully equipped on-campus laboratory and is designed to enhance students' aural skills through the comprehension and analysis of authentic materials, that is, samples of language produced by a real user of that language for a real audience (Gilmore, 2007), thus developing idiomatic competence, since the language is contextualized through real-life situations (see the section "Interlingual Subtitling in the FL Classroom"). As discussed later, the project activities, which include classwork and independent practice, cover different steps of the subtitling process from the "reading" of a video in Italian to the production of the target text (in English) in the form of subtitles.

Learners' Background

At the University of Liverpool, learners of Italian language can start their program as absolute beginners or at intermediate level (identified in some UK institutions as advanced, B1/B2). After a biennium where the two cohorts follow different pathways, with four weekly hours of contact time for beginners and three for intermediate learners, students generally spend their third year abroad. On their return, both sets are merged for the final year module, which, in line with the national Subject Benchmark Statement for Languages, Cultures and Societies, prepares students to reach a level of proficient linguistic and cultural competence of at least C1 (AQA, 2019).

The Italian program, which combines language modules with "content" modules taught in English, develops a broad range of Italian language skills from linguistic competence—through historical, cultural, and transnational studies (including literature and film)—to practical, digital, and mediation skills. The whole program includes elements of translation in both directions (FL>L1; L1>FL): Didactic exercises to enhance language acquisition are introduced early, and from Year Two elements of translation and interpreting are incorporated into language modules to develop linguistic awareness and mediation and intercultural skills.

It must be emphasized that the aims of the program are those of a language and culture undergraduate university course, which means that it includes an introduction to a variety of employability skills with a specific focus, for the language component of the program, on translation and interpreting, but the course is not designed to train professionals in this field—only to provide basic competence and knowledge in the translation sector, while the main objective remains FL education.

Italian classes for finalist undergraduates at LCF include on average 9–12 students per year, and because of their relatively small size, relations among peers and between learners and tutors are generally amicable and collaborative. This furnishes an appropriate background for teaching innovation and data analysis and makes this project possible. Most students who take part have English as their first or main language, and it is very common for participants to study at least one other language, in which they tend to be more proficient.

In their final year, students are not directly taught grammar in dedicated sessions, and classes do not focus mainly on specific skills, for example, writing and reading, or speaking and listening. Instead, module components are based on short "projects" aimed at developing a combination of competence, skills, and knowledge.[3] The module also includes a weekly class dedicated to translation. The following section gives an outline of the learning and teaching aims of the Learn Italian with Subtitles project.

Learning and Teaching Aims

Following a fortunate encounter with Dr. Raffi from an Erasmus+ partner institution (University of Macerata, Italy), a series of workshops on subtitling in language education was organized at the University of Liverpool, including teachers' development days and the Annual 2019 Translation Lecture, which Dr. Raffi delivered. These initial contacts inspired the creation of a subtitling course, which has become integrated into the final year Italian language module. The learning and teaching aims of this project are primarily linguistic and cultural, as well as interlinguistic and intercultural, because it is essentially a language module in which translation activities are included (Borghetti, 2011; Borghetti & Lertola, 2014).

As anticipated, the project activities, which include classwork and independent practice, cover different steps of the subtitling process. First of all, it must be noted that at this pilot stage of the project, a decision was made not to work with reversed subtitling but only in the direction of Italian (FL)>English (L1).[4] The benefits of using any form of translation in language education has been widely investigated and, especially in the field of Italian language pedagogy, several studies have affirmed and reinforced a full "rehabilitation" of translation techniques in language education after decades of "ostracism" (Balboni, 2010).[5] For this specific project, it was agreed to use FL>L1 activities for three main pedagogical reasons. First of all, finalists in Italian mainly start as beginners, and at the end of the program their linguistic competence, as well as their confidence, is still developing. Additionally, the translation class in the first semester is taught in the opposite direction (L1>FL). Finally, in the second semester, the translation class "changes direction" (FL>L1), while interpreting replaces the subtitling sessions. Therefore, a variety of translation tasks and activities are offered in both directions, which helps to make student performance more balanced.

Choosing this direction of translation (FL>L1) also offers advantages: When students "read" an authentic text (i.e., clip, video, podcast) in their language of study, they can learn to appreciate the complexity of both the linguistic content and the cultural system in which that text is embedded. Furthermore, the exercise of creating a target text in the form of English subtitles strengthens linguistic and interlinguistic competence among students even in their first or stronger language (Lertola, 2015). This allows them to better focus on comprehension of the source text with all its nuances; the process of translating a text, which includes evaluating meaning and expression, negotiating choices, finding solutions; the subtitling task, thereby learning new skills that enhance digital fluency. How this translates into classroom practice and how these aims are met will be discussed in the following section.

Learn Italian with Subtitles: A Proposal

The semester 1 final year Italian course lasts for 12 weeks with a total of 150 hours of study time per module, including classwork and independent study time. Contact time is three hours per week, one of which is dedicated to subtitling.

Each class of the subtitling course includes a theoretical part focused on subtitling rules and guidelines, and a practical one. The first classes focus on establishing the basis of the subtitling process, providing students with information about the sector and possible career opportunities, in line with the institution's recommendations. In addition to Dr. Raffi's support both as an academic specializing in (AVT) translation studies and as a professional audiovisual translator, at the University of Liverpool we also benefit from the support of a technician with expertise in subtitling software, video-making, and both Mac and MS operating systems. Being able to rely on separate training, especially on the use of the selected software and technical problem solving, in the form of ad hoc video tutorials, allowed us to free more class time to focus on the actual activity of subtitling.

In the pilot year of the project, once the chosen guidelines were agreed and basic rules established, students were introduced to a subtitling software tool. We opted for free, easy-to-use software, Subtitle Edit, which was downloaded onto all machines in an equipped language laboratory on campus. However, since not all operating systems support this software, when classes moved online we introduced a second subtitling tool, Aegisub, which helped us cater to all students. Switching to online classes meant that students had to ensure that they could download and install the software onto their personal computers at home. This was also an opportunity for students to refresh and expand their digital skills and to learn how to access and run new programs, while keeping their machines "healthy" and up-to-date.

The project activities cover all aspects of the subtitling process, and classes generally follow the pattern inspired by the LU model globalizing/analyzing/synthesizing/reflecting formalized for Italian by Balboni.[6] The activity starts with "reading" an original audiovisual text. A variety of sources are used, including movie trailers, web series, and clips.[7] Given the learners' proficiency level, it was decided not to provide subtitles (neither in English nor in Italian). After an initial viewing, followed by a discussion (based on comprehension, analysis of linguistic and cultural traits, identification of potential challenges), students are provided with the full transcript: This allows the tutor to choose a more complex text, which can, for instance, highlight linguistic variations, use of jargon, idiomatic expressions, and irony. Then, a sequence of the text is assigned to the class for independent (or group, in some cases) subtitling practice. This is the "reacting" stage: Students use the software to create subtitles for the chosen extract. At the end of the class, a student is asked to share their attempt; this can be done anonymously, by sending the task to the tutor, or, if appropriate, the student can share their screen (working online has eased this procedure). The class is asked to comment on the translation choices made, to offer alternatives, and eventually to negotiate a final proposal as a group. Finally, at home, students complete the set video, or work on a new clip that the tutor has previously selected, and then email their work to the tutor. Feedback is either sent back via email or used as a starting point during the next class.

It must also be noted that, although a deeper analysis of this topic would require a more extensive discussion, students undergo a summative assessment on completion of a subtitling test, which currently constitutes 30% of the final module mark. The set task for the test is similar to those used for class practice, and in the weeks running up to the assessment a mock test is set to help students become accustomed to exam conditions (see this chapter's appendix for an example). The tasks used over the years in the subtitling tests constitute a form of authentic assessment that, while appropriately reflecting the knowledge and skills that need to be tested, mirror authentic tasks that students can expect to undertake outside of academia and that require the real-life thinking processes that experts use to solve the problem in a real context (Gielen et al., 2003; Gulikers et al., 2004).

PRELIMINARY RESULTS

We are in the early stages of examining our results, and data collection and analysis are still in progress, which means that it is not yet possible to present a final evaluation of the project. These preliminary reflections are intended to comment on the evolution of the project so far, including students' performance and satisfaction, as well as tutors' feedback. A survey will be used to test our hypothesis, and students' results will be studied diachronically, and also in comparison with former laboratory tests, as well as other assessments (e.g., speaking tests) to determine whether introducing subtitling tasks has had a substantial and consistent impact over the years.

Informal data, which include the initial reading of students' module feedback and performance, seem to point positively toward the direction outlined. The numerous advantages of using subtitling activities in language education, suggested by previous studies and projects (see the section "Interlingual Subtitling in the FL Classroom"), seems in fact to have been confirmed by the class practice. It has been noted that students have adopted a more active role during the set tasks and in their learning experience, with increased motivation enhanced by opportunities to practice in their independent learning time and to receive timely feedback. Moreover, subtitles and captions are nowadays largely available and observable in everyday life. Since out-of-class exposure to subtitled AVT products assists FL learning (Lindgren & Muñoz, 2013;

Peter & Webb, 2018), this authentic experience has offered students a fresh perspective on the practical application of their learning, as well as a continuous and varied source of stimuli and inputs.

As with all innovations, especially those with a digital focus, the integration of subtitling tasks into the language course has also presented some challenges. First, tutors need to be trained. The level of expertise required clearly depends on the course learning outcomes that are set in the first place. Investments must be made, especially in terms of time for training and technical equipment. As stated previously, this specific project has greatly benefited from external expertise regarding the theoretical framework and professional advice, as well as internal support, thanks to a patient and reliable technician. Institutions willing to introduce such innovations must be aware of these needs and their implications.

Finally, it must also be acknowledged that, especially at the beginning, the setting of subtitling tasks can be time-consuming. As with all text-based activities, material selection requires time, and in the case of these tasks, it can also involve additional video-cutting and conversion, while transcripts need to be searched for or drafted. This is the case for assessment as well, whether formative or summative, as providing accurate feedback involves not only linguistic, cultural, and mediation skills but also digital and sector competence, supported by the appropriate technical equipment and the assistance of a tutor whose first language is English, given the direction of the translation. Needless to say, large cohorts can therefore generate a discouraging workload.

However, the tutors' evaluation of the project so far is highly favorable. On top of the positive outcomes suggested above, students have shown an increased level of collaboration, supporting each other with technical hiccups or linguistic queries, sharing linguistic resources, and slowly gaining increased confidence. Despite the disruption caused by the lockdowns in 2020 and 2021, which affected two out of the three cohorts that took part in the project, this opportunity to learn new skills and delve deeper into Italian language and culture has given students a more optimistic view of their learning and of their future as linguists, which has also created a palpable sense of achievement and progress within the class.

FINAL REMARKS

Since the 1970s, AVT modalities have attracted the considerable attention of scholars in the field of foreign language and teaching. The first studies were considered pioneering in their successful efforts to provide students with new tools and learning experiences, but these researchers interestingly viewed interlingual subtitles as obstacles to language learning and teaching (see Wegner, 1977). This attitude changed in the 1980s, when the potential of interlingual subtitling as an additional language-learning tool was fully discovered and applied in FL classrooms (see the section "Interlingual Subtitling in the FL Classroom"). Its potential has recently increased even more and as O'Sullivan (2013) remarks, in today's multimodal environment translators must take into account various signifying codes, not just written elements.

As the preliminary results of our project demonstrate (see previous section), by actively producing subtitles, that is, tangible outputs, students become aware of and make decisions about communicative, sociolinguistic, and pragmatic aspects of both languages, while also learning a variety of transferable and soft skills that enhance their employability, particularly in the audiovisual and translation fields (Díaz Cintas & Remael, 2021); students are thus producers and not just consumers of knowledge. In addition, introducing subtitling tasks to a language class helps develop translation and mediation skills with a special focus on digital awareness (Ávila-Cabrera & Corral Esteban, 2021).[8]

Therefore, the project has been enhancing the students' learning experience, with a specific focus on the University of Liverpool Curriculum Framework (University of Liverpool, n.d.): digital fluency (i.e., using digital platforms to problem-solve, create, collaborate, and communicate), confidence (i.e., being able to adapt and apply knowledge in new contexts), and global citizenship (being active members of the community). The project also has been helping teaching staff to further incorporate Liverpool Hallmarks, also part of the Liverpool Curriculum Framework, into learning and teaching, creating activities that are research-connected and incorporating active learning as well as authentic assessment. All this is underpinned by the core value of inclusivity, which means providing activities that are accessible to as many students as possible. In fact, in addition to increasing students' participation, the use of subtitles in the language classroom helps all groups of students better comprehend the videos, including students who have difficulties with speech or auditory elements.

To conclude, with this chapter we hope to have increased awareness of the advantages of applying AVT modalities to the learning and teaching of Italian as a FL. The project we have presented, which is still running and expanding, could pave the way to a better understanding of the benefits and good practices of AVT in FL teaching and learning.

APPENDIX A:
AN EXAMPLE OF A SUBTITLING TASK
FOR SUMMATIVE ASSESSMENT

Marking criteria and instructions were shared via the institutional Virtual Learning Environmental Platform (VLE) with the students at the beginning of the semester as follows:

The subtitling test will take place during our normal class time in Week 12.

It will be preceded by a mock test in Week 10, also during class time.

For the subtitling test, you will have 50 minutes to subtitle at least 1 minute of video (depending on the source). At the end of the test, you will need to submit your task on [VLE instructions].

Marking criteria:
60% TRANSLATION: you will translate from Italian into English. You will be assessed on:

(1) comprehension of the source text (e.g., meaning, pertinence, omissions)
(2) linguistic accuracy (e.g., register, style)
(3) ability to convey a cohesive and coherent message
(4) production of a functional and effective text
(5) ability to transfer cultural and connotative aspects of the source text

40% TASK: you will need to complete at least 1 minute of a given audio-text (see above). You will be assessed on:

(1) temporal dimension (e.g. time-in/time-out, synchronisation, scene changed, line numbers)
(2) punctuation and other conventions (e.g. punctuation, dialogues dash, use of Italics)
(3) segmentation (e.g. line breaks within subtitles, line breaks across subtitles)
(4) linguistic/translation issues (e.g. condensation, omissions, reduction)

Notes: use of dictionaries and linguistic support IS allowed for this test. Use of machine translation systems (Google Translate and similar) IS NOT allowed and will be verified.

You will have the script in Italian.

On the day of the test, conducted online in the last two academic years, the task is released on the VLE. It consists of an mp4 in VLC format, supported by the subtitling software in use, and the clip transcript, with a brief synopsis and—if appropriate—explanatory notes. An example of audio text is available at this link, from minute 01:48: it is a clip by Italian comedy group The Jackal, famous for their funny videos about modern life: https://www.youtube.com/watch?v=CCe2IZVoU8g&ab_channel=TheJackal.

NOTES

The authors made equal contributions to the conception and writing of this chapter. In particular, Rosalba Biasini is responsible for the sections "The Learn Italian with Subtitles Project" and "Preliminary Results." Francesca Raffi is responsible for the sections "Introduction," "Interlingual Subtitling in the FL Classroom," and "Final Remarks."

1. It must be noted that this project and the corresponding research are still in the initiation phase. The results collected so far and presented here are therefore partial, hence the project description outline should be considered the basis for a more extended analysis that will follow in a further study.
2. In this section, the focus is on interlingual studies and projects, in line with the nature of the Learn Italian with Subtitles project at the University of Liverpool (UK). Intralingual subtitling (or captioning) has also been extensively investigated and used in the FL classroom. For further references, see *Bibliography: Intralingual Subtitles (Captions) and Foreign/Second Language Acquisition*, available at http://www.fremdsprache-und-spielfilm.de/Captions.htm.
3. In the first semester, for instance, one of these projects explores the language of literature, and students work toward writing a literary review. In the second semester, the focus is on the language of advertising, and via the creation of an advertisement, students develop not only language and cultural competencies but also soft skills, related for example to digital fluency and communication.
4. Reverse subtitling is where the soundtrack/audio language and the subtitle language are different, but in this case the former is the L1 and the latter is L2. For instance, the soundtrack language is English and the subtitle language is Italian for viewers whose L1 is English.
5. For a summary of this theoretical discussion, see Biasini (2016).
6. In English, see Balboni (2007), especially pp. 39–52.
7. Over the years, varied resources were chosen to offer a broad range of cultural and linguistic elements. We used, e.g., trailers for the documentary *Come il peso dell'acqua* (Segre, 2014) and the film *Domani è un altro giorno* (Spada, 2019) and episodes of the web series *Genitori vs Figli* (Centro Sperimentale di Cinematografia, 2015). Some of these samples also involved off-screen voices, which helped introduce new elements to the subtitling task.
8. Incidentally, due to the unfortunate outbreak of the COVID-19 pandemic, followed by several national or local lockdowns that imposed remote learning, students had to rely even further on their digital skills.

BIBLIOGRAPHY

AQA. (2019). Subject benchmark statement: Languages, cultures and societies. Accessed November 22, 2022. https://www.qaa.ac.uk/docs/qaa/subject-benchmark-statements/subject-benchmark-statement-languages-cultures-and-societies.pdf

Ávila-Cabrera, J. J., & Corral Esteban, A. (2021). The project SubESPSKills: Subtitling tasks for students of business English to improve written production skills. *English for Specific Purposes*, 63, 3–44. https://doi.org/10.1016/j.esp.2021.02.004

Baker, R. G., & Damper, R. I. (1986). Educational aspects of television subtitling in deaf education." *Behaviour & Information Technology*, 5, 227–36.

Balboni, P. (2010). La traduzione nell'insegnamento delle lingue: Dall'Ostracismo alla riscoperta. In F. De Giovanni & B. Di Sabato (Eds.), *Tradurre in Pratica. Riflessioni, Esperienze, Testimonianze* (pp. 179–200). Naples: ESI.

Baños Piñero, R., & Sokoli, S. (2015). Learning foreign languages with ClipFlair: Using captioning and revoicing activities to increase students' motivation and engagement. In K. Borthwick, E. Corradini, & A. Dickens (Eds.), *10 years of the LLAS elearning symposium: Case studies in good practice* (pp. 203–13). Dublin: Research-publishing.net. https://doi.org/10.14705/rpnet.2015.000280

Beltramello, A. (2019, April). Exploring the combination of subtitling and revoicing tasks: A proposal for maximising learning opportunities in the Italian language. *International Journal of Language Translation and Intercultural Communication*, 8, 93–109. https://doi.org/10.12681/ijltic.20279

Biasini, R. (2016). Per una rivalutazione del ruolo della traduzione nella didattica dell'Italiano LS. In P. Mazzotta & R. Abbaticchio (Eds.), *XXI Congress AIPI Associazione Internazionale Professori di Italiano Vol. L'insegnamento dell'italiano dentro e fuori d'Italia* (pp. 37–50). Florence: Franco Cesati Editore.

Borghetti, C. (2011). Intercultural learning through subtitling: The cultural studies approach. In L. Incalcaterra McLoughlin, M. Biscio, & M. Áine Ní Mhainnín (Eds.), *Audiovisual translation subtitles and subtitling: Theory and practice* (pp. 111–37). Oxford: Peter Lang.

Borghetti, C., & Lertola, J. (2014). Interlingual subtitling for intercultural language education: A case study. *Language and Intercultural Communication*, 14(4), 423–40. https://doi.org/10.1080/14708477.2014.934380

Caimi, A. (2002). Cinema: Paradiso delle lingue: I sottotitoli nell'apprendimento linguistico. *Rassegna Italiana di Linguistica Applicata (RILA)*, 34(1–2), 19–51. Roma: Bulzoni.

Caimi, A. (2005). Subtitling in a cognitive perspective to encourage second language learning. In J. D. Sanderson (Ed.), *Research on translation for subtitling in Spain and Italy* (pp. 65–77). Alicante: University of Alicante.

Caldwell, D. C. (1973). Use of graded captions with instructional television for deaf learners. *American Annals of the Deaf*, 118, 500–507.

Chaume, F. (2012). *Audiovisual translation: Dubbing*. Manchester: St. Jerome.

Council of Europe. (2001). *Common European framework of reference for languages: Learning, teaching, assessment*. Cambridge: Press Syndicate of the University of Cambridge.

Danan, M. (1992). Reversed subtitling and dual coding theory: New directions for foreign language instruction. *Language Learning*, 42(4), 497–527. https://doi.org/10.1111/j.1467-1770.1992.tb01042

Davila, R. R. (1972). Effect of changes in visual information patterns on student achievement using a captioned film and specially adapted still pictures. Unpublished PhD diss., Syracuse University.

Díaz Cintas, J. (2001). *La traducción audiovisual: El subtitulado*. Salamanca: Ediciones Almar.

Díaz Cintas, J. (2006). La subtitulación y el mundo académico: Perspectivas de estudio e investigación. In N. Perdu Honeyman, F. García Marcos, E. Ortega Arjonilla, & M. Á. Garcia Peinado (Eds.), *Inmigración, cultura y traducción: Reflexiones interdisciplinares* (pp. 693–706). Tarrasa: Editorial Bahai.

Díaz Cintas, J. (2010). Subtitling. In Y. Gambier & L. Van Doorslaer (Eds.), *Handbook of translation studies* (Vol. 1, pp. 344–49). Amsterdam: John Benjamins.

Díaz Cintas, J. (2019). Audiovisual translation. In E. Angelone, M. Ehrensberger-Dow, & G. Massey (Eds.), *The Bloomsbury companion to language industry studies* (pp. 209–30). London: Bloomsbury.

Díaz Cintas, J., & Remael, A. (2021). *Subtitling: Concepts and practices*. New York: Routledge.

Gambier, Y. (2013). The position of audiovisual translation studies. In C. Millán & F. Bartrina (Eds.), *The Routledge handbook of translation studies* (pp. 45–59). Abingdon: Routledge.

Gielen, S., Dochy, F., & Dierick, S. (2003). Evaluating the consequential validity of new modes of assessment: The influence of assessment on learning, including pre-, post- and true assessment effects. In F. Dochy, M. Segers, & E. Cascallar (Eds.), *Optimising new modes of assessment: In search of quality and standards* (pp. 37–54). Dordrecht: Kluwer Academic.

Gilmore, A. (2007, April). Authentic materials and authenticity in foreign language learning. *Language Teaching*, 40(2), 97–118. https://doi.org/10.1017/S0261444807004144

Gulikers, J. T. M., Bastiaens, T., & Kirschner, P. (2004). A five-dimensional framework for authentic assessment. *Educational Technology Research and Development*, 52, 67–85.

Incalcaterra McLoughlin, L., & Lertola, J. (2014). Audiovisual translation in second language acquisition: Integrating subtitling in the foreign language curriculum. *Interpreter and Translator Trainer*, *8*(1), 70–83.

Lambert, W. E., Boehler, I., & Sidoti, N. (1981). Choosing the languages of subtitles and spoken dialogues for media presentations: Implications for second language education. *Applied Psycholinguistics*, *2*(2), 133–48. https://doi.org/10.1017/S0142716400000904

Lertola, J. (2013). *Subtitling new media: Audiovisual translation and second language vocabulary acquisition*. Galway: National University of Ireland.

Lertola, J. (2015). Subtitling in language teaching: Suggestions for language teachers. In Y. Gambier Yves, A. Caimi, & C. Mariotti (Eds.), *Subtitles and language learning* (pp. 245–67). Bern: Peter Lang.

Lertola, J. (2019). *Audiovisual translation in the foreign language classroom: Applications in the teaching of English and other foreign languages*. Voillans: Research-publishing.net.

Lindgren, E., & Muñoz, C. (2013). The influence of exposure, parents, and linguistic distance on young European learners' foreign language comprehension. *International Journal of Multilingualism*, *10*, 105–29.

McKenzie, R. (2018). Subtitling in the classroom: Il secondo tragico Fantozzi (1976). *Neke—The New Zealand Journal of Translation Studies*, *1*(1). https://doi.org/10.26686/neke.v1i1.5160

O'Sullivan, C. (2013). Introduction: Multimodality as challenge and resource for translation. *Journal of Specialised Translation*, 20, 2–14.

Paivio, A. (1986). *Mental representations: A dual coding approach*. New York: Oxford University Press.

Peter, E., & Webb, S. (2018). Incidental vocabulary acquisition through viewing L2 television and factors that affect learning. *Studies in Second Language Acquisition*, *40*(3), 551–77. https://doi.org/10.1017/S0272263117000407

Talaván, N. (2006). Using the technique of subtitling to improve business communicative skills. *RLFE, Revista de Lenguas Para Fines Específicos*, 11–12, 313–46.

University of Liverpool. (n.d.). Liverpool curriculum framework. Accessed November 22, 2022. https://www.liverpool.ac.uk/centre-for-innovation-in-education/curriculum-resources/

Venuti, L. (1995). *The translator's invisibility: A history of translation*. London: Routledge.

Wegner, H. (1977). *Teaching with film*. Bloomington: Phi Delta Kappa.

8

TEACHING ITALIAN THROUGH PODCASTING

Pedagogical Rationale, Implementation,
and Student Evaluation of the Podcast Project
Dagli Inviati sul Campus

Elisabetta Ferrari, Riccardo Amorati, and John Hajek

This contribution discusses the podcast project *Dagli inviati sul campus*, developed at the University of Melbourne (Australia), aimed at incorporating experiential and project-based learning (PBL) (Kolb, 2015; Lee, 2015; Park & Hiver, 2017; Stoller, 2006) into an intermediate-level Italian language subject. After presenting the project, we discuss its aims and theoretical foundations, offer a detailed description of its mechanics (inclusion in the subject, internal organization, role of the teacher, assessment methods), and present an overview of the podcasts produced by students. Finally, we discuss some empirical data on students' evaluation of the activity, in an effort to encourage future implementations of the project in Italian and in other languages across different delivery modes and university contexts. This chapter also includes an overview of subsequent COVID-19 pandemic-related changes applied to the project, due to the online learning and teaching delivery mode, and some initial findings on its online application.

THE PODCAST PROJECT: *DAGLI INVIATI SUL CAMPUS*

The podcast project *Dagli inviati sul campus* was first implemented in 2018 as a pilot activity for students taking an intermediate-level Italian subject and was offered again the following year with some minor refinement. As part of the project, students enrolled in the second semester subject Italian 4 (ITAL10002 and ITAL20008) are required to produce, in small groups (3 to 4 students), short podcasts in Italian for potential broadcasting. Podcasts are scripted by students and then recorded in a professional recording studio (available at the university). They are then subsequently edited by professional staff to optimize sound quality and, if necessary, can include prerecorded interviews or music. Students are also required to produce a short version of the podcast (about 1 minute) for submission to SBS Italian Radio (a national broadcasting service that targets Italian speakers in Australia through radio and podcasting) as part of a collaboration to give students direct industry contact as well as appropriate work-related skills relevant to media production.

Podcasts produced as part of the project are used both for assessment purposes and as listening material shared in class for learning purposes. As part of the project each group is responsible for overseeing and completing the whole podcast's production: choice of themes, research, interviews, script writing and editing, and podcast recording. In 2020 and 2021, as teaching and learning activities shifted online due to the COVID-19 pandemic, the podcast project was once again offered, with minimal changes, as an online group activity and assessment.

AIMS AND THEORETICAL FOUNDATIONS OF THE PROJECT

The learning module underpinning the podcast project was informed by scholarship on three key pedagogical foundations or drivers, which are displayed in Figure 8.1, together with subthemes related to each. Due to space limitations, in this chapter we will only elaborate some aspects of these foundations before listing the specific aims and expected outcomes of the project.

Podcasts as a Learning Tool

Podcasts are increasingly being included in language classroom settings as a learning tool (e.g., Edirisingha et al., 2007; Samperi Mangan, 2008). There is a reasonable body of research literature that focuses on the implementation and inclusion of podcasts in the language curriculum as a means to improve listening skills and competence as well as to provide authentic material in the teaching and learning of a second language (L2) (e.g., Abdulrahman et al.,

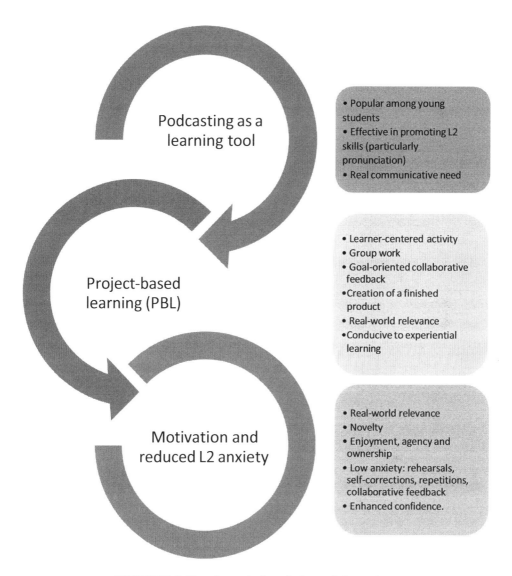

FIGURE 8.1. Key thematic foundations of the project.

2018; Kavaliauskienė & Anusienė, 2009). Less attention has, to date, been given to students' production of podcasts as a learning tool and its subsequent use in class. The idea to include an assessment task focusing on the production of podcasts by students emerged from various considerations: a need to move away from a "traditional" form of oral assessment; a focus on student-centered activities that could lead to the inclusion of co-creative aspects in the curriculum; and the possibility of reaching out to a wider audience/community outside the classroom. As noted previously, a collaboration with SBS Italian

Radio has also been established as a type of industry engagement that enables students to hear firsthand from experts in the industry in an effort to equip them with work-oriented skills as part of the project.

Podcasts are considered a familiar medium by students and they are supported by increasingly accessible technology that also allows for facilitated self-production. The latter point was confirmed for the current project. Although in the first two editions of this project students' podcasts were recorded in a professional studio, the online shift imposed by COVID-19 restrictions demonstrated that the project could easily be transferred online and completed with readily available everyday technology tools (e.g., mobile phones, Zoom recordings, Teams meetings, etc.).

Rethinking Oral Activities and Assessment from a PBL Perspective

This project seeks to readdress the way in which L2 oral activities and oral assignments are included and evaluated within the subject curriculum by creating novel student-centered, project-based, and experiential-learning activities that are engaging and foster students' self-confidence as well as their proficiency in the use of the language.

The complexity and variety of assessment for language learning have been widely studied. Chapelle and Brindley (2010) note, nevertheless, that little attention has been given to the pedagogical role of assessment, although they also report a shift away from more "traditional" forms toward approaches able to closely align performance assessment with curriculum and instruction. Among these alternative forms of assessment we can find, for instance, project work, peer-assessment, and learning journals. These are examples of assessment that can help increase students' self-motivation, involvement in learning trajectories, and independent learning (Chapelle & Brindley, 2010). This rationale fully aligns with the pedagogical and innovative aims of the podcast project, which intends to include PBL elements in both language oral activities and assessment tasks.

In the context of language education, PBL is considered an appropriate tool to foster communicative language learning (CLL) (e.g., Mitchell, 1994; Pachler, 2000). CLL emphasizes the importance of creating learning opportunities where the language is used for a real purpose and promotes the inclusion of authentic texts and tasks in the language classroom. The focus is on the ability to use the target language (TL) to communicate personal meaning rather than on knowledge about the TL. In this approach there is an emphasis on active participation of learners and language use outside the classroom.

According to Seidel, Aryeh, and Steinberg (2002), PBL is most often characterized by activities that are linked to an outcome and that are not only confined to the classroom, while at the same time having defined goals linked to various interrelated dimensions (academic, social, and metacognitive). The same authors also underline the necessity for ongoing assessment and feedback from instructors, peers, and the public, as well as self-assessment. The way in which PBL can be applied in the classroom and especially in the context of foreign language acquisition is wide and varied (Parker, 2020).

The PBL podcast project devised also provides students with an experiential, that is, hands-on learning opportunity as well as the opportunity to co-create/design part of the subject curriculum. This process allows students to have a more active and meaningful collaboration with their teachers and peers and an authentic learning experience while also moving from a more traditional top-down model of curriculum design to a participatory bottom-up collaborative approach (Gravett et al., 2019).

Motivation and Language Anxiety

The devised project has also been informed by considerable research that addresses issues of student well-being, anxiety, and motivation in second language acquisition (Dörnyei, 1994, 2001; Gkonou et al., 2017; Lambert et al., 2017). One of the most difficult challenges for language learners, at first- and second-year levels in particular, is to achieve confidence when using the target language. Students typically experience feelings of insecurity and anxiety when faced with oral activities and oral assessment conducted in class. Students often describe oral activities, in addition to provoking feelings of apprehension, as impacting on their confidence and motivation in the use of the target language (Lemos Tello, 2012). Furthermore, oral components (both assessed and not assessed) also increase students' fear of negative peer evaluation (e.g., Gkonou et al., 2017). The production of podcasts allows students not only to reflect on their competences but also to successfully create a finished product centered on their oral skills without the pressure usually associated with on-the-spot classroom presentations.

EXPECTED OUTCOMES AND AIMS OF THE PROJECT

The project is directed at enhancing students' confidence and motivation while using an additional language. There is an emphasis on participation and teamwork during class activities as well as collaboration between students and tutors/lecturers. One of the project's aims is also to foster co-creation activities for inclusion in the subject curriculum. Students will therefore improve communication/oral skills, allowing them to confidently use the language in an authentic real-life situation. This increases experiential learning as part of a first/second year subject. Furthermore, the project is designed to implement oral activities aimed at reducing student anxiety.

Students also develop digital literacy skills as the project focuses on providing an effective, intellectually stimulating experience at the undergraduate level that takes them out of the classroom and into a novel work-type context. The project can also potentially serve as a model for student-focused experiential learning for all languages offered at the university level.

IMPLEMENTATION OF THE PROJECT AND INCLUSION IN THE CURRICULUM

As mentioned previously, the podcast project, *Dagli inviati sul campus*, was implemented as part of the oral component of a first- and second-year intermediate-level Italian subject. The University of Melbourne degree structure allows students to complete the study of a language as part of a major/minor/diploma, and also as single units within the so-called breadth subject component for students completing degrees both inside and outside the humanities field. This flexible model allows for a very diversified cohort of students studying an L2, resulting in a variety of studies' approaches, range of skills, range of expectations, and career pathways. The project was therefore conceived taking into account the varied composition of students' backgrounds and personal motivations in the study of the TL.

Curriculum and Project Structure, Methodology and Role of Teachers

The subject, Italian 4, includes 4 weekly hours of in-class teaching (for a duration of 12 weeks per semester) involving both seminars and a practical class. Within this curriculum structure teaching and learning activities follow a mixed-mode pedagogical approach and teaching modes (text analysis and discussion, explicit grammar instruction, etc.) with a program that centers on Italian culture, history, and contemporary literature. In editions of the subject before the inclusion of this project, subject assessment included a "traditional"

TABLE 8.1. Semester Plan for Practical Class (Divided into Three Phases)

Structure of the practical class over the semester	Activities
Part 1 (weeks 1–4)	Exposure to professional podcasts with listening comprehension activities, awareness-raising of genre-specific conventions, and general conversation on a variety of topics Workshop on Italian phonetics (how to sound more natural) Guest visit from SBS Italian radio staff
Part 2 (weeks 5–9)	Practical class activities (1) First half: students work half an hour in class on their podcasts (research, drafting of script) (Students' main podcast work is conducted outside class contact hours) (2) Second half: general conversation on a variety of topics Each week one or two groups record their podcasts (in a professional university recording studio) with another teacher instead of attending the practical class
Part 3 (weeks 10–12)	Listening activities on podcasts produced by students

oral presentation in Italian on an assigned topic. The podcast project substituted for this oral assignment and was incorporated in the practical class component of the subject, constituting 20% of the overall subject assessment (a further 10% is assessed as part of the subject's final examination).

The organization of the project follows the dynamic learning organization structure of PBL identified by Thi Kim (2019): identify the learning project topic; make a plan; implement the learning project; present the results; and then assess the results.

The phases of the project are summarized in Table 8.1. The project begins at the start of the semester with an initial experiential phase, where students are exposed to the use of podcasts (listening and comprehension) and engage with staff from SBS Italian Radio to gain a deeper understanding of the medium. Students are then grouped into teams to begin their own podcast's productions, and by the end of the semester they also become the main users and consumers of these.

During the pandemic-related online teaching and learning period, as mentioned earlier, the project structure was slightly modified, shifting most of students' group work outside class contact hours through independently organized Zoom/Team online meetings. Additionally, as access to the recording studio was unavailable due to COVID-19 restrictions, students were also required to complete their own recordings and were offered the choice to have them edited by professional technical staff from the university or to complete their work independently. Many groups were able to oversee the sound editing of their podcasts (adding music, background noise, etc., with available programs), delivering a surprisingly good-quality product without the need for specialized assistance.

Although the first few weeks of the semester are focused on familiarizing students with podcast activities, most of the project revolves around group work conducted outside class contact hours as an independent student activity. The actual production of students' podcasts can be divided into five main steps:

- Topic research—Students are required to identify a theme (which must then be approved by the teacher), conduct research and/or interviews (teachers are available to facilitate interviews through first contact or letter of support). (For a comprehensive list of topics see Table 8.3.)
- Podcast script writing—Podcasts scripts are written by students in groups and sent to the teacher for editing. Students are encouraged to use a dialogue style in their script to achieve a more natural use of language while recording.
- Podcast script editing—Teachers edit the podcast and return corrections and suggestions to the students for final script submission. The final script is then used as a transcript aid during class activities and podcast listening activities.
- Podcast recording and audio file editing—These are undertaken in a professional recording studio at the university or by individual groups during online teaching and learning mode.
- Use of podcasts among other groups—Podcasts are used in class among students (of all groups) and associated listening and comprehension activities are prepared by teachers.

During the organization of the project, which involves a shift from a more traditional teacher-centered approach, much consideration was given to the role of teaching staff. The aim was to be able to provide enough support in activities that were conceived as student-centered, while maintaining a focus on independent, self-directive work and team collaboration. While teachers remain available during the whole project to direct, facilitate, and guide students in their research, their major role is performed during the third and

TABLE 8.2. Assessment Structure and Marking Criteria

Material produced by students	Marking criteria
ASSESSMENT 1 1. First draft podcast script (group submission) 2. Final podcast script, after revisions (group submission) 3. Personal reflection on the experience and on teamwork (individual submission)	Use of language and vocabulary, structure of podcast—60% (group mark) Research, data collection, accuracy of details and information—20% (group mark) Personal reflection on podcast project—20% (individual mark)
ASSESSMENT 2 Recorded podcast	Voice recording as per final podcast registration (accuracy, vocabulary, pronunciation)—60% (individual mark) Presentation of podcast, as per final podcast recording—20% (group mark) Coherence and teamwork, as per final podcast recording—20% (group mark)

fourth phases of podcast script editing and as facilitator/coach in the recording studio.

Assessment Methods and Learning Outcomes

The assessment of the podcast project takes into consideration the various aspects of learning outcomes expected by students that have been discussed previously. Students are assessed on their recorded podcasts in terms of accuracy, vocabulary, pronunciation, and on their podcast script (see Amorati et al., 2022). Hence the project entails both oral and written assessment. Finally, students are asked to reflect on their personal and group contribution. Table 8.2 summarizes the two assessment components.

Overview of Podcasts Produced

For this project students receive broad direction in the selection of podcast themes, leaving the main responsibility for the choice of topics and research to individual groups. As previously noted, students are invited to cover themes that could be of interest to fellow students of Italian and to the broader Italian community in Australia (i.e., students' experience, university life, topics studied, Italian community events, etc.). Students are also asked to include only factual themes conveying real information (as opposed to invented scenarios or events). Additionally, students are encouraged, when relevant, to conduct and include interview excerpts.

Over the years in which the project has been offered, students have tended to investigate topics close to their personal interests as learners of an L2, sharing personal motivations for their choice in learning Italian. Various events and/or historical facts related to the local Italian community have also been extensively researched and used as main themes.

Table 8.3 shows a selection of themes chosen by students in their podcasts throughout the implementation of the project:

The sample topics listed in Table 8.3 highlight a common interest among students to research and focus on the reasons for studying a language and also on their personal or community connection with the history of the local Italian migration. Not surprisingly, during the pandemic, students tended to focus on the impact of COVID-19 on their personal and academic lives. This theme, which was explored through different points of view, offers an important insight into both students' well-being and personal experiences during an unprecedented event.

SELECTED FINDINGS ON STUDENTS' EVALUATION OF THE PROJECT AS AN ON-CAMPUS ACTIVITY

To study and understand the effectiveness and reception of the project, data have been collected since its first implementation through online questionnaires eliciting both quantitative and qualitative data as well as through the use of interviews and focus groups. In this section, we present selected findings on students' evaluation of the project as an on-campus learning activity, as well as the problems that some have encountered. Our main goal here is to offer some insight on key aspects that educators should keep in consideration when implementing the project. The data presented in this section were collected from students who completed the subject on campus in 2018 and 2019. The sample consists of 24 questionnaire respondents (only 20 answered some of the questions presented here) and 7 interviews with participants. Due to space limitations, the reader is referred to Amorati, Ferrari, and Hajek (2022) for a detailed overview of the study design as well as of the demographic background of the sample.

Among the questions asked in the survey, we were interested in exploring how students perceived aspects of the project relating to the use of Italian for a real purpose, the incorporation of a research component, and finally the use

TABLE 8.3. Selection of Themes Chosen by Students for Podcasts

Year	Topics
2018	Students' life and experiences • The experiences of international students on campus • Students' music preferences Podcasts related to Italian culture / history / events in Australia • Comparing migration from Italy to Melbourne from post-WWII to the present • Italian festa event in Melbourne • Italian Film Festival (presented in Melbourne by Palace Cinemas) General topics of interest • Teaching and learning languages at the University of Melbourne • Bilingual education in an increasingly monolingual Australia
2019	Students' life and experiences • Studying Italian and music at university • The advantages and disadvantages faced by international students in Melbourne, and some suggestions • Advantages and disadvantages of studying science and Italian Podcasts related to Italian culture / history / events in Australia • Cinescapes: a cinema retrospective presented by the Italian Institute of Culture in Melbourne • A photographic event organized by Co.As.it. (local institution in Melbourne) • Italian Film Festival (presented in Melbourne by Palace Cinemas) • Second-generation Italians and how to maintain the Italian language and culture in Melbourne
2020 Online edition	Students' life and experiences (Focus on life during the pandemic) • Distance education for students during COVID-19 • Studying Italian during COVID-19 • How to feel like you are in Italy while in lockdown • How to survive lockdown Students' life and experiences • Reasons for studying Italian Podcasts related to Italian culture / history / events in Australia / or on Italian culture • History of Italian community in Melbourne • The cinema of Federico Fellini
2021 Online edition	Students' life and experiences (Focus on life during the pandemic) • Living with COVID-19 • Studying a language during COVID-19 • Negative and positive aspects of studying online during COVID-19 Students' life and experiences • Reasons for studying Italian Podcasts related to Italian culture / history / events in Australia / or on Italian culture • Italian migration and food in Melbourne • Garibaldi and Australia • The life and work of Raffaello

TABLE 8.4. Questionnaire Items Relating to Key Aspects of the Project

Question	Strongly disagree	Disagree	Not sure	Agree	Strongly agree	Total
1. Creating and recording a podcast enabled me to use the language in a real way[i]	0% (0)	8.3% (2)	8.3% (2)	41.7% (10)	41.7% (10)	24
2. The podcast project allowed me to complete further research on Italian related topics	0% (0)	0% (0)	20.8% (5)	50% (12)	29.2% (7)	24
3. The podcast project was a good way to complete the oral assessment for the subject	0% (0)	8.33% (2)	4.17% (1)	20.83% (5)	66.7% (16)	24

Response rates are given in percentages and raw numbers (in parentheses). The most common response is highlighted.

i. Please note that this item has also been presented in Amorati, Ferrari, and Hajek (2022), where the focus was more on students' perceptions of the impact of the project on L2 proficiency rather than on their experience of the learning activity.

of the activity as part of the assessment. Questionnaire items are displayed in Table 8.4.

As response rates in relation to the first item show, the opportunity to use Italian to produce a final tangible product was highly valued. As we have noted elsewhere (Amorati et al., 2022), the presence of such a product that could be potentially broadcast contributed to students' long-term investment in the activity and also enabled them to use the language in a "real way," that is, for spoken discussions, rather than for more formal academic writing in the form of essays. This was for many a novel experience: "I enjoyed the podcast because it was unlike any other assignment I have completed" (Participant 1).

The research component included as part of the project was also generally appreciated. The largest portion of respondents agreed (50%) or strongly agreed (29.2%) that the activity allowed them to complete further research on Italian related topics (item 2). One of the key aspects contributing to students' enjoyment of the activity was the fact that they could research topics that they were interested in and that they perceived as having world relevance, while also exploring aspects of Italian culture: "The podcast project allowed me to research a topic which I had an interest in and allowed me to gain a more in-depth understanding of the Italian culture" (Participant 2).

Students were also asked whether the project was a good way to complete the oral assessment for the subject (item 3). As can be seen, respondents were overwhelmingly in agreement with the statement. This was also confirmed by qualitative comments: "I loved the assessment for this project. I felt at ease, it didn't feel like an exam. Also, the reflection was good too" (Participant 3).

There was additionally general agreement that the project was more enjoyable than an oral presentation, mainly because it entailed an element of creativity while still having a clear structure. In addition, the project was perceived as less anxiety-inducing, as students worked in groups and had the opportunity to repeat sentences in case they made mistakes. The following quotes illustrate these findings:

> I like when there's an actual purpose to the assessments and when some level of creativity is provided while still having a relatively clear structure. I definitely preferred this over an oral presentation in front of class. (Participant 4)

> I really liked this assessment. I had never recorded a podcast prior to this so it was a very rewarding experience and I learnt a lot more regarding the use and control of the Italian language than I would have from the standard oral presentation format. (Participant 5)

> I was nervous but at the same time there were four of us in there and we were all sort of like helping each other . . . in terms of the group, you were there . . . it was a lot easier I think, because we could redo it if it wasn't right. (Participant 6)

Students were also asked if they had encountered any problems during the project, as our aim was to determine which aspects needed further improvement in future iterations (see Table 8.5). Of the 20 participants who answered this question, 55% (n = 11) responded affirmatively.

The respondents who encountered problems were asked to specify what they struggled with. They could select as many answers as they wished from a list and could also add any other response that was not included. Respondents were also encouraged to leave comments to explain their answers if they wished (n = 7). Results are presented in Table 8.6.

As can be seen, the main issue appeared to be related to group work (28.6%). Participants mostly referred to other group members not meeting

TABLE 8.5. Respondents Report Whether They Encountered Problems during the Project

Did you encounter any problem when carrying out the tasks?	Answer	% (Raw number)	Count	Total respondents
	Yes	55% (11)	11	20
	No	45% (9)	9	

TABLE 8.6. Respondents Report Which Problems They Encountered

	Answer	% (Raw number)	Count	Total
What problem(s) did you encounter? Please explain your answer in the comments.	1. The project was time consuming	21.4% (3)	3	
	2. Group work was difficult	50% (7)	7	
	3. My language skills were not up to the required standard	28.6% (4)	4	14
	4. I did not receive enough support	0% (0)	0	
	5. Other (Please specify)	0% (0)	0	

Percentages are calculated on the total number of responses.

deadlines and impacting the quality of the final work: "We had a member of our group who did not complete the task(s) agreed to and failed to work as a team player nor respond to feedback. This made our project very difficult as her lack of commitment and effort affected the overall product" (Participant 7).

Group work issues are often unavoidable in activities that require teamwork, as some participants acknowledged: "This is always a problem in group work" (Participant 8), and students are likely to encounter similar issues not only during their studies but also in their professional lives (see also Amorati et al., 2022, for further discussion on this). A possible way to reduce these issues would be to encourage students to assign clear roles within groups, including supervisory roles (e.g., one student being responsible, among other things, for deadlines being respected and for reporting the issue to the teacher if the problem persists).

In the design of the project we have attempted to manage the time commitment by allowing students to work in class on their podcast drafts. However, as shown in Table 8.6, some participants indicated (21.4%) that the time required was still an issue. This was not completely unexpected, as this is a common problem associated with the implementation of PBL (Larmer et al., 2015). Complex projects generally require more time investment than more traditional classroom activities: "Writing, editing and creating the podcast in tandem with others did take quite a lot of time" (Participant 9).

In particular, some students indicated in the qualitative comments that they would have liked to have had more time to rehearse with a teacher before the recording: "It might be good to have a bit more time on the project, especially for the recording aspect. Maybe more info/practice recording?" (Participant 10). This could be easily integrated in future iterations of the project, with some consultation sessions being organized before the recording session.

Some respondents also indicated that their language skills were not up to the required standards (28.6%). In our experience, however, even students with lower proficiency were able to successfully complete the project. While—as noted previously—working in groups can have disadvantages, it has the clear advantage that different team members can bring different skills and compensate for one another's weaknesses.

As we have noted elsewhere, students also appreciated listening to other groups' podcasts, but sometimes complained that they lacked specific vocabulary to fully understand them. For this reason, in future iterations of the project, we aim to ask students to submit a glossary with useful vocabulary relevant to their podcast together with their script.

SELECTED FINDINGS ON STUDENTS' EVALUATION OF THE PROJECT AS AN ONLINE ACTIVITY

Some initial data collected on students' perceptions of the online version of the project show very similar findings in terms of students' positive perception of the activity as a way to use Italian for a real purpose as part of an assessment task. Similarly, problems related to group work and the time-consuming nature of project-based work also emerged.

During this second evaluation of the project students were asked to comment specifically on the benefits of the project as an online activity. Students commented, for example, on how the project created an opportunity for social/peer interactions, highlighting a new important aspect of the activity, especially in an online learning environment: "Meeting new people. Connection with students on topic, in depth discussions in Italian leading to better oral skills" (Participant 11); "A strong connection with other students. I really enjoyed this activity" (Participant 12).

As previously mentioned, topics chosen by students during the two years of online learning tended to focus on the effect of the pandemic on students and the wider community. Students were asked to comment on the opportunity that the project gave them as a space to talk about their own experience with COVID-19. All answers show that this opportunity was considered useful as noted in the comment: "Yes it allowed not only our team but the rest of the students in our class to hear about our experiences and perspectives as well as let us hear about others and we all gained a wider understanding of how different this has been for everyone" (Participant 13).

These initial data demonstrate that the podcast project has strong application potential even in an online learning environment and that additionally it offered an opportunity for peer engagement and teamwork across a different mode of delivery.

OUTCOMES AND CONCLUSIONS

In this chapter we have outlined how the oral component of an intermediate Italian language can be successfully transformed through a project-based learning activity focused on podcast production by students.

The curriculum change we discuss has multidimensional implications and consequences for students' experience of language learning. The project has a direct positive outcome on students' confidence in speaking skills by addressing student anxiety and stress normally associated with oral production, by allowing them to work collaboratively in small groups, and by giving them the opportunity to edit their oral work and strengthen their oral skills. At the same time, by asking students to have an active role in choosing the topics to be investigated for their podcasts, and producing the podcast for a potential broadcast around Australia, the project also allows them to learn and apply skills in a real-life work situation and therefore enhance students' employability, while also improving their proficiency and ability to conduct tasks in Italian.

BIBLIOGRAPHY

Abdulrahman, T., Basalama, N., & Rizky Widodo, M. (2018). The impact of podcasts on EFL students' listening comprehension. *International Journal of Language Education*, *2*(2), 23–33.

Amorati, R., Ferrari, E., & Hajek, J. (2022). Podcasting as project-based learning and its effect on the acquisition of linguistic and non-linguistic skills. *Language*

Learning in Higher Education, *12*(1), 7–28. https://doi.org/10.1515/cercles-2022-2036

Chapelle, C. A., & Brindley, G. (2010). Assessment. In N. Schmitt (Ed.), *An introduction to applied linguistics* (pp. 247–67). London: Routledge.

Dörnyei, Z. (1994). Motivation and motivating in the foreign language classroom. *Modern Language Journal*, *78*(3), 273–84.

Dörnyei, Z. (2001). *Motivational strategies in the language classroom*. Cambridge: Cambridge University Press.

Edirisingha, P., Rizzi, C., Nie, M., & Rothwell, L. (2007). Podcasting to provide teaching and learning support for an undergraduate module on English language and communication. *Turkish Online Journal of Distance Education—TOJDE*, *8*(3), 87–107.

Gkonou, C., Dewaele, J.-M., & Daubney, M. (2017). *New insights into language anxiety: Theory, research and educational implications*. Bristol: Multilingual Matters.

Gravett, K., Medland, E., & Winstone, N. E. (2019). Engaging students as co-designers in educational innovation. In S. Lygo-Baker, I. M. Kinchin, & N. E. Winstone (Eds.), *Engaging student voices in higher education: Diverse perspectives and expectations in partnership*. Cham, Switzerland: Palgrave Macmillan.

Kavaliauskienė, G., & Anusienė, L. (2009). English for specific purposes: Podcasts for listening skills. *Coactivity: Philology, Educology*, *17*(2), 28–37.

Kolb, D. 2015. *Experiential learning: Experience as the source of learning and development*. Upper Saddle River, NJ: Pearson Education.

Lambert, C., Philp, J., & Nakamura, S. (2017). Learner-generated content and engagement in second language task performance. *Language Teaching Research*, *21*(6), 665–80.

Larmer, J., Mergendoller, J., & Boss, S. (2015). *Setting the standard for project based learning: A proven approach to rigorous classroom instruction*. Alexandria: ACSD.

Lee, C.-J. (2015). Project-based learning and invitations: A comparison. *Journal of Curriculum Theorizing*, *30*(3), 63–73.

Lemos Tello, N. C. (2012). On air: Participation in an online radio show to foster speaking confidence: A cooperative learning-based strategies study. *Profile*, *14*(1), 91–112.

Mitchell, R. (1994). The communicative approach to language teaching: An introduction." In A. Swarbrick (Ed.), *Teaching modern languages* (pp. 33–42). London: Routledge.

Pachler, N. (2000). Re-examining communicative language teaching. In K. Field (Ed.), *Issues in modern foreign language teaching* (pp. 26–41). London: Routledge.

Park, H., & Hiver, P. (2017). Profiling and tracing motivational change in project-based L2 learning. *System*, *67*, 50–64.

Parker, J. L. (2020). Students' attitudes toward project-based learning in an intermediate Spanish course. *International Journal of Curriculum and Instruction*, *12*(1), 80–97. http://ijci.wcci-international.org/index.php/IJCI/article/view/254/153.

Samperi Mangan, J. (2008). Podcasting and iPod in teaching and learning Italian language, culture and literature: A research study at Université de Montréal." In E. Occhipinti (Ed.), *New approaches to teaching Italian language and culture: Case studies from an international perspective* (pp. 210–24). Newcastle: Cambridge Scholars.

Seidel, S., Aryeh, L., & Steinberg, A. (2002). *Project-based and experiential learning in after-school programming*. Report. Harvard Graduate School of Education. https://files.eric.ed.gov/fulltext/ED481931.pdf

Stoller, F. (2006). Establishing a theoretical foundation for project-based learning in second and foreign language contexts. In G. H. Beckett & P. Chamness Miller (Eds.), *Project-based second and foreign language education: Past, present, and future* (pp. 19–40). Greenwich: Information Age.

Thi Kim, O. D. (2019). Organizing experiential learning activities for development of core competences of technical students in Vietnam. *Universal Journal of Education Research*, 7(1), 230–38.

9

A CASE STUDY ON CHINESE EXCHANGE STUDENTS IN ITALY

Issues, Adaptation Strategies, and a Culture-Shock Management Syllabus

Shuang Liang, Pietro Amadini, Alessandro Macilenti

Until COVID-19 broke out, Italian universities hosted an increasing number of foreign students, and an increasing number of students from the People's Republic of China (PRC) selected Italy as a study destination (Bonvino & Rastelli, 2011; Statista Research Department, 2021). This trend is likely to resume after the pandemic wanes. However, studies investigating the effectiveness of student exchange programs—such as the Erasmus or Overseas programs, or other private agreements between universities—are, in contrast to the number of students involved in these initiatives, scarce. Given the increasing economic and educational importance of Sino-Italian exchange programs, the aim of this case study is to update the Italian and Chinese teaching communities on how to mitigate the adverse effects of culture shock and optimize the academic outcome of future cohorts of exchange students. Specifically, this chapter explores issues and problems encountered in short-term university student exchange programs. These only last a single semester, are arranged through direct arrangements between the interested universities, and allow Chinese students majoring in Italian and Italian students majoring in Chinese to spend time abroad without needing to certify their target language fluency.

Many international students arrive in Italy as a part of student exchange programs provided by private agreements between universities and not by consolidated protocols such as the Erasmus Program in Europe (Li et al., 2019). Because of linguistic and cultural differences and the fact that most of them have no international experience (Lin & Chen, 2019), a large percentage of Chinese exchange students report high levels of stress that impact their academic performance in the host country as well as diminish the benefit they could reap from this critical and often unrepeatable chance to familiarize themselves with Italian culture (Bonvino & Rastelli, 2011; Brenna, 2019; Lan, 2020; Tagliavini, 2015).

The literature on this topic mostly concentrates on long-term students who enroll in bachelor or master's programs, or in one-year exchange programs for high school students (Brenna, 2019; Li et al., 2019; Sinigaglia, 2014; Xue, 2010). Other studies focus on the Marco Polo and Turandot projects, which aim to prepare Chinese students for Italian higher education (Bagna & Carbonara, 2019; Bonvino & Rastelli, 2011; Canini & Scolaro, 2020; Li et al., 2019).[1] Studies focused on the difficulties of Chinese students in Italy are even rarer. Celentin (2013) offers an interesting contribution on Erasmus students in Italy. However, Celentin's contribution only marginally touches on issues specific to Chinese students. Li Baogui et al. (2019) exhaustively investigate the characteristics, challenges, and countermeasures of China-Italy higher education cooperation and exchange under the background of the Belt and Road Initiative,[2] providing detailed data on Chinese universities offering an Italian major and on students involved in the programs. However, their study does not investigate short-term exchanges in Italy. This chapter is also indebted to Brenna (2019) and Yu Xiaoping (2001). Brenna (2019) is an interview-based qualitative study exploring accounts of culture shock among Italian exchange students in China. Yu Xiaoping (2001) provides a reference for the design structure of the questionnaire and the follow-up interview, and also investigates the specific issues faced by Chinese students studying abroad—although with a focus on the UK, it offers insight on Chinese students in other European countries. Xue (2010) and Chen (2014) study the phenomenon of culture shock in Chinese students abroad. Lin and Chen (2019) explore the construction of Chinese students' identity while studying abroad. Finally, Chen (2004) compares Chinese and European higher education systems and the impact of the two educational philosophies on Chinese students' lives, studies, and social activities abroad.

QUESTIONNAIRE AND INTERVIEWS

The research subjects (henceforth RSs) of this study were part of a cohort of 27 undergraduates aged 19–23 and attending the third year (out of a total of four) required to obtain the Chinese equivalent of a bachelor of arts in one of the main Italian departments of a university in the PRC's Northeast. Of these, 19 students (i.e., the RSs) spent a semester as exchange students at the Università Ca' Foscari (in Venice), while the remaining 8 (all female students) decided not to travel abroad. All of those who went to Italy agreed to take part in this study and, among them, 9 agreed to be interviewed. Two of the authors (Dr. Alessandro Macilenti and Dr. Pietro Amadini) were the RSs' lecturers of Italian studies before their departure and after their return, while the third, Dr. Shuang Liang, tutored the RSs in Italy.

After spending five to six months in their exchange program, RSs informally reported minimal improvements in their language proficiency. We assumed that their failure to improve their language skills was due to the stress of being thrown for the first time into a radically different social and academic landscape. However, it was found that conditions such as course selection and lack of familiarity with academic culture were more serious causes of the RSs' learning difficulties. In November 2020, the 19 RSs were invited to fill in an online questionnaire and participate in one-on-one interviews. The authors' decision to use a questionnaire followed by an interview replicates the statistical study method observed in similar studies, considered the most suitable approach to analyze and integrate heterogeneous and often conflicting data and opinion (Bagna & Carbonara, 2019; Brenna, 2019; Lan, 2020; Sinigaglia, 2014).

The questionnaire items were tested on a number of students from previous years in order to ensure clarity, meaningfulness, and coherence. The questionnaire included 50 questions in Chinese covering all aspects of the RSs' life and experiences in Italy, 20 of which yielded answers meaningful enough for inclusion in this study. To increase the number of students completing the questionnaire, a small monetary incentive (400 Chinese yuan or about €55 in total) was offered to the group after all eligible students completed the form, using a function of the WeChat app that allows sharing a sum of money within a chat group. Because the authors were in Italy and travel to the PRC was impossible due to COVID-19, the questionnaire was made available online using the forms.office.com website and shared as a link. In order to prevent duplicated entries and make sure all the RSs answered the questions, the authors asked the students to provide their identity with their responses. After collection and cleansing, the data were anonymized. To make it easier for the RSs to provide answers, no long-form questions were included. Instead, the questionnaire consisted almost exclusively of multiple-choice questions (in Chinese) about various aspects of the RSs' experience in Italy, divided into 6 thematic categories (see Appendix A of this chapter).

Based on existing literature, we decided to employ multiple tools to monitor consistency in order to try to work around the RSs' reticent and disenchanted relationship with academic authority (Canini & Scolaro, 2020).

First, we reassured the RSs in writing as well as in informal conversation that anonymity would be preserved and that this study was not in any way linked to or commissioned by the RSs' home university. Second, the questionnaire included two mechanisms to verify whether RSs understood the questions and carefully answered them: a timer to monitor how long the RSs took to fill in the questionnaire and a number of common-knowledge questions among the data-gathering questions, as per Appendix A.

Completion time varied between 1 and 26 minutes, with an average of 12.33 minutes. Completion time of 1 minute was disregarded: it is clearly impossible to answer all the questions meaningfully in such a short period of time. However, the authors noted that some RSs provided noncommittal, group-approved, or otherwise canned answers when asked to share personal opinions and a potential critical view of academic authority. Possible explanations could include lack of trust in the ultimate goal of the study or even the fear of informants. Eight RSs provided 1 or more incorrect answers to the common-knowledge questions and two RSs were excluded from the final results because of multiple wrong common-knowledge questions.

Table 9.1 summarizes the answers received from the RSs. Summaries are provided as averages (rounded up to the second decimal) for scale-type questions and as the number of times each answer was chosen overall for the multiple-choice questions (key to questions in Appendix A).

A few weeks after RSs completed the questionnaire, the authors asked them to take part in a follow-up interview, and a total of 9 students (all women) accepted. The interviews, led by Dr. Shuang Liang, were conducted in Chinese, conversational in form, about 20 minutes in duration, and included between 10 and 15 questions. On this occasion, students were not offered any kind of incentive, monetary or otherwise. Interviews touched on multiple aspects of the RSs' experience as exchange students and included questions that had already been asked in the questionnaire to verify that answers were consistent and, if they weren't, understand why. In addition, we included questions meant to further investigate the students' adaptation level to life and study in Italy while, at the same time, exploring in depth the main causes of their maladjustment.

The interview questions were customized to the answers of the RSs' questionnaires. Some of the most frequently asked questions are reported in Appendix B.

TABLE 9.1. Synthesis of Survey Replies

Question	Arithmetic mean or summary of replies
S.1	2.84
S.2	2.95
Q.1	2.05
Q.2	3.68
Q.3	4.32
F.1	No spare time: 1 Less than half day: 3 About half day: 9 More than half day: 4
F.2	Played video games: 4 Practiced team sports: 5 Went to the gym or practiced other solo sports: 2 Other extracurricular activities: 9 Took walks on my own: 9 Socialized with Chinese friends: 17 Socialized with Italian friends: 9 Socialized with people from other nationalities: 2
F.3	I had no friends: 5 I had 1 or 2 friends: 9 I had between 3 and 5 friends: 5 I had between 6 and 10 friends: 0 I had more than 10 friends: 1
T.1	None: 0 1: 0 2 or 3: 1 4 to 6: 7 More than 6: 11
T.2	None: 5 1: 0 2 or 3: 0 4 to 6: 5 More than 6: 6
T.3	By myself: 3 With my partner: 3 With classmates: 10 With Chinese friends: 14 With Italian friends: 1

(*continued*)

TABLE 9.1. (*Continued*)

Question	Arithmetic mean or summary of replies
C.1	Other Chinese institutes: 18 Other Asian countries: 8 Other European countries: 13 Africa: 0 North America: 4 South America: 3
C.2	Italian: 18 English: 14 Chinese: 10
C.3	3.10
A.1	3.42
A.2	3.68
A.3	4.37
A.4	4.58
A.5	Answering questions from the teacher: 13 Presentations: 11 Group activities: 12 Individual activities: 8 Note-taking: 13

A comprehensive analysis of the results goes beyond the scope of this chapter. Instead, an executive summary of recurring responses that have emerged from the interviews is offered here as provisional conclusions. The answers have been classified according to the same thematic groups already employed in the questionnaire, with the addition of two groups: "Learning methods and exams" and "Feedback."

- ◇ Access to basic services: 3 students declared having encountered difficulties in handling various procedures upon their arrival in Italy. Their main difficulties involved the complex and time-consuming procedures required to obtain a residency permit.
- ◇ Quality of life: 2 students pointed out that life was difficult at the beginning due to their insufficient language proficiency; 2 other students specified that they managed to adjust to life in Italy only toward the end of their stay.

- Free time: Traveling around and exploring the city of Venice were the main leisure activities of 3 students.
- Classroom socialization: 7 students declared that their Italian language partners had a significant effect on their language proficiency and ability to adapt to the Italian lifestyle.
- Academic achievement and satisfaction: 5 students expressed their satisfaction with this experience and thought that their Italian language proficiency had improved, while 3 students admitted that there was no significant improvement in their language proficiency while in Italy.
- Learning method and exams: 4 students thought that the traditional note-taking method generally adopted by Chinese students was more efficient compared with the method of taking notes with computers adopted by most Italian students. In addition, 2 students addressed stress-related issues that appeared in oral exams, which are common in Italy but not in China, while 2 students indicated that they preferred the flexibility of oral exams over sitting for written exams.
- Feedback from students: 5 students pointed out that a semester-long exchange was too short, hoping that the project time would be extended, while 2 students opined that the program time was sufficient.

DISCUSSION

After the RSs returned from their experience abroad, the authors noticed that the students' fluency had not improved as hoped. As already mentioned, in the interviews RSs themselves commented on their lack of improvement, and several even complained about having to leave Italy just as they were beginning to settle down and their use of Italian was beginning to improve. Based on previous research to date, the authors first hypothesized that the RSs' failure to improve their language skills was due to the stress of being exposed for the first time to a radically different social and academic environment. Indeed, while it is true that Italian academic institutions provide guidance to exchange students, interviews demonstrate that the RSs were often unaware of the support being offered. According to the results, RSs suffered from varying levels of stress during their stay in Italy. Nevertheless, the mean self-reported anxiety level was relatively light, with an average of 2.05 out of 5 (Table 9.1: Q.1). Anxiety as one of the main causes of suboptimal academic performance was therefore ruled out. Cumbersome bureaucracy and administration were also considered as plausible reasons why the ability of RSs to adapt to Italian society was hindered (Vedovelli, 2011). Indeed, interviews revealed students found Italian bureaucracy hard to navigate:

> I've requested the residence permit in Italy. You had to go early to the Police Headquarters and there was a very long queue. The Post Office was inefficient, and I had to go there twice. The first time, after a long while, I found out they had run out of residence permit forms. I've studied the procedure with my classmates. It was hard in the beginning. (RS3)

However, this was only a problem for the first few days of the RSs' permanence in Italy, as newcomers have to apply for a residence permit within 10 days of their entry in Italy. RSs report that the volume and complexity of the paperwork needed to legally stay in Italy, as well as the time spent queuing at a police station to take fingerprints, caused them a great deal of stress, which unfortunately corresponds with the time they first needed to navigate their Italian host university, its courses, and its classrooms. This initial stress, however, soon subsided and gave way to a relatively stress-free day-to-day routine.

The data shows that the RSs' difficulties with adjusting to the academic environment were closely linked to course selection (as in Canini & Scolaro, 2020). The interviews and the questionnaire show that RSs gave unclear answers as to who was responsible for their course selection. While some claimed that their head teacher simply recommended courses (e.g., RS1), others offer a different account: RS2 and RS5 state that at least the course Storia economica del Mediterraneo was chosen by their head teacher and that they would have preferred to choose their courses themselves. Indeed, a scan of the courses RSs have been enrolled in shows that some of these courses delve into specialized topics that RSs could not follow because they lack the required academic or language foundations. One example is the aforementioned course, which RSs had been enrolled in despite their rudimentary grasp of Italian history, and which was almost universally deemed too difficult partially because it was taught in English, a language most RSs are not fluent in (as reported by RS2, RS6, and RS8). Another example of a problematic course selection was Letteratura italiana, which includes content unsuitable to Chinese students whose proficiency in the Italian language reaches at best the Common European Framework of Reference for Languages (CEFR) level B1. In the interviews, RS5 pointed out that she would not have understood the contents of the literature class had it not been for her Chinese-speaking tutor, while RS6 complained that she could only grasp a fraction of what the professor was teaching. In addition to causing stress and confusion, inadequate course selection ate into the time RSs could devote to learning Italian: attending content courses reduced the time for their language courses. In fact, RSs reported only attending four hours of formal Italian language classes weekly. Furthermore, some RSs pointed out that the content of the Italian language courses in Italy was the same as in their home university (B1 level), so they considered language classes more of a revision than progression. In addition to formal language classes, once a week RSs attended a master's-level Lingua cinese course, not only finding themselves at ease in a Chinese-speaking environment, but using the time to learn Italian through a grammar-translation method. The Chinese literature class also provided the RSs with an opportunity to meet Italian language buddies who were also Chinese learners, and it was generally agreed that speaking with Italian buddies helped them improve their language proficiency. Nonetheless, their language skills did not significantly improve during their permanence.[3]

Another common grievance voiced by the interviewees involved the differences between the Italian and the Chinese teaching approaches (although this primarily concerns content classes as opposed to language classes) because the Italian teaching style differs radically from what Chinese students are used to (Cao, 2018; Celentin, 2013; Chen, 2004; Consalvo, 2012).[4] Since childhood, Chinese students have been exposed to teacher-centered, step-by-step teaching methods and have been deeply influenced by Chinese collectivist values. Therefore, they usually regard challenging others or taking a critical stance as an infringement on the dignity of life (Xue, 2010). Because of these cultural values, Chinese students tend to be taciturn, introverted, appear unwilling to learn, seemingly lack independent thought, and strictly abide by rules and regulations (Xue, 2010; Yu, 2001). In fact, RS5 and others were troubled by the flexibility of teaching methods and the learning freedom granted to students in Italy, finding themselves more motivated within Chinese academia, where they must follow a ready-made and standardized academic path. Academic staff in Italian universities also enjoy more teaching freedom than their PRC peers and can choose teaching content and materials independently. According to RSs, courses in Italy are somewhat less structured. RS9 points out that Italian teachers rarely make learning material available in advance and expresses a preference for the Chinese way that allowed her to consult learning materials beforehand. Moreover, exams in the RSs' home university are mostly written and mostly a formality, whereas RSs report that exams they took were for the most part oral. Although some of the RSs were happy with the flexibility that came with conversational examinations (see Lei, 2016), this brought tension and anxiety to others. For example, RS9 lamented that oral exams made her feel anxious and that she was unable to organize her thoughts and articulate her answers in such a setting.

We also found that the RSs were unfamiliar with differences between the Chinese and the Italian academic environments (Celentin, 2013), leading to missed opportunities. First, unlike in Chinese universities, lectures in Italy are open-access and signing up is required only in order to sit for exams. However, RSs incorrectly assumed that they were not allowed to attend any extra classes: RS6 claims that she felt that the university offered too few courses and found herself with too much time on her hands. RS5 claimed that she would have liked to attend more courses than the ones she had been enrolled in. A second peculiarity of Italian universities is that they provide students with long term breaks to allow time for self-study, causing RS7 to complain that classes were available for only three months out of her five-month stay.[5] Also, due to the number of available offerings in Italy, timetables might clash, potentially forcing students to drop classes or split attendance. RS5 pointed out that most of the classes were crammed in one day of the week, which made it impossible to even have lunch on that day. Due to these organizational circumstances and the lack of structured activities, RS5 found herself lacking motivation, feeling bored, and as a consequence, eschewing social contact. RS8 complained that the workload in Italy was too light and lectures too sparse. Because of this, she found she could not properly absorb the study material. Moreover, data from both the questionnaire and interviews shows that RSs chose not to take advantage of teaching staff's office hours, probably due to the fact that this option was not available at the RSs' home university. Instead, as a response to the pressure, RSs tended to gather in tightly bound study groups, often created even before leaving the PRC. Within these study groups, they supported each other in collating and comparing notes and helped each other when faced with learning difficulties (as in Celentin, 2013). Belonging to such subgroups, however, limited the RSs' ability to integrate into the host society and ended up determining the RSs' academic and life choices (even in relation to housing, sociality, and elective courses). Furthermore, being fettered to these Chinese-speaking groups led to an inability to establish meaningful informal relationships with locals and, consequently, to familiarize themselves with the Italian language and culture outside the academic setting. Due to lack of confidence in their language proficiency and lack of understanding of cultural differences, a vicious circle was established whereby RSs spent more time with Chinese students, making it harder for them to improve their language skills.

CONCLUSIONS

The authors of this chapter detected unsatisfactory improvements in their students' Italian language skills after they spent a semester in Italy. They wanted to explore whether this was due to the same problems and pressures afflicting Chinese students participating in longer exchange programs, which have been more extensively investigated. However, interviews indicate that issues faced by long-term exchange students and the RSs are only partially superimposable. It was found that neither stress nor bureaucracy can explain the RSs' difficulties in integrating and their unsatisfactory academic performance. Moreover, it became apparent that, although the RSs realize that they are taking part in an important cultural experience, they fail to translate it into an actual improvement in language proficiency. The authors would argue that a review of both home and host university learning offers is in order. In contrast to private initiatives (such as the Marco Polo and Turandot programs), short exchange programs like the one considered here require no minimum language fluency to sit for exams, and it thus would be desirable that host universities provide access to intensive Italian language courses for foreigners mirroring the Chinese offer. Another option would be to coordinate joint programs with the exchange students' home institutions. It is critical that short-term Chinese exchange students are offered a more structured, more focused, and more substantial Italian language curriculum during their stay abroad, even where this might mean sacrificing other content teachings.

It is our hope that, when Italian and Chinese institutes resume their exchange programs as the pandemic subsides, this chapter can provide clues as to how to enhance the overall quality of the learning outcomes for Chinese short-term exchange students. Specifically, this chapter provides Italian universities hosting exchange students from the PRC with indispensable insights to better understand and meet their needs, therefore enhancing material support and better tailoring the academic offer. The authors are only too aware that consistently replicating the same program in very different teaching and learning systems and environments is challenging, and they also know that relationships between universities are based on the principle of reciprocity in relation to study programs (see Li et al., 2019).[6] For these reasons, a syllabus has been included (Appendix C) to provide a blueprint for a propaedeutic short course to be delivered by the home university in the months preceding the students' departure. In addition, the authors plan to deliver the proposed syllabus to a cohort of students going on exchange to Italy whom they will also test and interview after their return in order to gauge their satisfaction and compare their pre- and postexchange language skills. It is to be noted, however, that the emergence of the COVID-19 pandemic has interrupted all academic exchange programs between Italy and the PRC for the foreseeable future. Even though the future of relationships between institutes remains uncertain, the authors believe that once the pandemic has subsided, exchange agreements will be reestablished and hope that the findings presented in this chapter will inform the way in which they are run.

APPENDIX A:
DATA-GATHERING QUESTIONS

1. Access to basic services:
   S.1. 取得居留的难度: 1 (很复杂) - 5 (很简单) (On a scale Between 1 (very hard) and 5 (very easy), how difficult did you find obtaining a "permesso di soggiorno" [residence permit]?)
   S.2. 在意大利办理各类手续有多困难: 1 (很复杂) - 5 (很简单) (On a scale between 1 (very hard) and 5 (very easy), how difficult did you find dealing with Italian bureaucracy?)
2. Quality of life:
   Q.1. 许多人在国外生活时会感到焦虑, 你在意大利时感觉如何: 1 (毫不焦虑) - 5 (非常焦虑) (Many people experience stress or unease when spending extended periods abroad. On a scale between 1 (almost nothing) and 5 (very much), how stressed did you feel while living in Italy?)
   Q.2. 很多人认为国外的生活消费水平偏高, 你认为意大利情况如何: 1 (消费低) - 5 (消费高) (For many students, living abroad can be expensive. On a scale between 1 (very cheap) and 5 (very expensive), how did you find living in Italy?)
   Q.3. 从个人经历而言(不考虑学业和语言水平), 你对去意大利的交流满意吗: 1 (很不满意) - 5 (非常满意) (From a personal point of view, on a scale between 1 (not at all) and 5 (very much), how satisfied are you with your exchange in Italy?)
3. Free time:
   F.1. 你在工作日里有多少闲暇时光?: (How much spare time did your typical day include?)
   选项: 没有闲暇时光; 少于半天; 半天; 大半天; 一整天 (Possible answers: none whatsoever; less than half day; about half day; more than half day; the whole day)
   F.2. 你业余时间都会做什么? (Which of these activities did you choose to do more often in your spare time?)
   选项: 团队运动; 去健身房或独自运动; 和中国朋友出去玩; 和意大利朋友出去玩; 独自探索城市; 打电子游戏; 其他 (Possible answers: team sports; individual sports including gym; going out with Chinese friends; going out with Italian friends; exploring the city on my own; playing video games; other.)
   F.3. 除同学外, 你经常与多少意大利朋友见面? (Besides your classmates, how many Italian friends did you choose to see more often?)

选项: 0个; 1-2个; 3-5个; 6-10个; 10个以上 (Possible answers: None; 1–2; 3–5; 6–10; more than 10.)

4. Travel

    T.1. 你参观过多少个意大利城市 (威尼斯除外)? (Excluding Venice, how many Italian cities did you visit during your stay?
    选项: 0个; 1个; 2-3个; 5-6个; 6个以上 (Possible answers: None; 1; 2–3; 4–6; more than 6.)

    T.2. 你参观过多少个欧洲 (意大利除外) 城市? (How many European (non-Italian) cities did you visit during your stay?)
    选项: 0个; 1个; 2-3个; 4-6个; 6个以上 (Possible answers: None; 1; 2–3; 4–6; more than 6.)

    T.3. 你和谁一起旅行? (With whom did you travel?)
    选项: 一个人; 和男/女朋友; 和同学; 和中国朋友; 和意大利朋友 (Possible answers: By myself; with my partner; with classmates; with Chinese friends; with Italian friends.)

5. Classroom socialization:

    C.1. 你的同学都来自哪里 (除了吉林外国语大学的同学)? (Think back about your Italian class classmates (excluding your colleagues from your university). Where did they come from?)
    选项: 其他中国学校; 其他亚洲国家; 其他欧洲国家; 北美; 南美; 非洲 (Possible answers: Other Chinese institutes; Other Asian countries; Other European countries; Africa; North America; South America)

    C.2. 你用哪种语言和外国同学交流? (Which languages did you use to communicate with your non-Chinese classmates?)
    选项: 意大利语; 英语; 中文 (Possible answers: Italian; English; Chinese)

    C.3. 刚到威尼斯时, 与班上其他同学相比, 你的意大利语水平怎么样: 1 (差很多) - 5 (好很多) (On a scale between 1 (much less fluent) and 5 (much more fluent), how fluent were you in Italian compared to your classmates?)

6. Academic achievement and satisfaction:

    A.1. 你认为回国后意大利语水平提高了多少: 1 (没提高) - 5 (提高很多) (On a scale between 1 (very little) and 5 (very much), how did your fluency in Italian improve during your stay in Italy?)

    A.2. 去上课时的心情: 1 (很沮丧) - 5 (很幸福) (On a scale between 1 (mostly negative) and 5 (mostly positive), how were your feelings while you were in class?)

A.3. 从学业角度上来看, 你对在意大利交流学习的经历满意吗: 1 (很不满意) - 5 (很满意) (From an educational point of view, on a scale between 1 (not at all) and 5 (very much), how satisfied are you with your exchange in Italy?)

A.4. 你会建议学弟学妹也去意大利交流学习吗: 1 (绝对不会) - 5 (肯定会) (On a scale between 1 (very unlikely) and 5 (very likely), how likely are you to recommend other students from your university to go on an exchange to Italy?)

A.5. 你经常参加哪些课堂活动? (What activities did you participate in?)
选项: 回答老师提问; 小组活动演讲; 独自活动; 记笔记; (Possible answers: Answering questions from the teacher; Group activities; Presentations; Individual activities; Note-taking)

COMMON-KNOWLEDGE QUESTIONS

- 7+6+9 等于多少? (7 + 6 + 9 equals?)
  Free short answer
- 意大利国旗的颜色是? (What are the colors of the Italian flag?)
  选项: 红色; 黄色; 绿色; 白色; 蓝色; 棕色; 紫色; 橙色 (Items: Red; Yellow; Green; White; Blue; Brown; Purple; Orange)
- 按照由大到小的顺序, 对以下动物进行排序 (Order these animals from the smallest to the biggest:)
  鲸鱼; 牛; 狗; 青蛙; 蚂蚁 (Items: Whale; Cow; Dog; Frog; Ant)
- 端午节的特色饮食是? (What special food is associated with the Dragon Boat Festival?)
- 威尼斯大学在哪个城市? (In which city is Ca' Foscari located?)
  Free short answer
- 9乘以4 等于多少? (9 * 4 equals?)
  Free short answer
- 中国国旗的颜色是? (What are the colors of the Chinese flag?)
  红色; 黄色; 绿色; 白色; 蓝色; 棕色; 紫色; 橙色 (Items: Red; Yellow; Green; White; Blue; Brown; Purple; Orange)

APPENDIX B:
COMMON INTERVIEW QUESTIONS

1. 你觉得在意大利办理各种手续困难吗? (Do you find it difficult to go through bureaucratic formalities in Italy?)
    1. 你在意大利有没有意大利朋友? (Did you have Italian friends in Italy?)
2. 你更喜欢跟意大利朋友还是中国朋友一起玩? 为什么? (Did you prefer to play with Italian friends or Chinese friends? Why?)
3. 你在意大利每天如何安排时间? (How did you organize your day in Italy?)
4. 你喜欢威尼斯大学的课程吗? 如果喜欢为什么会觉得它们很难? (Did you like the courses at the University Ca' Foscari of Venice? If you liked them, why did you find them difficult?)
5. 你最喜欢哪门课? 为什么喜欢那门课? 那门课与其他课程有何不同? (Which course do you like best? Why do you like it? How is that course different from other courses?)
6. 你上课会经常回答老师提问吗? (In class did you often answer the teacher's questions?)
7. 你认为意大利教学方法和中国的教学方法是否有差异? 差异是什么? 你更喜欢哪个? 为什么? (Do you think there are differences between Italian teaching methods and Chinese teaching methods? What are the differences? Which one do you prefer and why?)
8. 中国和意大利的意大利语课有哪些差异? (What are the differences between Italian language courses in China and Italy?)
9. 你上课时喜欢用哪种学习方法? 为什么? (Which learning method did you prefer to use in class? Why?)
10. 在学习时遇到问题你会如何处理? (How did you deal with problems while studying?)
11. 你认为意大利学生和中国学生的学习方法是否有差异? 差异是什么? (Do you think there are differences in the studying methods of Italian students and Chinese students? What are the differences?)
12. 你去意大利交流的主要目的是什么? 目的达到了没有? (What was the main purpose of your exchange in Italy? Has the purpose been achieved?)
13. 请你整体评价一下你在意大利的经历, 哪些方面你最满意, 哪些方面你最不满意? (Could you please rate your experience in Italy as a whole, which aspects are you most satisfied with and which aspects are you least satisfied with?)
14. 对此次交流学习项目有何建议? (What are your suggestions for this exchange program?

APPENDIX C:
CONOSCERE L'UNIVERSITÀ ITALIANA E OTTENERE IL MASSIMO PROFITTO DAL TUO SEMESTRE IN ITALIA

Luglio, 2022
Dipartimento di italianistica
Corso facoltativo
Lezioni serali extrascolastiche

Dr. Bianca Bianchi
Italiano L2
bianca.bianchi@università.mail
Ufficio Italianistica, blocco A, primo piano
Orario: 16:15 – 17:45 (da lunedì 4 a venerdì 8)

Partecipanti

Il corso è rivolto a tutti gli studenti che il prossimo semestre partiranno per l'Italia.

Materiali

Gli studenti sono invitati a portare in classe il proprio *notebook* o, in mancanza di questo, il proprio smartphone. Fotocopie e moduli in fac-simile saranno consegnati a lezione.

Descrizione

Questo corso è di fondamentale importanza per gli studenti che vorranno iscriversi all'università italiana. Esso fornirà le basi per superare ogni ostacolo burocratico, guadagnare tempo prezioso e raggiungere più velocemente gli obiettivi di apprendimento. In cinque lezioni lo studente imparerà a: capire il sistema universitario italiano, conoscere le caratteristiche specifiche dell'università ospitante, muoversi in città velocemente e in sicurezza, integrarsi nelle nuove dinamiche sociali. Alla fine del corso i partecipanti sapranno programmare il proprio percorso formativo, selezionare un corso, comprendere il metodo didattico e le dinamiche della classe, iscriversi ad un esame, comunicare con l'università. Oltre a questo, gli studenti impareranno a compilare tutti i moduli necessari per il permesso di soggiorno e a riconoscere gli uffici di riferimento.

Indice delle lezioni

Lunedì 4: Scegli le materie che più ti piacciono.

Navigare nel sito web dell'università; analizzare il programma di un corso; scegliere il proprio percorso formativo; perché, quando e come iscriversi a un esame.

È richiesto l'uso del *laptop*.

Martedì 5: In aula.

Cosa aspettarsi dai professori e dai nuovi compagni; corsi teorici e lezioni di lingua; il laboratorio linguistico; un diverso approccio alla didattica.

Lezione simulata: preparatevi a prendere appunti!

Mercoledì 6: Conosciamo la città.

Usare i mezzi di trasporto (treno, autobus, tram, vaporetto); ottenere un abbonamento studentesco; raggiungere le aule partendo dalla sede del dipartimento di italianistica; le regole del dormitorio.

È richiesto l'uso del *laptop*.

Giovedì 7: vita sociale.

In dipartimento, in biblioteca, al bar: frequentare gli amici italiani senza spendere soldi in aperitivi. Il progetto *Tandem*. La comunità di scambio italiano-cinese di WeChat.

Seminario: dibattito libero coordinato dal professore.

Venerdì 8: Il permesso di soggiorno.

Compilare i moduli per il permesso di soggiorno; raggiungere le Poste Centrali e la Questura; come comportarsi agli sportelli.

La lezione prevede un esercizio scritto e simulazioni di dialogo (a coppie).
È richiesto l'uso del *laptop*.

Perché

Viaggiare e conoscere culture diverse dalla nostra è un'esperienza formativa entusiasmante. Tuttavia, la permanenza in un paese lontano dai modelli di vita ai quali siamo abituati, e dove il sistema scolastico è molto diverso dal nostro, può essere difficile. Conoscere a fondo la città nella quale andrai a vivere e l'università che frequenterai è fondamentale per affrontare al meglio la tua esperienza in Italia.

Esercitati a usare gli strumenti multimediali, ad affrontare moduli e burocrazia, a prendere appunti e a interagire con compagni e professori senza alcuna paura.

NOTES

1. The Marco Polo/Turandot programs began as an initiative of the Conferenza dei Rettori Italiani (Italian Deans' Conference) by request of the Italian presidency of the republic. Its goal is to increase the number of Chinese students enrolled in Italian universities. It facilitates Chinese students obtaining a study visa after enrolling in Italian universities, conservatories, and art schools. In order to access Italian universities, applicants are required to attend a ten-month Italian language course at an Italian university.
2. The Belt and Road Initiative (BRI) is a project aimed at building a major worldwide network of overland and maritime commercial routes linking China, the Middle East, and Europe. It is primarily planned and sponsored by the PRC.
3. It is to be noted that the experience of the Italian exchange students in their home university is diametrically opposite, since they are offered intensive and structured daily Chinese language classes in addition to elective courses. Consequently, Italian students that researchers had the chance to interview report high levels of academic satisfaction and achievement.
4. Chinese students reside within the university campus and are assigned from day 1 to cohorts composed of 20–30 students. Each cohort attends the same classes, performs the same routines, and often shares the same living spaces. The coordination follows a strict top-down hierarchical structure: study, leisure times, and activities are all regulated. Conversely, Italian universities generally lack a campus: faculties and services are diffused within the city, sometimes at considerable distance from each other. Students enjoy more freedom in personalizing their course of study and tend to work independently of each other, choosing whether and when to take exams. With the exception of language tutorials, Italian universities offer lectures with dozens or even hundreds of students attending at the same time.
5. Another cause of concern among RSs was that, in Venice, floods could force the university to cancel classes for days on end.
6. 面对"全球化"发展日益深化和复合型人才紧缺的社会环境，为深度挖掘留学"红利"，两国政府采取了一系列措施，旨在以双方合作为"基点"，带动周边国家在高等教育领域的互通互联，从而综合提升中意两国高等教育在世界范围内的竞争力和吸引力。" (Faced with the increasingly deepening development of "globalization" and the shortage of compound talents, the governments of the two countries have adopted a series of measures in order to deeply discover the "bonus" of studying abroad, which are aimed at promoting the interconnection of neighboring countries in the field of higher education based on bilateral cooperation, so as to comprehensively enhance the competitiveness and attractiveness of higher education of China and Italy in the world.)

BIBLIOGRAPHY

Bagna, C., & Carbonara, V. (2019). *Le lingue dei centri linguistici nelle sfide europee e internazionali: Formazione e mercato del lavoro* (Vol. 1). Pisa: Edizioni ETS.

Bonvino, E., & Rastelli, S. (2011). *La didattica dell'italiano a studenti cinesi e il Progetto Marco Polo: Atti del 15. Seminario AICLU, Roma, 19 febbraio 2010*. Pavia: Pavia University Press.

Brenna, M. (2019). *Shock culturale negli studenti italiani in Cina: Come affrontare il problema*. MA diss., Università Ca' Foscari di Venezia. http://dspace.unive.it/handle/10579/14752

Canini, G., & Scolaro, S. (2020, April). I Programmi Marco Polo e Turandot in Cina: Voce ad insegnanti e studenti. *Bollettino Itals*, no. 83, 85–97. www.itals.it/sites/default/files/pdf-bollettino/aprile2020/Canini_Scolaro.pdf

Cao, J. (2018). *Italiano L2 per apprendenti Sinofoni: Problemi e proposte*. MA diss., Università degli Studi di Padova. tesi.cab.unipd.it/60905/1/Cao_Ju_2018.pdf

Celentin, P. (2013, March). Italiano L2 a studenti Erasmus incoming: Quali priorità? *EL.LE*, *2*(1), 111–25. https://edizionicafoscari.unive.it/it/edizioni/riviste/elle/2013/1/italiano-l2-a-studenti-erasmus-incoming-quali-prio/

Chen, S. 陈素燕. (2004). Yingguo nuodinghan daxue zhongguo liuxuesheng liuxue tiyan diaoch 英国诺丁汉大学中国学生留学体验调查 [A survey on the experience of Chinese students studying abroad at the University of Nottingham, UK]. *Quanqiu jiaoyu zhanwang* 全球教育展望, *33*(10), 73–76. https://kns.cnki.net/kcms/detail/detail.aspx?dbcode=CJFD&dbname=CJFD2004&filename=WGJN200410021&uniplatform=NZKPT&v=NuDFHC6oeOySykLHbQBnchn_bexhW3aJuq8fBEvrP6ub7GD4m6ZN-1BRM9_Wy7lr

Chen, X. 陈雪芬. (2014). Zhongguo liuying xuesheng xueshu wenhua xiuke wenti fenxi 中国留英学生学术文化休克问题分析 [Analysis on the academic culture shock of Chinese students studying in the UK]. *Jiaoyu pinglun* 教育评论, (10), 79–81. https://kns.cnki.net/kcms/detail/detail.aspx?dbcode=CJFD&dbname=CJFD2014&filename=JYPL201410026&uniplatform=NZKPT&v=rpdU9nqxytQ69NGpx02iGBjZ0ksyff_p5t-rZpNg6_SbibsUXXR9SbMMz2C5DjuK

Consalvo, G. (2012, July). L'influenza delle differenze culturali nell'apprendimento dell'italiano L2 da parte di sinofoni: Il metodo di studio e l'apprendimento della lingua straniera in Cina. *Italiano LinguaDue*, *4*(1), 31–45. doi:10.13130/2037-3597/2269

Lan, S. (2020). Youth, mobility, and the emotional burdens of Youxue (Travel and study): A case study of Chinese students in Italy. *International Migration*, *58*(3), 163–76. *Wiley Online Library.* https://.org/10.1111/imig.12676

Lei, Q. (2016). *Evaluation of the Italian teaching in the Chinese classroom among the young adult beginners*. MA diss., Università Ca' Foscari di Venezia. http://dspace.unive.it/bitstream/handle/10579/9061/853238-1198193.pdf

Li, B., 李宝贵, et al. (2019). Yidaiyilu beijing xia zhongyi gaodeng jiaoyu hezuo jiaoliu de tedian 一带一路'背景下中意高等教育合作交流的特点、挑战与对策 [The characteristics, challenges and countermeasures of China-Italy higher education cooperation and exchange under the background of the Belt and Road Initiative]. *Xiandai jiaoyu guanli* 现代教育管理, (11), 18–23. https://kns.cnki.net/kcms/detail/detail.aspx?dbcode=CJFD&dbname=CJFDLAST2019&filename=LNGD201911004&uniplatform=NZKPT&v=CnsZxCW6jCpIXKHZm2bqBuKAhX-scp1P8T9v_bza_qX3j9QEuW7AKXcvqz5p3Plc

Lin, X. 林煦丹, & Chen, X. 陈晓亮. (2019). Kuaguo jiaoyu liudong zhong de keban yinxiang yu shenfen jiangou—yi zai mei zhongguo liuxuesheng weili 跨国教育流动中的刻板印象与身份建构—以在美中国留学生为例 [Stereotype and identity construction under the background of transnational educational mobility: A case study of Chinese international students in the United States]. *Renwen dili* 人文地理, *34*(3), 68–74. https://kns.cnki.net/kcms/detail/detail.aspx?dbcode=CJFD&dbname=CJFDLAST2019&filename=RWDL201903011&uniplatform=NZKPT&v=x_e2JmK888jb9hZuAiKHTUEOwnLutI4T3styVC7JqUdAUk4MaxCMfZ6O_HPAyC9u

Sinigaglia, V. (2014). *Una proposta metodologica per l'approccio con gli studenti cinesi in Italia e la didattica a loro rivolta*. MA diss., Università Ca' Foscari Venezia. http://dspace.unive.it/handle/10579/5567

Statista Research Department. (2021, March). Leading countries of origins of foreign students enrolled at university in Italy in the academic year 2019/2020. *Statista*, 6. Online data. www.statista.com/statistics/572639/total-number-of-foreign-university-students-by-country-of-origin/

Tagliavini, A. (2015). *Lo shock culturale. Integrarsi in nuove culture. Uno sguardo sul contesto cinese*. MA diss., Università degli studi di Urbino. www.tesionline.it/tesi/lingue-e-letterature-straniere/lo-shock-culturale-integrarsi-in-nuove-culture-uno-sguardo-sul-contesto-cinese/52935

Vedovelli, M. (2011). Marco Polo, l'internazionalizzazione, la non-politica linguistica italiana. In E. Bonvino & S. Rastelli (Eds.), *La didattica dell'italiano a studenti cinesi e il Progetto Marco Polo: Atti del 15. Seminario AICLU, Roma, 19 febbraio 2010* (pp. 1–18). Pavia: Pavia University Press.

Xue, H. 薛惠娟. (2010). Wenhua shiying yu guoji jiaoyu zhong xueye chenggong zhi yanjiu—zhongguo xuesheng liuying jingli kaocha 文化适应与国际教育中学业成功之研究 —中国学生留英经历考察 [Acculturation and academic success in international education—A study of Chinese students undertaking UK higher education]. *Jiaoyu xueshu yuekan*, 教育学术月刊, *12*(3), 50–53. https://kns.cnki.net/kcms/detail/detail.aspx?dbcode=CJFD&dbname=CJFD2010&filename=YANG201012015&uniplatform=NZKPT&v=exDBft8RODMaW3y7mjDlzCZNCtvN_vpJjrSq1OjjLFqaEILQM5Pzh-2sq-8yrnh5

Yu, X. 郁小萍. (2001). Zhongguo xuesheng liuying xuexi tiyan diaocha 中国学生留英学习体验调查 [An investigation into the learning experiences of the Chinese students in UK universities]. *Xiandai hanyu* 现代外语, *93*(3), 317–23. https://kns.cnki.net/kcms/detail/detail.aspx?dbcode=CJFD&dbname=CJFD2001&filename=XDWY200103011&uniplatform=NZKPT&v=Uln8KmZObBcEhKcxrHrRU79pC1xd2NL0zzLQyeji5Wk9AaItk4w-7vnBloKT_LxJ

10

TANDEM LEARNING IN AN ITALIAN PROGRAM

A Study of Perceived and Measured Gains in Language Proficiency and Cultural Competence

Louise Hipwell

This article outlines the results of a study on the learning outcomes of a Virtual Exchange between the Department of Italian at Georgetown University and the University of Salento in Italy. The program is modeled on the Teletandem approach developed by Telles and Vassallo and put into practice at the Department of Spanish and Portuguese at Georgetown through an Initiative on Technology-Enhanced Learning (ITEL) project spearheaded by professor Michael Ferreira.[1] The article provides background on the Teletandem exchange, the rationale behind its implementation, the course design, and assessment. Then, using qualitative and quantitative data, the article discusses the impacts of the exchange on learning outcomes, perceived and actual, as well as key language-learning enhancers such as confidence-building, engagement, intercultural awareness, and personal connections.

BACKGROUND

Though Virtual Exchanges in Foreign Language Learning have been around for a long time, Mark Warschauer discusses technology-enhanced exchanges or "Virtual Connections" as far back as 1996 (Dooly, 2022, pp. 113–27). This article will focus specifically on Teletandem as outlined by Telles and Vassallo in their Teletandem Brazil: Foreign Languages for All project created in 2006

(Vassallo & Telles, 2011). We were fortunate to have João Telles, one of the foremost scholars of computer-assisted language learning (CALL), share his experience with telecollaborative methods when he joined the Department of Spanish and Portuguese at Georgetown as a visiting professor in the fall semester of 2010.

Teletandem is a synchronous exchange that aims at improving communicative skills and developing cultural knowledge and awareness. The exchange occurs between two students, learners of one language who are native or proficient speakers in the other (Vassallo & Telles, 2006). The approach is based on three principal tenets, the first of which is equality. Each session is divided into two equal parts with the same amount of time dedicated to both languages, and during each segment of the exchange languages are kept separate to allow equal amounts of practice for each one. Reciprocity is the second fundamental principle of Teletandem. During each session students can be both the language expert and the language learner, and this relaying of roles mitigates learners' sense of vulnerability as they interact with a native speaker for the first time. Autonomy is the third guiding principle of the exchange, in that participants decide when to meet and the order in which the languages will be spoken. They also decide how and when to give each other feedback on their language performance. The context of the exchange is flexible; as well as practicing free conversation, students can work on collaborative projects or complete assigned tasks together, depending on the context of the collaboration (Cavalari & Aranha, 2019). The three principles of Teletandem are linked since "reciprocity assists the separation of languages in the pursuit of practical equality of opportunity of participants. It is also part of a collaborative kind of autonomy, which is co-constructed in peer interaction" (Gontijo & Salomão, 2019, p. 131). The combined principles of reciprocity and autonomy fundamentally ensure that learning occurs in tandem. Both members of the partnership in this student-directed activity are responsible for each other's learning, and they must decide how best to collaborate and assist each other to achieve their learning goals (Costa et al., 2018).

The American Council on the Teaching of Foreign Languages (ACTFL) World-Readiness Standards see language and culture as inextricably linked to prepare students to participate effectively and competently in the multicultural and globalized world in which we live.[2] Educators must prepare students to speak proficiently in the foreign language (L2) but also provide opportunities for them to interact with authentic culture, create meaningful connections and communities, and foster comparisons between their own and other cultures. It is commonly accepted that Virtual Exchanges can have a positive effect on these learner outcomes (O'Dowd, 2021). A Virtual Exchange can enhance students' awareness of the language-learning process, helping them to "plan, monitor, and evaluate their learning" (Guedes Evangelista & Salomão, 2019, p. 157). It offers the opportunity to develop oral competence (Lopes Messias & Ferreira, 2018). It can also help overcome anxiety, instilling confidence in students' abilities as communicators in their studied language (O'Dowd, 2021). As well as these practical outcomes, using the language for this authentic purpose can bring students to engage in the L2 in a more meaningful way, allowing them to achieve their learning goals but also to develop cultural knowledge and awareness. Studies have shown how a Virtual Exchange can involve students in "genuine processes of negotiation, in scaffolding for constructing experience, knowledge and their conception of the L2 culture" (Leone, 2014, p. 45). It can also bring them to adjust stereotypes and gain critical cultural awareness as they reflect on cultural perspectives through comparisons with their own culture (Dugartsyrenova & Sardegna, 2018).

PROJECT FORMAT

The Department of Italian at Georgetown has experimented with Teletandem in a variety of ways. Following the ITEL project mentioned earlier, Prof. Fulvia Musti tested Teletandem as an integrated part of two first-year Italian courses in 2016.[3] It is currently an integrated part of a 200-level conversation course for students who have completed the language program and a 1-credit add-on course open to all students who have completed the first semester of ITAL:011 Intensive Basic Italian.[4] Typically between the two courses an average of twenty-three students participate in the language exchange each fall semester.[5] This study focuses on the 1-credit Teletandem course, as its self-contained structure can be easily adapted into any language program.[6]

The telecollaborative partnership with Professor Elena Manca at the Department of the Humanities at the University of Salento in Apulia began in fall 2016.[7] This partnership came about after a visit to our campus by Professor Paola Leone, a scholar who focuses on Virtual Exchanges and computer-mediated communication (CMC) in language learning at that institution. Students who participate in the program in Italy are offered credit for participating in the exchange as part of their Translation and Mediation Studies course, and just as for the students at Georgetown, it is a voluntary activity for them. At the beginning of the semester, both the Italian and American participants complete an online shared document and are paired based on their interests.

Students meet with one partner of roughly the same age for free discussion on cultural topics for the duration of the semester. For most of the Georgetown students the cost of the credit is covered by basic tuition, and no fees are exchanged between the institutions.

The setup of this self-directed course is straightforward. Using Zoom, students complete and record eight one-hour sessions with their partners, dedicating 30 minutes to Italian and 30 minutes to English each time. Beyond the one-hour exchange, students are also instructed to give each other feedback on their language performance. This exchange of feedback usually lasts 5–10 minutes. As a group, students are required to attend three mediation sessions, as they are called by Telles (Telles, 2015), with their teacher during the semester (week 1, week 6, week 13), and besides attending these meetings, they are responsible for organizing their own schedules, uploading recordings of each session, and completing feedback assignments and surveys available on the Canvas Learning Management System (LMS). (See Appendix A for a sample course syllabus.)

The first of the mediation sessions is crucial to lay out the project design, clarify expectations, discuss the logistics of the exchange, and allow students to define their learning goals. The importance of this mediation is to maximize the benefits of the exchange and make students aware of "all the factors conducive to their decision making, like objectives, habits, opportunities, preferences, etc." (Costa et al., 2018, p. 30). Students are provided a series of questions or conversation starters as well as some functional language expressions to facilitate their first Teletandem session. Sample activities they can carry out with their partners are also suggested. These can be as simple as collecting photos of the important people, places, or things in their lives to share with their partners; choosing a current news item, article, tweet, movie, TV show, song, or poem to discuss; or giving a live tour of their city, campus, or dorm, all activities that can function as catalysts for their conversations. A list of conversation topics is provided for students, though they are free to choose whether or not to follow it. In preparation for the second mediation session, which occurs midway through the semester, students are asked to reflect on their learning by completing a chart on which they rate their perceived learning gains using a Likert scale. The chart focuses on learning outcomes such as confidence in speaking, listening comprehension, grammar accuracy, vocabulary knowledge, and cultural knowledge. They are then asked to recall examples from their sessions that are indicative of these five learning outcomes. With the help of the teacher, they identify strategies going forward to improve performance in the areas to which they have attributed low scores. (See Appendix B for a sample survey.) The final mediation session is a moment to reflect on the overall Teletandem experience, on the connections and community they have built with their partners, and on their growth as language learners over the course of the semester.

ASSESSMENT

To promote self-efficacy and motivation, assessment in the course is not based on performance but on self-reflective assignments that focus on students' learning strategies and practice. Once students start their sessions, they upload their recordings to Canvas and complete reflections after sessions 1, 2, 3, 5, and 7. The types of reflective assignments vary, but they are generally ACTFL-style Can-Do Statements and video or written recaps of their sessions.[8]

The Study: Perceived and Measured Learning Gains

The qualitative data of this study is based on two items from two sections of the course completed in fall 2016 and in fall 2021. A total of twenty-one

TABLE 10.1. Total of 18/21 Student Responses

Question 1: Yes/No question
On the whole, did you enjoy your Teletandem sessions this semester?

	Yes	No
Student responses	18	0

Question 2: Rate on a scale of 1–5
How satisfied are you with your performance in Italian during your 8 sessions?

Scale	1	2	3	4	5
Student responses		1	3	11	3

Question 3: Yes/No question
Do you think the Teletandem sessions had a positive impact on your spoken Italian this semester?

	Yes	No
Student responses	18	0

Question 4: Yes/No question
Did you encounter any difficulties with your ZOOM sessions (technical, logistical, other)?

	Yes	No
Student responses	6	12

students registered in these courses, but the data is based on the work of the eighteen students who completed all the items selected for the analysis and gave their permission for their work to be included in the study.

The first item is an anonymous survey completed at the end of the final mediation session. The survey results, posted in Table 10.1, show positive feedback from students. Although a third of the students encountered some logistical issues such as problems with WIFI connectivity, overall, the survey shows that they enjoyed the Teletandem experience, were relatively satisfied with their performance, and felt the exchange had a positive impact on their language competence.

To provide more context to the survey, the second item studied is a two-page reflection paper that students wrote as part of their final portfolio. The assignment is designed as a comparison between two five-minute video clips of their choosing, one from their first session and one from their last session. Though they had freedom to focus on any aspect of their interactions, it was interesting to note that a series of themes emerged, which are indicated in Table 10.2. The numbers in the third column show how often these themes were identified.

Here, as in the anonymous survey, in the final overview of the Teletandem experience, students overwhelmingly report that they have made progress in their language ability. Out of the sixteen papers that mention this theme, two describe the improvement as minimal while the rest perceive the improvement as significant. The fourteen students who saw marked improvement in language ability mention a number of areas of improvement. They discuss noticeable improvement in their vocabulary acquisition, specifically in the use of filler words and connectives. They notice how over time their ability to explain context and use circumlocution allowed them to express their complex thoughts even in cases where they were lacking a specific vocabulary word. They express the ability to put into practice the "difficult" grammar concepts they have formally studied, mentioning specifically the conditional tense and the subjunctive, and they also notice improvements in basic grammar structures such as the use of articles and noun/adjective agreements. Due to corrective feedback received from partners, they feel their pronunciation has improved and that they have gained the ability to speak more fluidly and naturally. Students remark on how in their first sessions their partners spoke slowly, taking care to enunciate each word to ensure their comprehension, but that this changed over the course of the semester, and in their final sessions their partners were speaking at natural speed; and they see this as an indication of how their oral comprehension skills improved over time. The examples

TABLE 10.2. Themes in Reflection Papers

Theme	Sample citation	Number of reflection papers containing this theme (out of 18)
Language improvement	• The clips that I have chosen show growth with my speaking but not as much as I would have liked • I found that I was unable to discuss my ideas in depth and could only ask her about things that interested her; there was an impenetrable wall of language that I was unable to rise above, that was blatantly obvious at the time. . . . Within the second video, I feel that it is much clearer that I am comfortable with X and with Italian. My transitions are smoother, my ability to verbally repost was better and I was able to use a new verb that X taught me: one that I struggled with for quite some time • There was a session where I met X's mother. She appeared on screen out of nowhere and presented herself. Next thing I knew, the conversation was with her and she began sharing her viewpoints on the topic we were currently discussing. It was an incredible way to practice my formal speaking, interact with yet another native speaker and realize how comfortable I was feeling while speaking my fourth language. The progress I have made with these sessions is remarkable • The related reason I offer a reflection on the use of poetry in the semester is the connection to learning new vocabulary evidenced in the contrast between the two clips. Developing robust session themes and content that allowed for significant discourse beyond everyday topics was a crucial enabler of this. Our session content literally advanced from speaking about everyday topics like the weather in the first session to being able to discuss poetry in the last. Not only my ability to express myself in this regard but my abilities to understand my partner were also augmented significantly through this process	16
Confidence	• I'm really happy with my progress in the language. I think the most important difference is that I have much more confidence in my abilities. I feel sure that I will be able to communicate effectively with native speakers • I'm not as scared to speak because of my fear of making a mistake but rather I have become comfortable speaking and learning along the way • The clip from the 8th session shows a marked improvement in both my confidence in speaking Italian and a higher level of speaking ability	6

(continued)

TABLE 10.2. (*Continued*)

Theme	Sample citation	Number of reflection papers containing this theme (out of 18)
Positive personal connection	• Overall, our interactions culturally and linguistically were positive. I am glad I have a new friend also :) • I distinctly remember our conversations being slightly tense and awkward at the start, it is blatantly clear to me that we became actual friends throughout our Teletandem sessions • I became close friends with my partner and plan to keep up with her • In the second clip it is noticeable that we are a lot more comfortable. Our postures are a bit more relaxed and we are smiling, laughing, and joking around a lot more. Since we were more comfortable we were a lot more comfortable interrupting each other so there was a lot more overlapping speech and overlapping questions	12
Deeper understanding of culture and gaining perspective	• On more than one occasion, we presented one another with critiques of both American and Italian approaches to things like politics, economics, and overall lifestyles. . . . As someone who loves to exchange conflicting ideals and discuss controversial topics, I found this discourse to be healthy and informative • I was able to expand my perspective of the world to include a more European and less American view. This learning outside of the classroom helped me to understand how important globalization is and how small the world has become • During my Teletandem experience, I learned a lot about Italian culture and traditions and during the course I taught X about life in America • Now I feel that I have a good understanding about life in Italy and how it is similar and different to life in the United States • Then X said that in Italy, they will not sit down to eat if there are 13 people at the table. They would rather find someone else to join them than eat with 13 people, which I though was strange at first. Then though I thought of some of the weird superstitions that Americans hold.	15
Engagement	• It's different to being in class because you learn about the daily life of somebody your own age. It's not like learning from a textbook or watching films and learning literature • Each session was random, to the point where you can say there was no theme. Instead of the sessions losing value for not having a sense of direction, they gained meaning and personal appreciation through spontaneity • Often in more traditional courses, I have to balance my intrinsic desire to learn with the necessity to score a high grade, as they do not always go hand in hand. With Teletandem, however, I was able to work on my language skills worry-free	8

provided in the table are indicative of how motivated students were to improve their language proficiency. One student mentions how enthusiastic they were to speak to their partner because of their shared interests in video games and anime. This was the principal motivating factor for this student "to rise above the impenetrable wall of language" that they experienced in their first session. Another student discusses how the spontaneity of the sessions allowed them to practice language functions that are often not given space in the classroom setting. In this case, the surprise appearance of the Italian student's mother on screen gave the student a sense of accomplishment at being able to use the formal register appropriately in this improvised interpersonal encounter. Another example shows how students felt their ability to improve their language was based on the freedom to select session topics. In this partnership, students shared an interest in poetry, and this allowed them to both develop a more sophisticated level of language based on the acquisition of thematic vocabulary and improve oral comprehension.

Moving on to the next theme, six of the students reported that the sessions had an impact on their confidence in speaking the language due to the variety of topics they were able to confront during their conversations. These students remarked that they felt reduced anxiety because they could share their vulnerabilities as language learners with their partners, and by the end of the semester they felt more comfortable interacting in the language. Two of the students noted that the experience brought them to feel confident enough to undertake a direct matriculation study-abroad experience.

Another theme that emerged from the papers centered on the important personal connections, the sense of community, that participants were able to develop with their partners. One student mentions how the conversations moved from being slightly awkward at the beginning to becoming dates on the calendar that they looked forward to, and in fact nine of the students used the word "friend" to describe their partners by the end of the program. As they rewatched their final videos, four of the students note how they laugh, joke, and tease one another, showing the ease with which they came to interact. In short, the picture that emerges from the papers shows that students viewed their sessions as particularly meaningful because of the deep interpersonal connections they forged with their partners.

In fourteen of the papers, another important theme that can be identified relates to the cultural learning that took place during the sessions. Students considered the sessions an important source of authentic information about Italian culture and how contemporary life is for young Italians today. Their discussions hinged on topics such as stereotypes, traditions, holidays, lifestyle, food, and education, but they also mentioned the importance of the deeper understanding and the context they gained from their partners' own personal experience in relation to more delicate issues such as immigration, politics, labor, the European Union, and the economy. Two of the students mention how they were not afraid to approach these difficult topics and enjoyed being able to debate conflicting stances with their partners. Discussions on stereotypes and superstitions led them to a greater self-awareness about their own culture and brought them to look at their own cultural norms with a more critical eye.

A final theme that appeared through the self-reflections was engagement. Students note how they felt engaged in their learning because the sessions took place outside the formal setting of the classroom. They felt challenged by the interactions that they considered a true test of their abilities as they were interacting with a native speaker as opposed to listening to peer language-learners in the classroom. One student noted how in-class speaking is always monitored by the instructor and is being evaluated, and they found it engaging and refreshing to practice in a stress-free environment where they did not have to self-censor in order to get a good grade. Another factor of engagement came from the freedom to discover and make use of colloquial expressions not typically taught in the classroom.

As the five themes show, students overall had a positive perception of the impact of the Teletandem sessions both on the linguistic and the cultural dimensions of their learning.

To add more context to the qualitative data, the final part of the study is an analysis of student recordings to examine whether their self-perceptions of learning can be corroborated by markers of improvement in their recordings.

This part of the study focuses on the recordings of the Italian segment of the conversation of two sessions for each student: one recording from the beginning and one recording from the end of the semester. A total of eighteen students (nine from fall 2016 and nine from fall 2021) are included in this study for a total of about eighteen hours of speech analyzed.

Three performance indicators (PI) were tracked: percentage of time spoken by the student in the L2 during each session, breakdowns per minute (the number of times per minute of conversation in the L2 when the student reverted to English because of the inability to use circumlocution to express their thoughts), and miscomprehensions (instances per minute of conversation when the student clearly misunderstood their partner's speech, leading to confusion during the exchange). These three markers were considered indicative of students' confidence in speaking the L2, their ability to use circumlocution, and their oral comprehension.

PERFORMANCE INDICATORS (PI)

Average percentage of time spoken in L2 (Figure 10.1): The number of minutes spoken in the target language were timed and compared to the total number of minutes of the Italian segment of the session. From the 44.2% of the first session, the analysis shows there is improvement to 44.9%, which, though minimal, is trending toward the desired 50% mark.

Average communication breakdowns per minute in the L2 (Figure 10.2): The average rate of breakdowns is lower (from 0.61 to 0.52 breakdowns per minute), suggesting that the students have improved their ability to circumlocute and use context to express their thoughts without reverting to English.

Average instances of miscomprehension per minute (Figure 10.3): This analysis focused on oral comprehension and tracked instances when the students clearly misunderstood their partners' speech, leading to confusion during the exchange. It is observable from the figure that the average rate of miscomprehension is lower in the seventh session, decreasing from 0.043 to 0.036 episodes of miscomprehension per minute.

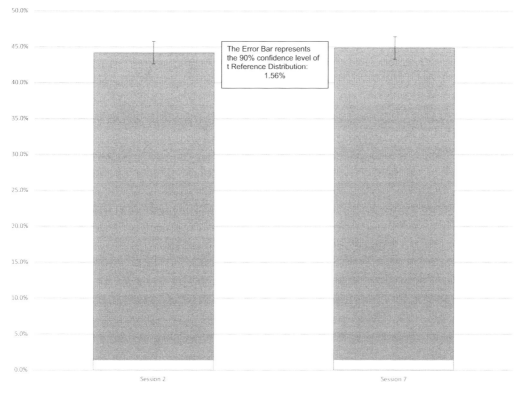

FIGURE 10.1. Column graph that represents the average percentage of time spoken in L2 per session with included error bars.

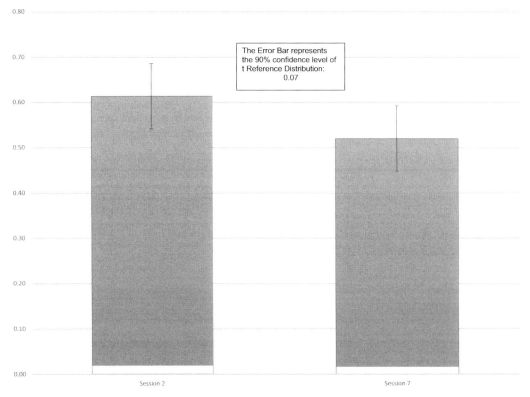

FIGURE 10.2. Column graph that represents the average breakdown per minute of time spoken in L2 with included error bars.

CONCLUSION

This study shows that integrating Teletandem into the language curriculum can bring numerous benefits to students. It can increase students' self-perception of learning as well as key language-learning enhancers such as confidence-building, engagement, intercultural awareness, and personal connections. As well as this, three positive trends in the students' actual language gains can be observed. The performance indicators in all areas show an improvement even if *t*-tests with a 90% confidence are not conclusive on the statistical validity of the results. It is important to note that the level of difficulty of the topics that students discussed toward the end of the semester may have had an impact on their performance in Session 7, though this possible variable was not considered in the data. A larger sample of recordings is needed to confirm these very encouraging data trends. In the future, the findings of this study will be applied to a larger sample of students to confirm the results.

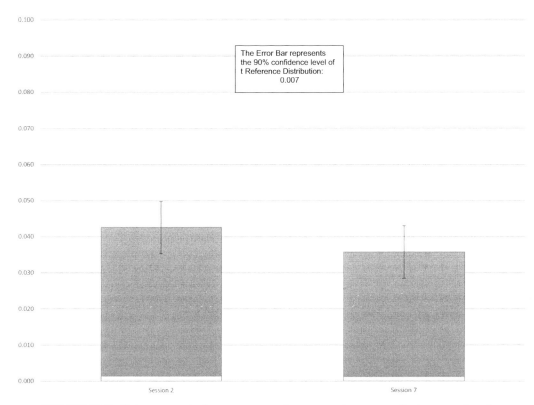

FIGURE 10.3. Column graph that represents the average instances of miscomprehension per minute of conversation with included error bars.

Adding Teletandem to the curriculum in the format of a 1-credit course makes it logistically easier to integrate into any program, and concentrating assessment on self-reflective assignments means that the course can be offered to students at all levels of proficiency at the same time. The 1-credit option allows students who may not have space in their schedules for a more intensive language class to maintain contact with the language in a manageable way. It is interesting to note that some students report that they have maintained contact with their partners long after the program has ended and they have graduated from university, showing the impact the program can have on creating an affective connection to Italy and Italian that outlasts their college experience.

There are two fundamental factors that contribute to Teletandem as a positive learning experience for students. The first is to find a collaborator at a partner institution who is willing to assign credit in some way to the program. Though all students start the program with great enthusiasm, Teletandem may move down on their list of priorities as the semester progresses. Assigning credit for the program on both sides of the partnership ensures that students will complete all of their sessions despite other pressing demands on their time.

The other essential factor is the involvement of the instructor of the course as mediator. The mediation sessions not only allow students to reflect on their learning but allow them to share any difficulties they may be encountering with their partner, giving time to the instructor to mitigate any possible negative experience. Though students generally report positively on their Teletandem experience, there are times when partners do not get along or do not show up to scheduled meetings. This can cause frustration and it's important to be able to intervene to find a new partner or reach out to the partner instructor to revisit the requirements of the course with all students enrolled in the program.[9]

Teletandem is becoming ever more popular in Italian programs today, and to attest to its success one need only look at the Teletandem program set up by the University of Trento in the fall of 2021. This program involved the participation of over 140 international students (including from the United States) during the first call for participation.[10]

APPENDIX A

ITAL 409: ITALIAN CONVERSATION PRACTICUM

Teletandem for 1 credit

Instructor:
This Teletandem course offers you the opportunity to interact with a native speaker of Italian at an Italian university. You will meet your Italian partner at least 8 times during the semester for about one hour and you are encouraged to meet once per week. During each session, you will speak for 30 minutes in Italian and 30 minutes in English, and the session will have an additional 5–10 minutes of language feedback. You will record and upload your video chat sessions to the instructor on Canvas, and complete self-assessment assignments, written and video-recorded reflections. To enroll in this course, you must have completed ITAL 011 Intensive Basic Italian. This course is intended for all intermediate and advanced level students who wish to improve their oral proficiency, maintain their contact with the language, and especially for those planning a semester abroad in Italy.

Objective: improve oral speaking and comprehension, gain opportunity to develop intercultural competence

Implementation:
- ◇ You will have 3 meetings during the semester with your instructor and the other students in the class. The instructor will send out an e-mail to schedule these meetings on ZOOM prior to the beginning of the semester.
- ◇ You will video chat at least 8 times using ZOOM with an Italian partner at the University of Salento, in Lecce, Italy.
- ◇ Each session will be a minimum of 65 minutes long, 30 minutes in English, 30 minutes in Italian, with 5–10 minutes of language feedback.
- ◇ Sessions will begin as soon as possible. Please add the requested information to the shared Google Doc so the appropriate partner can be found for you.
- ◇ Once you have connected with your Italian partner, you will set a date and time for your first session. It is advisable that you settle on a day and time that will work well with your schedules throughout the semester to avoid scheduling difficulties later on.

Assessment:
- You must upload a recording of 8 complete video chats after your Teletandem sessions, you will complete post session surveys or video recaps as indicated on Canvas.
- At the end of the semester, you will submit a Teletandem Portfolio. The portfolio will contain the following items:
- A 5-minute video excerpt from your first Teletandem Session
- A 5-minute video excerpt from your final Teletandem Session
- A 2-page self-assessment written in English or Italian in which you discuss how the two clips you have chosen are indicative of how successfully (or not) you have reached your language-learning goals.
- A 5-minute video recording in Italian in which you describe your Teletandem partner, reflect on your cultural learning during the semester, and give general feedback on the experience.

APPENDIX B

FINAL MEDIATION SESSION

1. Think back over the sessions you have completed since our last meeting.

On a scale of 1 to 5, how much do you feel you have improved in these areas? (1 = little improvement / 5 = marked improvement)					
Confidence in speaking	1	2	3	4	5
Listening comprehension	1	2	3	4	5
Grammar accuracy	1	2	3	4	5
Vocabulary knowledge	1	2	3	4	5
Cultural knowledge	1	2	3	4	5

2. Now, think of moments during your conversations or episodes that are examples of why you have rated yourself and your performance in this way.

Area of ability	Example
Confidence in speaking	
Listening comprehension	
Grammar accuracy	
Vocabulary knowledge	
Cultural knowledge	

3. Following our mid-semester meeting, what were some of the strategies you thought would help you make the most of your sessions in the second part of the semester? Which of these strategies did you employ and how did they work for you?

APPENDIX C

Post-Session Self-Assessment to Be Completed after Session 1

After your first Teletandem session, complete the following survey. To make the most out of every session, it is important to reflect on what went well and what needs work. The first 10 questions are simple multiple choice but for question 11 you must comment on your answers to the previous 10 questions. So, for example, you can list the new vocab that you learned, or the words that you had difficulty pronouncing, or the grammar points that you feel need more of your attention...

Answer choices = YES, NO, SOMEWHAT

Question 1
In this session I was able to understand most of my partner's speech without having to interrupt him/her.

Question 2
In this session I was able to discuss an everyday topic.

Question 3
In this session I was able to express my opinions.

Question 4
In this session I was able to speak using correct grammatical structures.

Question 5
In this session I was able to pronounce my words clearly.

Question 6
In this session I was able to use appropriate fillers in Italian. (For example: beh, allora, così, cioè, ecco, voglio dire, niente, diciamo . . .)

Question 7
In this session I was able to explain my thoughts or ideas when I didn't know the exact vocabulary in Italian.

Question 8
In this session I was able to learn new vocabulary, expressions, or grammar structures.

Question 9
In this session I was able to discuss aspects of Italian culture without reinforcing stereotypes.

> **Question 10**
> In this session I was able to mentor my partner, providing appropriate feedback on language usage and content.
>
> **Question 11**
> Are you generally happy with your performance in Italian during this session? What do you hope to do better next time? How will you prepare for the next session? Add notes here on the answers you gave to the multiple-choice questions above.

Video-recap to be completed after Session 2

> Che cosa hai discusso durante questa sessione? Com'è andata la discussione? Hai imparato dei vocaboli o delle strutture nuovi? Hai imparato fatti culturali interessanti? Record a 5-minute recap in Italian of your session and upload here.

Post-session feedback to be completed after Session 3

> Dopo aver completato Sessione 3, riascolta la tua registrazione e poi **scrivi un'analisi (in inglese o in italiano) della tua prestazione linguistica**. Hai notato qualcosa in particolare a cui devi prestare attenzione? Cosa puoi fare per evitare di fare gli stessi errori in futuro? Delinea i tuoi obbiettivi per migliorare la tua performance linguistica. Write at least 200 words.

NOTES

1. This project was inspired by the work of professor Michael Ferreira from the Department of Spanish and Portuguese at Georgetown who began to utilize this virtual learning exchange in his classes in 2008 in collaboration with Dr. João Telles who taught at the time at the State University of São Paulo at Assis in Brazil. In 2015 professor Ferreira launched a new university-funded ITEL project (Initiative on Technology-Enhanced Learning) at Georgetown University that sought to study the impact of Teletandem in other language departments, and though the Italian Department did not benefit from the funding for this project, it certainly benefited from the expertise of several colleagues from different departments who were directly involved in that project. Special thanks to professor Ferreira and professor Alissa Webel (French) for being so willing to share their experience.
2. ACTFL World-Readiness Standards for Learning Languages. Retrieved February 26, 2022, from https://www.actfl.org/resources/world-readiness-standards-learning-languages.
3. I am extremely grateful to my Italian Department colleague Fulvia Musti. Her knowledge and experience have been essential to the successful integration of Teletandem into our program at Georgetown.
4. This intensive language course consists of 70 hours of language instruction. Students who have completed this course are given the option to register for the Teletandem course, though they typically wait until their second year of language study to enroll.
5. In the fall of 2016 when the project began, a total of 19 Georgetown students were enrolled in Teletandem, and in the fall of 2021 this number had grown to 28. Since the fall of 2016, 115 exchange partnerships have been created by the program.
6. Students are permitted to take the 1-credit Teletandem course twice during their studies as undergraduates at Georgetown. Originally this credit counted only toward their overall number of degree credits, but recently 1-credit courses have been added to the Italian curriculum. Three separate 1-credit courses now count toward the major and minor in Italian.
7. For the Teletandem collaboration to be successful, it is essential to work with a teacher at the partner institute who shares the same learning-centered goals. Professor Elena Manca at the University of Salento has been a wonderful partner in this project, and I am extremely grateful for her collaboration over the years of this exchange.
8. The first survey is modeled on an ACTFL Can-Do Statement, and this survey is a modified version of a survey created by Viviane Furtoso given at a presentation at Georgetown in 2015. See Appendix C for a sample survey.

9. Many thanks to the students who gave their permission for their work to be analyzed in this study and to all my colleagues at the Department of Italian who are a constant source of encouragement and support. Very special thanks go to Alessandro Giorgioni, Georgetown University graduate in Italian and linguistics, for the countless hours of work dedicated to analyzing the recordings for the quantitative portion of this study.
10. University of Trento, Tandem Language and Culture Exchange, accessed November 18, 2022. https://www.cla.unitn.it/en/2184/tandem-language-and-culture-exchange.

BIBLIOGRAPHY

ACTFL. (n.d.). *World-readiness standards for learning languages.* Accessed February 26, 2022. https://www.actfl.org/resources/world-readiness-standards-learning-languages

Cavalari, S., & Aranha, S. (2019). The teacher's role in telecollaborative language learning: The case of institutional integrated Teletandem. *Revista Brasileira De Linguística Aplicada*, *19*(3), 555–78. https://doi.org/10.1590/1984-6398201913576

Costa, L., Salomão, A. C., & Zakir, M. (2018). Transcultural and transcontinental telecollaboration for foreign language learning: Proposals and challenges. *Revista Do GEL*, *15*(3), 26–41. https://doi.org/10.21165/gel.v15i3.2434

Dooly, M. (2022). The evolution of virtual exchange and assessment practices. In A. Czura & M. Dooly (Eds.), *Assessing virtual exchange in foreign language courses at tertiary level* (pp. 113–27). Research-publishing.net. https://doi.org/10.14705/rpnet.2022.59.1407

Dugartsyrenova, V., & Sardegna, V. G. (2018). Raising intercultural awareness through voice-based telecollaboration: Perceptions, uses, and recommendations. *Innovation in Language Learning and Teaching*, *13*(3), 205–20. https://doi.org/10.1080/17501229.2018.1533017

Gontijo, V., & Salomão, A. C. (2019). Students' voice on learning in Teletandem: Expectations and self-assessment. *Portuguese Language Journal*, 13, 129–43. https://www.portugueselanguagejournal.com/_files/ugd/02e26d_d7942d44fdcc47b48b1a165022fe1de9.pdf

Guedes Evangelista, M. C., & Salomão, A. C. (2019). Mediation in Teletandem: From face-to-face sessions to reflective journals. *Pandaemonium Germanicum*, *22*(36), 153–77. https://doi.org/10.11606/1982-88372236153

Leone, P. (2014). Teletandem, video-recordings and usage-based tasks: Developing a socially situated scenario for learning. *International Journal of Learning, Teaching and Educational Research*, *9*(1), 41–50. https://www.ijlter.org/index.php/ijlter/article/view/203

Lopes Messias, R. A., & Ferreira, M. J. (2018). Oral communicative competence development in PFL: Focusing on Teletandem. *Revista Do GEL*, *15*(3), 134–54. https://doi.org/10.21165/gel.v15i3.2412

O'Dowd, R. (2021). What do students learn in virtual exchange? A qualitative content analysis of learning outcomes across multiple exchanges. *International Journal of Educational Research*, 109, 1–13. https://doi.org/10.1016/j.ijer.2021.101804

Telles, J. (2015). Learning foreign languages in Teletandem: Resources and strategies. *DELTA: Documentação de Estudos em Lingüística Teórica e Aplicada*, *31*(3), 603–32. https://doi.org/10.1590/0102-4450226475643730772

University of Trento. *Tandem language and culture exchange.* Accessed November 18, 2022. https://www.cla.unitn.it/en/2184/tandem-language-and-culture-exchange

Vassallo, M. L., & Telles, J. A. (2006). Foreign language learning in-Tandem: Theoretical principles and research perspectives. *ESPecialist*, *27*(1), 83–118. https://revistas.pucsp.br/index.php/esp/issue/view/426

Vassallo, M. L., & Telles, J. A. (2011). Foreign language learning in-Tandem: Teletandem as an alternative proposal in CALLT. *ESPecialist*, *27*(2), 189–212. https://revistas.pucsp.br/index.php/esp/article/view/1629

11

BLM AND ə

Introducing Diversity in the Syllabus Design

Valentina Abbatelli

For twenty-first-century higher educators, the commitment to diversity has become one of the main priorities (Miles et al., 2013), with the benefits of this initiative extending beyond the classroom experience. Engaging with diversity not only means representing an increasingly heterogenous world (reflected in the student population) but also proves to be an effective pedagogical tool through increasing cognitive sophistication and critical thinking skills, reducing prejudice, and appreciating different racial and cultural backgrounds. Additionally, this pedagogic turn to consider diversity contributes to the development of leadership skills, cooperative intergroup behavior, and openness to considering alternative views (Lee et al., 2012).

By engagement with diversity, I refer to its definition as the "active, intentional, and ongoing engagement with differences in people, in the curriculum, in the co-curriculum, and in communities in ways that increase one's awareness, content knowledge, cognitive sophistication, and empathic understanding of the complex ways individuals interact within systems and institutions" (Clayton-Pedersen et al., 2009, in Lee et al., 2012, p. 6). From this definition, it is clear how engaging with diversity goes hand in hand with two main objectives in the language classroom: first, the development of students' intercultural understanding based on cognitive knowledge and awareness; second, the enhancement of intercultural competence, which involves the ability to communicate effectively in specific intercultural contexts, "whether in words or actions" (Reynolds et al., 2017, p. 49).

This chapter aims to provide an example of how themes from the movement Black Lives Matter (BLM) in Italy and from the debate on inclusivity in the Italian language can be integrated into the Italian language syllabus to challenge cultural stereotypes and to foster students' critical thinking when engaging with global phenomena. In this way, the contribution will draw on pedagogical examples and strategies used to design two learning units (LU) of an Italian language module, with a specific focus on writing skills, for final year students. I will explain the context in which I taught these two LU and outline the visual and written resources and activities employed. I will then analyze a few students' outputs in light of the learning outcomes and suggest further material that expands on the topics of BLM and inclusivity. Ultimately, I present these two cases from my classroom to potentially offer one means of configuring a more diverse syllabus of Italian language modules for advanced-level students.

I will argue that cultural themes related to diversity and inclusivity can be successfully embedded in the language curriculum. Lessons centered around these themes improve linguistic and intercultural competence while stimulating engagement among students in the Italian language classroom, provided that an intercultural and "glocal" approach to teaching and learning are employed.

The language classroom and this pedagogical approach prove to coproduce particularly fruitful environments when dealing with intercultural encounters. On the one hand, language teaching plays a pivotal role in the development of cultural and intercultural awareness, as the foreign language teacher not only introduces the learner to a new language but to other sociopolitical and cultural systems (Hennebry, 2014). On the other hand, a glocal approach, defined as "the interpretation of the global and the local resulting in unique outcomes in different geographic areas" (Ritzer & Dean, 2015, p. 73), links intercultural understanding and competency as it "raises student's critical language awareness and develops border-crossing communicative skills that enable [students] to actively and critically engage in diverse cultural, ethnic, racial and linguistic contact zones" (Kubota, 2011, p. 116).

A glocal approach to language teaching underpins the pedagogic choice to look at the Italian specificities of BLM in comparison with movements in the United States and United Kingdom after the murder of George Floyd in Minneapolis in May 2020 and the discussion on the debate on language inclusivity across different European languages.

This connection between global phenomena and local specificities "projects a world that is constantly in motion" (Mehta, 2018, p. 9), where understanding of the local specificities cannot take place without understanding the global and vice versa, as the complexity of the global phenomena is appreciated only through its local identities.

THE CONTEXT

I will now present two LU that I developed as part of the language module for final year students at the University of Warwick. Most of the students attending this module study two languages and have returned from their year abroad in Year 3, while a minority of them have been abroad in Year 2 or study three languages. All of them are expected to reach C1/C2 level of the CEFR (Common European Framework of Reference; Council of Europe, 2020). This module consisted of three weekly seminars that develop writing, oral, and translation skills.

The syllabi of the writing and oral seminars linked thematically organized cultural content learning and language learning to provide students with occasions to deepen their vocabulary and knowledge around a specific theme. Selected themes addressed current affairs and society in Italy, for example, politics, immigration/emigration, climate change, language, and social media. In the writing classes, themes were explored in connection to a specific genre of written text in order to integrate the development of language and culture through constructing an argumentative essay, a critical commentary, an opinion article, and an informative newspaper article.

Each LU of the writing classes to which I refer covered three 60-minute classes (three weeks of writing classes). The in-class activities carried out were propaedeutic to two formative written assessments: a 700–800-word critical commentary for the LU on BLM and an opinion article of the same length for the LU of "Inclusivity in Italian language." I designed the LU to constitute the main block of teaching of Term 1 and to be taught one after the other.

I will consider teaching writing holistically, encompassing its various pedagogic aspects in the second language (L2) class: learning to write (LW); writing to learn language (WLL); and writing to learn content (WLC).[1] Although WLC is usually associated with content and language integrated learning (CLIL) and not to L2 classes, in this case, students had to use the acquired knowledge on L2 language and also engage with a specific content. Assignments called on students to demonstrate their understanding of the themes covered through written output, which demonstrated their ability to comment on authentic written sources and support their opinion through a convincing and informed argument.

The overall learning outcomes of the writing classes were the following:

⋄ To familiarize students with different text types in terms of content and style while fostering their knowledge around current topics of Italian culture and society

- To familiarize students with a more formal register of written Italian and to broaden their vocabulary
- To polish students' written language focusing on anglicisms, false friends, issues of language contamination, and colloquialisms
- To consolidate problematic grammatical structures

In addition to the strictly linguistic objectives, the two LU units featured the learning outcomes that Abrams listed for the pedagogy of intercultural communication, as a means to "reflect on their own cultural practices and use their existing knowledge as a resource for learning about new cultures" and "gain knowledge about social groups in other cultures, including critical awareness of cultural, political, and ideological issues of language, power, and identity" (Abrams, 2020, p. 50).

The LU on BLM gradually presented the historical and political aspects and people playing a role in the movement in Italy, immigration, the second generation of Italians and the acquisition of Italian citizenship, the Italian colonial past, and protests against monuments celebrating colonialism. Students worked on summaries and reading and comprehension questions through analyzing visual and written authentic material, including material created by Black Italians, and through reflecting on the British colonial past. The LU on Inclusivity in Italian language started from recent debates on the use of masculine names for professions and moved to proposals for an inclusive language, also stimulating a meta reflection on the Italian language. Students worked on the titles of opinion articles, experimenting with figurative language, and expressed their opinions on the topics through a "written debate."

THE LU ON BLACK LIVES MATTER IN ITALY

The LU on BLM in Italy consisted of three writing seminars. In preparation for the first seminar students read Barresi (2020).[2] The article brought to the fore the core scope of the LU, as the author compares the United States and the Italian situations, articulating the specificities of racial discrimination in Italy.

After reading the article, students responded to open questions that asked them to reflect on the theme of the article, to pinpoint the differences between Italy and the United States around racial discrimination, and to summarize the article in 100 words (see Appendix A). This pedagogic activity connected content and language, being "a form of knowledge creation through language" (Byrnes, 2011, p. 145), and shifted the role of student from a reader to a creator of a text (Hood, 2008, in Byrnes, 2011, p. 145). The assignment also introduced the task of developing critical commentary, the output that students produced at the end of the three-week period, which featured a first paragraph summarizing the thesis of the text students are asked to comment on. The in-class activities included a discussion of students' reading and comprehension and a workshop-style activity on summaries along with the clarification of doubts, particularly around vocabulary, before continuing with the explanation of the formal features of the critical commentary.

In preparation for the second lesson, students read two interviews (Bonazzi, 2020; Redazione, 2020[3]) that helped to expand and deepen their knowledge on this topic. The interviews gave direct voice to three Italian women who struggled to receive recognition of their nationality from the Italian public due to their racialized differences. Students had already read works of one of the people interviewed, the Italian writer of Somali origin Igiaba Scego. Her books regularly feature in modules on Italian transnational literature at the University of Warwick. However, they did not know either Antonella Bundu, the Italian activist and first black woman to run for mayor in a major Italian city, or Bellamy, one of the founders of the digital platform AfroItalian Souls.[4] In this way, students explored multiple points of view on the theme of Italian citizenship and recognition of Black Italians, gained knowledge about social groups in other cultures, and became aware of cultural and political issues around power and identity (Abrams, 2020; Lee et al., 2012).

These interviews contributed two elements to the discussion on diversity in Italy: the Italian law on the acquisition of citizenship and a historical perspective on the problem of racism, positing the relationship between the United States and slavery on the one hand and Europe and colonialism on the other. After reading the interviews, students replied to a few comprehension questions and completed short research on jus soli, jus sanguinis, and jus culturae (see Appendix A). As this reading provided the class with further elements to assess the specific features of the BLM protests in Italy, they then wrote their own opinion on similarities and differences between the protests in the United Kingdom and in Italy in order for them to use "their experiential knowledge as an instrument of critical enquiry" (Lee et al., 2012, p. 74).

In preparation for the second class, the second homework assignment called on students to exercise their summary skills on a video (AfroItalian Souls, 2019), which outlined a historical overview of blackface and tackled this issue in correlation with a few recent Italian cases of blackface (see Appendix A). The in-class activities started with a discussion of the citizenship law in Italy before moving on to the students' sharing their findings on the two interviews and their views on BLM protests in the United Kingdom and Italy. A workshop-style activity followed where students compared their own summaries in groups. A final activity called on students to develop argumentative skills as they replied to selected real comments posted to the video on blackface on YouTube and post it on Padlet.

The colonial aspect of contemporary racism introduced by Scego's interview provided the core of the final lesson of this LU, which employed again an intercultural perspective among British students, perhaps building on their own experiences of witnessing the recent toppling of the Edward Colston statue in Bristol. Also in this case, the preparation for the class required students to consider a written and a visual input (see Appendix A). Students looked at the website Postcolonial Italy[5] and noted which monuments in Rome reflect a colonial heritage. Additionally, students read Fiandaca (2020), which discusses visual representations that sparked strong reactions in the BLM movement in the United States, United Kingdom, and Italy (e.g., the film *Gone with the Wind*, the statues of Edward Colston and Winston Churchill in the United Kingdom, and the statue of Indro Montanelli in Milan). Next, students responded to open-ended questions, which guided their reflection on the nuances of the protests in the three geographical contexts. A final question asked for students' opinions on the reasons why the BLM movement targeted the monuments and their role in cities and in citizens' perception of history (see Appendix A).

The final lesson of this LU opened with student discussions in pairs and then in plenum on their findings around the colonial heritage still visible in Rome and on the reading and comprehension exercises. Students then read a short excerpt of a news article reporting that a new metro station in Rome would be named after the Somali-born partisan Giorgio Marincola instead of Amba Aradam (Gennaro, 2020).[6] Students considered this event in relation to the materials they had prepared in advance and thought of any similar initiatives undertaken in a country that they knew. The session ended with a short writing activity on MS Whiteboard where students wrote their own opinions on the presence of colonial monuments or monuments celebrating the colonial past and their stance on the decolonization of cities. During these three sessions students worked on their reading and comprehensions skills, widened their knowledge and vocabulary on the topic, developed their summary and argumentative skills, and familiarised themselves with the critical commentary. They reflected on their own experience of the Black Lives Matter protests and on this movement in light of Italian history and contemporary society. The formative assessment required students to write a 700–800-word critical commentary on the newspaper article titled "Una nuova legge sulla cittadinanza essenziale per combattere il razzismo."

THE LU ON INCLUSIVITY IN THE ITALIAN LANGUAGE

The last session on BLM introduced the topic of inclusivity in the Italian language as students encountered the use of the asterisk in Gennaro (2020). This use was only briefly explained in class and left to the following LU for a more in-depth conversation. In preparation for the first class of this new LU, students read Piccinni (2020). The opinion article dealt with the debate on gendered terms for job titles sparked by the election of the first female chancellor at La Sapienza university in Rome. Through responding to open-ended questions about the article, students focused on identifying the stylistic features of this genre of text and the arguments that the author brings to support her thesis on the legitimate use of the feminine noun "rettrice" (see Appendix A). Therefore, students extrapolated the formal characteristics of the text that they would write in the final formative assignment, while strengthening their ability to analyze arguments and starting to become familiar with the debate on gendered names in the workplace.

As usual, the in-class activities started from a workshop-style task based on students' reading and comprehension. Students also worked in pairs to pinpoint the features of the opinion article and to suggest a structural scheme and main stylistic features. They discussed schemes and features in plenum and then compared their findings on this text with the model provided. The second part of the lesson delved more into the theme of inclusivity in language through the reading of Gheno (2020), a Facebook post in which the sociolinguist lists several ways to address the so called "moltitudine mista"[7] (e.g., the masculine plural, the asterisk, the double form masculine and feminine, and the schwa). Recognizing personal knowledge and experience as a means to enhance learning, students reflected on these solutions focusing on the issue of inclusivity and compared them to the situation in the English language. A specific question was asked about the students' familiarity with the schwa and its sound in the English language. Building on this last assignment and in order to acknowledge it, the homework assignment tasked students with writing a short piece on this topic in at least two languages they knew and posting it on Padlet. They also produced a group analysis of an opinion article on a topic of their choice (see Appendix A).

The second session started with a brief discussion in plenum on the Padlet posts, which gave an intercultural perspective on the theme of the LU mostly across French, Spanish, and English registers. The class continued with some group presentations on opinion articles to consider the main stylistic features of this genre. As students would have to choose a title for their formative opinion article, the second part of the lesson was devoted to the analysis of newspaper titles and to figurative language. The class considered some authentic titles and reflected on syntax, punctuation, and figurative language (mostly metaphors, simile, and hyperbole) used. Working creatively while engaging with the theme of this LU, students created a new title for Piccinni (2020), which they had read in preparation for the first session. A discussion in plenum and feedback on the titles took place at the end of the session.

In preparation for the last class of this LU, students completed a reading and comprehension exercise on Riyahi (2020) (see Appendix A). After a brief discussion in class on the assignment, which called on students to reflect on the efficacy of arguments made by others, the session continued with a written debate to practice and enhance students' argumentative skills (see Appendix A). During these three sessions students worked on their reading and comprehensions skills, widened their knowledge and vocabulary on the topic, and familiarized themselves with the opinion article and figurative language. They also developed their argumentative skills and reflected on their own experience of inclusive language across languages. The formative assessment required them to write a 700–800-word opinion article based on the information reported in Venturi (2020).

OBSERVATIONS AND CONCLUSIONS

Oral reports on these two learning units highlighted an extremely positive appreciation on the themes of these two LU, which were considered the most relevant of the module. The perception of diversity as an important theme for the classroom also played a key role in the motivation that students demonstrated in engaging with the writing activities suggested.

The glocal approach and the intercultural pedagogy employed fostered cultural self-awareness and intercultural knowledge. The article on colonial monuments sparked the liveliest conversation, with several students specifically debating in Italian the reasons why Churchill's statue had been vandalized and reflecting on the lack of awareness of British colonialism in the history curriculum at secondary school level. The theme of inclusivity allowed students to grasp how the schwa, a common sound in the English language, played a prominent role in the debate on inclusivity in Italy. But even more, only one student who was studying modern languages and linguistics was aware of the name and the sound of the schwa, while the others learned more about the schwa and thus their own native language in the L2 class.

Students' outputs and classwork confirmed that the linguistic learning outcomes have been fulfilled. Students were able to write two different genres of texts arguing their own position using supporting evidence and convincing arguments. For the commentary, students agreed with the thesis of the article, but the vast majority argued for the need for further measures beyond a change in the citizenship law to tackle systematic racism in Italy. As for the opinion article, all students praised Effequ's initiative to use the schwa for the "moltitudine mista" in their publication;[8] however, a quarter of them underlined the linguistic difficulties of such an implementation and maintained that that would not solve the problem of sexism in society. Samples of students' outputs confirmed their engagement with intercultural reflections involving other languages and cultures with which they were familiar and their continued interest in pursuing further research on the topic to support their opinions more convincingly (Appendix B). A general observation from students' critical commentaries, however, revealed that the majority of them tended not to compare the British situation around the citizenship law and institutional racism with the Italian situation. This lack of engagement with cultural self-reflection might have been due to the complexity of this process (Russell, 2020), especially when it has to be expressed in the target language. However, it might also have been due to the formative assessment's not specifically requiring students to contrast the British and Italian contexts, while the guiding questions on the in-class activities aimed at a more explicit self-reflection.

At a more formal level, it is interesting to note the attempt to experiment with Italian wording through the exercise in which students devised titles for the opinion articles (see Appendix B).

From my observation in class and in oral feedback, it can be reported that many readings were perceived as difficult, mostly in terms of vocabulary and particularly from students who started Italian as beginners at university. Although students prepared for the sessions by reading the texts at home, except for occasionally short pieces in class, they would have required more scaffolding and targeted activities around vocabulary for in-class discussions due to the mixed levels of the class.

In the academic year of 2021 to 2022, I ran these writing seminars again along with the oral seminars with the aim of making the material more accessible to students and, where possible, including resources written by authors involved firsthand in the debates. I kept most of the writing activities for the LU on BLM and inclusivity as they were, but I included more vocabulary and paraphrase exercises, which also allowed students who spent a limited time in Italy in the year abroad to read and understand the texts more easily than the previous year. Teaching the oral seminars in addition to the writing seminars allowed me to expand on the resources used in both seminars. For the LU on BLM, I introduced authentic resources created by a more diverse range of authors, such as the podcast *Sulla razza*, Nadeesha Uyangoda's (2021) book *L'unica persona nera nella stanza*, the web series *The Expats* by Johanne Affricot, and the Twitter account *D.E.I.—Futuro Antirazzista*. For the LU on inclusivity, I included two episodes from the podcasts *Con parole nostre* (episode 47, "Il sessismo nella lingua italiana") and *Podcast Italiano* (episode "Il dibattito intorno ai femminili professionali in italiano") and the two newspaper articles by Raffaele (2021) and Manera (2021).

Overall, the integration of language and culture and the employment of a glocal approach in the L2 classroom have proved to be particularly fruitful in engaging students in the suggested activities and developing students' linguistic skills. It has also been key in order to engage students who study Italian alongside other languages and cultures to develop their intercultural competencies. However, I consider these two LU only as a starting point on which to build a more diverse and inclusive curriculum for the Italian language classroom. There are several areas where this still proves to be a challenge, such as the firsthand creation of didactic material, the research of more inclusive authentic material, and a more balanced integration of diversity in the syllabus and curriculum, not just limited to sessions dealing with diversity as a content theme. This final aspect is particularly important to avoid reinforcing "the very marginalization that those embodying this diversity face in the real world" (Ford & Santos, 2022). A further aspect to be enhanced concerns the development of students' critical self-reflection. As a matter of fact, self-reflection is not only key to the development of intercultural competence but also to the possibility that the integration of diversity in the curriculum has an impact on social changes beyond the classroom walls.

APPENDIX A

LU on Black Lives Matter in Italy

In Preparation for Session 1
Reading and comprehension on Barresi 2020:

Qual è il tema di questo articolo?; Quali sono le differenze tra Italia e Stati Uniti riguardo alla discriminazione razziale? A chi si riferisce l'autrice quando parla di Black Lives Matter in Italia?; Come riassumeresti l'articolo in max 100 parole?

In Preparation for Session 2
a) Leggi l'intervista ad Antonella Bundu e rispondi alle seguenti domande:
   Chi sono le seconde generazioni? Cosa sono lo ius soli, lo ius sanguinis e lo ius e lo ius culturae? Prova a spiegarlo con parole tue. Se non ne hai mai sentito parlare puoi fare una breve ricerca su internet e riassumere i tre concetti.
   Quali sono le caratteristiche del movimento BLM in Italia? A quali problematiche si lega? Trovi dei punti in comune tra questo articolo e l'articolo che era da leggere per oggi?
   Secondo te il movimento BLM nel Regno Unito ha delle caratteristiche diverse o no? Perché?
b) Leggi ora punti di vista di Bellamy (1), una delle fondatrici di Afroitalian Souls, e della scrittrice Igiaba Scego (2) e individua cosa rafforzano e cosa aggiungono al dibattito.
c) Guarda il video 'Blackface è razzista?' Riguarda le line guida sul commento critico e prova a scrivere il primo paragrafo introduttivo di un commento critico a questo video. Scrivi poi alcune frasi del video con cui siete completamente d'accordo e altre (se ci sono) con cui non siete d'accordo.

In Preparation for Session 3
a) Reading and comprehension questions on Fiandaca 2020:
   Quali tipi di rappresentazioni visive sono state contestate negli Stati Uniti? Quali statue sono state prese di mira nel Regno Unito e perché?; Qual è il caso italiano di cui parla l'articolo?; Quali sono le due opinioni contrastanti sulla questione della rimozione delle statue?; Qual è la proposta di Banksy?; Perché, secondo te, il movimento BLM ha

deciso di rivolgersi anche alle statue? Qual è il loro ruolo nelle città e nella percezione dei cittadini?

b) Guardate queste mappa d'Italia postcoloniale (guardate Roma in particolare). Quali tipi di monumenti sono evidenziati? Useremo l'articolo e la mappa per discutere in classe della questione della presenza nelle città di monumenti e statue di eredità coloniale.

LU on Inclusivity in the Italian Language

In Preparation for Session 1

Reading and comprehension on Piccinni 2020: Secondo voi è un testo argomentativo o no? Giustificate la vostra scelta. Qual è la struttura di questo testo? Individuate l'idea principale di ogni paragrafo. Quali sono, secondo voi, delle caratteristiche importanti del suo stile?

In Preparation for Session 2

a) Esaminate le soluzioni proposte per una lingua inclusiva in almeno due lingue che conoscete (o anche di più) e scrivete un breve post su Padlet in cui confrontate le varie proposte.

b) Nei gruppi stabiliti scegliete un articolo d'opinione (su un argomento a vostra scelta) ed analizzatelo secondo lo schema nell'handout e secondo quello che abbiamo fatto in classe. Fate attenzione anche a come sono strutturati titolo e sommario e allo stile generale dell'articolo (portate degli esempi concreti dal testo). Presenterete poi l'articolo al resto della classe.

In Preparation for Session 3

b) Reading and comprehension questions on Riyahi 2020: Quale commento scettico vi sembra il meno convincente? Perché? Quale risposta vi sembra la più convincente? Quali sono secondo voi gli aspetti più importanti da sottolineare su quest'argomento?

IN-CLASS ACTIVITY SESSION 3

Decidi quanto sei d'accordo (1—non sono per niente d'accordo—5—sono completamente d'accordo) con queste frasi e scrivi la tua opinione su Padlet

a) È bene che un dibattito sul sessismo della lingua ci sia perché il linguaggio non soltanto rispecchia i cambiamenti in corso nella società, ma è anche in grado di modificare la nostra percezione di categorie e fenomeni sociali.

b) Oggi, con una politica e una società che non hanno argomenti validi di cui trattare né soluzioni per reali e concreti problemi della nazione, ci si perde in dibattiti che, anziché includere, escludono: escludono il nostro passato, escludono i significati, escludono la personalità dei parlanti e degli scriventi e la loro stessa libertà di espressione.

c) Il sessismo linguistico è una delle scemenze di questo secolo, all'insegna del politicamente corretto che ho sempre considerato una delle più grandi ipocrisie della storia.

d) Visto che la lingua si evolve grazie all'uso delle persone che la parlano, è molto probabile che soluzioni alternative al maschile e al femminile si diffonderanno nell'italiano nei prossimi anni.

e) È arrivato il momento di introdurre il genere neutro in italiano.

APPENDIX B: SAMPLE OF STUDENTS' OUTPUTS

Critical Commentary—Excerpts

'Quest'anno, Maty Fall Diba, una modella senegalese-italiana, ha fatto la storia, come la prima modella nera, che ha la cittadinanza italiana, ad essere sulla copertina di Vogue Italia. Accanto a lei c'erano le parole "Italian Beauty". Eppure, dopo la pubblicazione, Daniele Baschin, consigliere del partito Lega, ha affermato che Diba non potrà mai essere considerata "una vera bellezza italiana" a causa della sua pelle'.

'Secondo me, la legge è un buon inizio ma non possiamo permetterci da [di] pensare che è l'unica cosa che dobbiamo cambiare. Prova di questo si può ritrovare al nord delle Alpi. In Francia, dal 1889 esiste una legge che stabilisce il [lo] ius soli—la cittadinanza per tutti chi [quelli che] sono nati sul territorio. La legge francese è adesso molto più inclusiva rispetto alla corrispondente legge Italiana. Tuttavia, la Francia continua ad avere gravi problemi a tutti livelli con il razzismo e gli effetti del colonialismo francese.'

Opinion Article

Sample of students' titles:

Riempia il vuoto: car_ tutt_

Un nuovo, libero modo di esprimerci per permettere a chiunque di sentirsi parte del dialogo.

Dobbiamo parlare di come parliamo.

L'importanza della lingua neutra e la casa editrice che sta aprendo la strada per la lingua italiana più inclusiva.

Casa editrice? Scusa, volevo dire casa editore. No, intendo casa editə.

La casa editrice italiana effequ è la prima a introdurre lo "schwa" nelle sue norme editoriali.

Opinion articles—Excerpts

'[. . .] in inglese, lingua isolante, contrariamente all'italiano, pochissime parole hanno forme diverse a seconda del genere, visto che molte hanno anche un'alternativa gender-neutral (woman/man > person e brother/sister > sibling). Nel libro originale Star Wars: Last Shot, di Daniel José Older, infatti per Taka Jamoreesa vengono usati i pronomi they/them, forma inclusiva. Per la traduzione in italiano quindi è stato suggerito di utilizzare lo Schwa ed appaiono espressioni come "lə giovane pilota" e "questə ragazzinə". Guarda come funziona!'

'Le altre lingue romanze affrontano le stesse questioni su come creare un genere neutro invece dell'uso delle parole maschili o femminili. Questo mostra che il problema della mancanza della lingua non binaria è un problema internazionale e quindi sottolinea l'importanza di trovare una soluzione perché molte persone sentino [si sentono] escluse dalla loro lingua'.

APPENDIX C:
AUTHENTIC MATERIAL USED IN THE CLASSROOM

Affricot, J. (2016). "The Expats NY: Trailer." Last accessed November 15, 2022. https://www.youtube.com/watch?v=1y209ACdjyg

Afroitalian Souls. (2019). "Blackface in Italia: Perché è razzista." https://www.youtube.com/watch?v=9-tE0Y7ICgE

Anonymous. (2020, June 12). "Una nuova legge sulla cittadinanza per combattere il razzismo." *Vita.* http://www.vita.it/it/article/2020/06/12/una-nuova-legge-sulla-cittadinanza-per-combattere-il-razzismo/155847/

Barresi, V. (2020, June 16). Black lives matter. All lives matter. But who, really, matters? Italy, capisci? *La Voce di New York.* https://www.lavocedinewyork.com/news/primo-piano/2020/06/16/black-lives-matter-all-lives-matter-but-who-really-matters-italy-capisci/

Bonazzi, L. (2020, June 9). In Italia siamo antirazzisti solo quando succede qualcosa in un altro Paese? *MarieClaire.* https://www.marieclaire.it/attualita/news-appuntamenti/a32769754/george-floyd-razzismo-italia/

Con parole nostre. (2021). Il sessismo nella lingua italiana. Last accessed November 22, 2022. https://soundcloud.com/conparolenostrepodcast/ep-47-il-sessismo-nella-lingua-italiana

D.E.I.—Futuro Antirazzista [@dei_f_arazzista]. (2021, July 2). *Cosa vuole dire colorblind Pt 1* [Tweet]. Twitter. https://mobile.twitter.com/dei_f_arazzista/status/1411061494142410758

Fernando, N., Mancuso, M. C., & Uyangoda, N. (n.d.). *Sulla razza.* Last accessed November 15, 2022. https://www.sullarazza.it/

Fiandaca, R. (2020, June 12). La "caccia alle statue" del movimento black lives matter sarà la fine dei monumenti razzisti? *ElleDecor.* https://www.elledecor.com/it/lifestyle/a32830578/black-lives-matter-statue-razzisti-colonialisti/

Gennaro, A. (2020, August 2). Roma, vince la mobilitazione anti-razzista e la stazione della metro cambia nome: sarà dedicata al partigiano italo-somalo Marincola. *Open.* https://www.open.online/2020/08/02/roma-metro-c-marincola-partigiano/

Gheno, V. (2020, June 7). *Censimento: Soluzioni in uso per gestire la "moltitudine mista."* Facebook. https://www.facebook.com/wanderingsociolinguist/posts/10158190755040915.

Manera, M. (2021, October 29). Chi ha paura dell'evoluzione? Lo schwa non è l'apocalisse. *Domani.* https://www.editorialedomani.it/idee/cultura/chi-ha-paura-dellevoluzione-la-schwa-non-e-lapocalisse-gx72g90x

Piccinni, G. (2020, November 15). Una donna fa il rettore ma "rettrice" si usava già nel XIII secolo. *Globalist.*

Podcast Italiano. (2020). Il dibattito intorno ai femminili professionali in italiano. Last accessed November 22, 2022. https://www.youtube.com/watch?v=N3AsSg0K4BQ

Postcolonial Italy. (n.d.). Last accessed November 1, 2022. https://postcolonialitaly.com/

Raffaele, S. (2021, October 12). Lo schwa è il frutto dell'illusione sul potere della grammatica. *Domani*.

Redazione. (2020, June 8). Black Lives Matter in Italia. Intervista all'attivista Antonella Bundu. *Radiopopolare*. https://www.radiopopolare.it/black-lives-matter-in-italia-intervista-ad-antonella-bundu/

Riyahi, Y. (2020, November 23). L'inclusività della lingua italiana: Intervista (al contrario) a Vera Gheno. *Exibart*. https://www.exibart.com/personaggi/linclusivita-della-lingua-italiana-intervista-al-contrario-a-vera-gheno/

Uyangoda, N. (2021). *L'unica persona nera nella stanza*. Rome: 66thand2nd.

Venturi, V. (2020, October 17). È italiana la prima casa editrice che sostituisce il generico maschile con lo "Schwa." *Il Messaggero*. https://www.ilmessaggero.it/mind_the_gap/maschile_generico_schwa_casa_editrice_italiana_effequ-5529659.html

NOTES

1. On the purposes of teaching writing in L2 see Manchón (2013).
2. Authentic resources used in class are listed in Appendix C.
3. Only the paragraphs of the article that report Igiaba Scego's and Bellamy's points of view.
4. Bellamy is a content creator and the founder of *Afroitalian Souls*, a digital platform that promotes the voices of Black Italians and the African diaspora. Among the reasons that led Bellamy to create *Afroitalian Souls* was frustration around the representation of Black Italian people who are involved in the public discourse only to express their opinion on immigration, crime, and jus soli.
5. *Postcolonial Italy* is a digital project that "aims at capturing and documenting material traces that are visible in the public space and, thus, stimulating a public debate on Italy's silenced colonial history" (https://postcolonialitaly.com/the-project/).
6. Amba Aradam was a battle won by the Italian army against the Ethiopian army in 1936. Via dell'Amba Aradam is also one of the points highlighted in the interactive map of Rome in *Postcolonial Italy*.
7. A group of people made of subjects identifying with different genders.
8. Effequ is an independent publisher.

BIBLIOGRAPHY

Abrams, Z. I. (2020). *Intercultural communication and language pedagogy*. Cambridge: Cambridge University Press.

Byrnes, H. (2011). Beyond writing as language learning or content learning. In R. Manchón (Ed.), *Learning-to-write and writing-to-learn in an additional language* (pp. 133–57). Amsterdam: J. Benjamins.

Clayton-Pedersen, A. R., O'Neill, N., & McTighe Musil, C. (2009). *Making excellence inclusive: A framework for embedding diversity and inclusion into colleges and universities' academic excellence mission*. Association of American Colleges and Universities.

Council of Europe. (2020). *Common European framework of reference for languages: Learning, teaching, assessment*. Strasbourg: Council of Europe Publishing. Last accessed February 17, 2022. www.coe.int/lang-cefr.

Ford, J., & Santos, E. (2022). Decolonising languages: Ways forward for UK HE and beyond. *Languages, Society and Policy*. Last accessed November 25, 2022. https://www.lspjournal.com/post/decolonising-languages

Hennebry, M. (2014). Cultural awareness: Should it be taught? Can it be taught? In P. Driscoll, E. Macaro, & A. Swarbrick (Eds.), *Debates in modern languages education* (pp. 135–49). Hoboken: Taylor and Francis.

Hood, S. (2008). Summary writing in academic contexts: Implicating meaning in process of change." *Linguistics and Education*, 19, 351–65.

Kubota, R. (2011). Immigration, diversity, and language education in Japan: Toward a glocal approach to teaching English. In P. Seargeant (Ed.), *English in Japan in the era of globalization* (pp. 101–22). Basingstoke: Palgrave Macmillan.

Lee, A., Poch, R., Shaw, M., & Williams, R. D. (2012). *Engaging diversity in undergraduate classrooms: A pedagogy for developing intercultural competence. ASHE Higher Education Report*, *38*(2). Last accessed February 17, 2022. https://doi.org/10.1002/aehe.20002

Manchón, R. (2013). Learning and teaching writing in the foreign languages classroom: Fostering writing-to-learn approaches. In P. Driscoll, E. Macaro, & A. Swarbrick (Eds.), *Debates in modern languages education* (pp. 96–107). Hoboken: Taylor and Francis.

Mehta, S. R. (Ed.). (2018). *Language and literature in a glocal world*. Singapore: Springer Nature.

Miles, R., Hu, R., & Dotson, K. (2013). Perceptions of diversity in higher education. *Journal of Continuing Higher Education*, *61*(2), 74–82. Last accessed February 17, 2022. https://doi.org/10.1080/07377363.2013.796244

Reynolds, R., Ferguson-Patrick, K., & Macqueen, S. (2017). "Players in the world": Action for intercultural competence in classroom pedagogy. In S. Choo, D. Sawch, A. Villanueva, & R. Vinz (Eds.), *Educating for the 21st century* (pp. 47–71). Singapore: Springer.

Ritzer, G., & Dean, P. (2015). *Globalization: A basic text.* Chichester: John Wiley & Sons.

Russell, G. (2020). Reflecting on a way of being: Anchor principles of cultural competence. In J. Frawley, G. Russell, & J. Sherwood (Eds.), *Cultural competence and the higher education sector* (31–41). Singapore: Springer. https://doi.org/10.1007/978-981-15-5362-2_3

12

QUEERING THE ITALIAN AND MODERN LANGUAGES SYLLABI

Toward a Queer Language Pedagogy and Intersectional Teaching Practices

Luca Malici

Amid the COVID-19 pandemic, Italy witnessed an unresolved dispute that demonstrates how societies urgently need to address equality, diversity, and inclusion (EDI) more profoundly, particularly in the education sector. In October 2021, after almost three decades of political debates, and hailed by a stadium-like victory roar that made the headlines, the Italian Senate voted down the DDL Zan: "a bill that would have made violence against LGBT and disabled people, as well as misogyny, a hate crime" (Tondo, 2021). To date, Italy remains one of the few European countries lacking this specific antidiscrimination legislation, communicating its inability and ideological unwillingness to recognize and safeguarded women, disabled, and nonheterosexual minoritized groups. Besides, the growing surge of far-right extremism, populist movements, and neo-fundamentalist groups perceive diversity as an attack on national identity and traditional family values. Shielding the education sector from discourses on gender and sexuality under a—mistakenly understood and elusive—*ideologia* or *teoria gender* remains one of their pivotal concerns, yet this is also the case in France.[1] As a result, integrating inclusive themes in Italian schools and universities remains routinely contested. Should EDI themes and current debates enter the classroom? How can we make language teaching and learning more inclusive? What methods and resources are available to address these questions? What has been achieved in this area of pedagogy? And what further steps could we take?

One year before the debate in Italy, I had raised these questions during an online Continuing Professional Development, Teaching Diversity in the Italian Classroom conference organized by the University of King's College London. Drawing on seminal research on queer pedagogy (Bryson & de Castell, 1993) and links to teaching English as a second language (ELS, Nelson 2018), I introduced Queer Language Pedagogy (QLP), an innovative approach and discipline devoted to exploring the intersection between queer theory and critical language pedagogy, which can be applied to the mother tongue (L1), the acquisition of a second language (L2) in foreign language environments (FL), conventional learning settings (LS), as well as to different linguistic contexts.

In this chapter, after defining QLP, I examine the normativity of some pedagogical practices and resources available to language teachers. To demonstrate this, I scrutinize a sample of recently published coursebooks used to teach Italian language at the university level through an initial, small-scale, quali-quantitative survey. The results gesture toward a rethinking of the representations of ethnicity, ability, gender, and sexuality in commercially available teaching materials. In the second part of the chapter, I present and discuss practical and innovative practices for the language classroom, and I analyze a variety of resources that can make teaching more inclusive. In my attempt to bring together the research done in this field, I use a mixed methodology that includes field experience, discourse and data analyses. This chapter also answers a recent call for more interdisciplinary research on queer pedagogy and experiences in higher education (HE) communication classrooms (Atay & Pensoneau-Conway, 2019). Although this work is situated in the context of teaching Italian in UK universities, many of the insights and considerations could be extended to other modern languages and geo-local contexts.

TOWARD A QUEER LANGUAGE PEDAGOGY

The QLP theoretical framework departs from a sociohistorical critique of the discourses around sexuality, but it crucially extends, encompasses, and applies to other spheres of (in)equalities.

Along with other disciplinary institutions such as the church and the workplace, schools and universities have historically helped to regulate and limit alternative sexual and gender expressions in favor of behaviors considered more "normal" and "natural." For example, only twenty years ago in the UK, the law known as Section 28 (May 24, 1988–2003) would still prohibit any form of discussion that could "intentionally promote the teaching in any maintained school of the acceptability of homosexuality" (Ellis, 2007). In more recent times, however, legal protection for, and recognition of, bisexual, gay male and intersexed, lesbian, queer, and trans (BGILQT)[2] people have improved in order to create a more equal society for all. However, this is the case for countries in the "Northern" and "Western" parts of the globe.

In the UK, legislation had an important impact on the ways minorities are represented, protected, and included in the curriculum. The Equality Act 2010 is a crucial antidiscrimination law that promotes and enforces equality, and it ensures that universities are liable for the discriminatory acts of their employees (EHRC, 2014). Thanks also to this, HE institutions now offer dedicated EDI training to their staff, even though, from my experience, this is rarely compulsory and often a hasty box-ticking exercise. Despite this, institutions are increasingly committed to achieving further external recognition through gender (Athena Swan), LGBT (Stonewall), disability, and race equality charters. Although almost twenty years have passed since Mary Bryson and Suzanne de Castell pointed out that even simply being a nonheterosexual university faculty member was considered "a gross violation" (Bryson & de Castell, 1993, p. 287), some scholars maintain that even today there are institutional limitations to the array of sexual discourses that could enter HE (Baldo, 2019; Nelson, 2018). Calling for more research on the gatekeeping institutional policies, Cynthia Nelson claims that open discussions of sexuality in the university setting is still "dissuaded, whether overtly or subtly" (2018, p. 15). Often these constraints have economical, geo-cultural, and ideological motives and are based on assumptions that a segment of the international, overseas fee-paying student body could be offended by putatively deemed "sensitive," "upsetting," "not appropriate" topics.[3]

Language and words have vital importance if we are to accept that they play a fundamental role in articulating realities and producing identities. Since the 1990s, queer scholars and activists began to challenge the hegemony and privileges tied to adjectives like "male," "heterosexual," and "cisgender."[4] They question the dominance of men in social or cultural systems (patriarchy); the view that heterosexuality is by default the only normal and acceptable sexual identity (heteronormativity); as well as the assumptions that a person's gender identity and expression match their biological sex at birth (cisnormativity). The term cis-hetero-patriarchy summarizes well this system of power, historically based on the supremacy and dominance of cis-heterosexual men through the exploitation and oppression of women and BGILQT people. Crucially, queer theory is not only exclusively concerned with gender and sexuality but considers "thick intersectionalities" to reveal multiple identity layers and vectors of difference (Yep, 2016, p. 86). Within curricula and classrooms, my use of QLP serves to challenge cis-hetero-patriarchal discourses at large as well as a plurality of "isms" such as—in alphabetical order—ableism, ageism, antisemitism, classism, heterosexism, and racism, to name but a few.

My understanding of QLP chiefly postulates the crucial importance of language and representations in articulating identities as they can amplify, quieten, and resist discourses that could solidify into stereotypes and become biased prejudices. The language tutor is a pivotal actor and facilitator in bringing forward open messages of inclusivity, equality, and difference against any form of marginalization. I now explore the language classroom as an institutionalized site influenced by normative and discriminatory discourses, and I discuss how a QLP approach could intervene in dissipating them.

PEDAGOGICAL RESPONSIBILITIES, RISKS, AND PLEASURES

In preparing our students to be proficient linguists and culturally agile "glocal" citizens, the productive advantages of a QLP approach are numerous. A queer-informed language pedagogy allows all students to think critically and creatively about their own identities and positionalities, opening productive spaces to ponder historical, social, and cultural awareness in class. Heteronormative assumptions might be wrong as "students in language classrooms may be eager to engage with LGBT topics because they represent part of their lived experiences, either because of their own self-identification or though having queer acquaintances" (Paiz, 2017, p. 351). Crucially, we must not forget that learners might have future work colleagues or even supervisors who happen to identify as BGILQT, therefore QLP might also assist with their future employability and work life.

On the other hand, scholars warned that maintaining a cis-hetero-patriarchal status quo in class has damaging effects as it encourages "bullying" (Paiz, 2017, p. 353) and limits "our collective efforts to foster multilingualism and multiliteracies" (Nelson, 2006, p. 1). Upholding even involuntarily normative discourses in class while excluding queer perspectives and other marginalities can, in effect, be "a way of enforcing compulsory heterosexuality" (Nelson, 2006, p. 7). From my personal experience and through conversation with colleagues, language tutors can often find themselves in awkward instances or "queer moments" in the classroom.[5] These instances include asking learners to talk about their significant other, presupposing their heterosexual relationship; correcting feminine endings while a male student describes his boyfriend; marking down a student's family exercise because it does not match heterosexual norms. These situations might all reveal a potential, latent cis-hetero-patriarchal bias, even when it "may manifest in seemingly benign ways" (Paiz, 2017, p. 353). In these cases, tutors assume that the student has not learned the grammar, when in fact the mistake pertains to the teacher. As a result, to correct their instructors, learners are often unwillingly forced to come out, generating potentially harmful moments of disclosure in the classroom. Alternatively, they are compelled to pass as cis-heterosexual (Djavadghazaryans, 2020). After all, allowing students to comfortably learn and use the language to talk about themselves with others is the fundamental premise of the communicative approach to language learning that most HE institutions pride themselves on using. De Vincenti et al. aptly state that "teachers may either contribute to the preservation of normative positions in regard to dominating social practices, or they can challenge them" (2007, p. 60). I believe that we have a crucial responsibility as language instructors, potentially queer-informed pedagogues, and teachers to think more openly about assumptions and privileges as well as to acknowledge—intersectional, queer—possibilities in our classrooms.

While applying QLP we must also take some precautions. First, we must be mindful of our learners from minority backgrounds so as not to tokenize or universalize their individual experiences for the sake of our inclusive lessons. We must consider our international learners, who might experience multiple layers of oppression, or those who might not wish to discuss certain topics as they are considered taboo in their culture. More research thus should be directed toward these conflicting classroom dynamics. Nevertheless, among the attributes we wish to pass on to our students are critical thinking, internationalization, and the ability to adapt to and move comfortably across different cultures; therefore all learners should be able to confront challenging issues such as misogyny, heterosexism, and xenophobia. As we apply QLP, we should also treat these themes with depth to avoid having heterosexually identified students see "this kind of 'border crossing' [as] a colonizing kind of 'intellectual tourism'" (Bryson & de Castell, 1993, p. 300) or suggest that inclusive classes can produce new forms of exclusivity and exclusion.

A queer-informed pedagogical approach might also help to revitalize the HE sectors, particularly Modern Languages, that are increasingly hit by financial cuts, reduction of programs, and palpable decreases in enrollment. For example, Nelson notices how "given the challenges LGBT language learners often encounter in class, it is not surprising that some opt out of formal education" (2018, p. 10). Francesa Calamita and Roberta Trapè maintain that languages departments could even capitalize on EDI pedagogy, reconsidering the profession of language educators as "cross-cultural mediators" who could help rebuild a more diverse postpandemic world (2021, pp. 9–10). To do this, however, practices and resources used in the language classroom must be reconsidered. In the following section, I examine the commercially available language textbooks and their often normative and outdated approaches and representations.

CIS-HETERO-PATRIARCHAL AND UN-QUEER TEXTBOOKS

As well as the classroom, textbooks and curricula can also be sites of biased power relations and struggles. Learning manuals are imbued with the ideology of the people who put them together, review, and publish them. Paiz claims that "no textbook can be ideologically neutral" and that "commercial publishers play a key role in maintaining the heteronormative environment that may exist in many language classes" (2017, p. 353). This is crucial because language textbooks often have a pivotal role in university programs, and they set the agenda affecting what is represented and discussed in class as well as what is excluded.

There is consensus among scholars who have reviewed and problematized stereotypical images in commercially available learning materials that there is a paucity of varied and inclusive representations, particularly concerning the underrepresentation of the BGILQT population (De Vincenti et al., 2007; Gray, 2013; Nemi Neto, 2018). This research, however, pertains mainly to ESL resources and is not always theorized or substantiated by data (Nelson, 2018).

In a few Italian language publications, there have been some timid attempts at inclusivity in higher levels (B1-C2), yet the situation at lower levels is still understudied. For an initial investigation of Italian language textbooks used at university level in the UK, I have examined a sample of five recently published coursebooks (2014–2022) aimed at complete beginners (A1 CEFR), three of which were launched in 2019. I identified the four most popular textbooks in use among the twenty-two UK universities that offer an Italian degree and/or institution-wide language programs (IWLP).

Table 12.1 shows the books and universities in which they are adopted. The sample includes one international publisher (Palgrave) and two well-known Italian companies (Alma, Edilingua), to which I added a recent publication by

TABLE 12.1. Inclusivity Scores of Selected Italian Language Textbooks

Year	Textbook	Universities adopting them	Inclusivity %
2014	*Nuovo Espresso 1: Corso Di Italiano A1* (Alma)	UCL, Royal Holloway, Leicester	3.69
2016	*Foundations Italian 1* (Palgrave)	Sheffield, Edinburgh, Southampton	22.50
2019	*Dieci. Lezioni Di Italiano A1* (Alma)	Reading, Edinburgh, Bristol	7.40
2019	*Nuovissimo Progetto Italiano A1* (Edilingua)	Imperial College, Warwick, York	2.26
2019	*Ls. Corso Interattivo A1* (Loescher/Bonacci)	—	2.06

Loescher/Bonacci as it remained unrepresented among the most recognized LS Italian publishing houses (Massimi, 2014). I used qualitative methodology to review inclusive representations in these textbooks, focusing on portrayals of families and professions; and quantitative analysis of all the images, drawings, and/or photos of individuals to gauge the variety of representations offered and the "thickness" of their intersectionalities.

The results reveal that, in order of publication, *Nuovo Espresso* (2014) has only 15 portrayals of nonwhite people out of 406 images, which represents less than 3.69% of the total. Although they are evenly spread between men (7) and women (8), their ethnic background is almost exclusively black. On a more constructive note, in the drawing of a family tree, Giovanni is married to Amina, and they have three biracial children (p. 131). The book mentions separation (p. 134), single mothers, de facto and extended families in a listening activity (p. 137); however, a cultural "infobox" still provides a rather normative account of Italian "modern" families (p. 198).

Foundations Italian 1 (2016) progressively presents an activity on Samantha Cristoforetti, the first Italian female astronaut (p. 14), a grandfather with a new partner, and a divorced uncle in a reading activity (p. 18). Compared to the previous textbook there are fewer images in total (151) but the proportion of its 34 varied drawings is the highest in this research with over 22.5%. Nevertheless, there is a noticeable imbalance between the 21 men and 13 women.

The most wide-ranging representations are found in *Dieci* (2019). Among a staggering total of 810 images, 60 of them (7.4%) pictured black (39), Asian (14), and South Asian (2) individuals, as well as people of Latin American

(3) and Middle Eastern (3) backgrounds. These portrayals are varied also in terms of gender (33 women and 27 men), ages (adults but also two elderly individuals, 2 children and 2 teenagers), and professions (e.g., two black male doctors). Regarding the debate on the feminization of professions, only *Dieci* mentions "architetta" but once only and at the end of the book (p. 162).

Despite *Nuovissimo Progetto Italiano* (2019) presenting itself as "the best-selling Italian textbook in the world" (p. 3) and having undergone a recent revision, out of the 487 images only 2.26% provide representations of non-white individuals. Among these 11 images there are 4 black males, 2 black females, 3 men and one woman from Latin America, as well one man of Moroccan and another of Asian descent.

The textbook that scored the poorest is *LS* (2019) with only 2.06% of varied representation, 13 out of 630, equally divided in terms of gender (6 women and 7 men) and including the images of Mahatma Gandhi and Che Guevara. In this textbook, the same photos are often repeated, which might suggest their limited budget for copyrighted photographs. This notwithstanding, publishers could opt for more affordable in-house drawings to provide more diverse and inclusive representations, as is the case for the Palgrave book. The representation of families in *LS* is also very traditional and, in the vocabulary section at the end of the book, most professions are presented only in their masculine form.

The fact that two of the three most recent publications analyzed are also among the less inclusive ones stands out as troubling. Furthermore, the numerical deviations between Italian publishers and the international publishing house Palgrave Macmillan demonstrate that the latter is more attentive to portrayals of different ethnicities and EDI. The analysis of the data gathered revealed that the representation of people with a disability is strikingly nonexistent, just like that of same-sex couples' relationships and BGILQT individuals. Despite some scant mentions of divorce and separations, families are still very much portrayed in a rather normative fashion as idealised, picture-perfect, nuclear white families like those once seen on TV adverts. For what concerns the Italian context, these findings seem to corroborate international research stating that at lower language levels, there are insignificant references to sexual identity, orientation, or alternative family formations and that families are routinely represented as predominantly white, with an average of two children (a boy and a girl, for grammatical convenience), while divorce, separation, adoptions, and other alternative family settings are rarely considered (Nemi Neto, 2018).

One must only look at some recent statistics on how Italian populations and families are changing because of sociopolitical advancements and migrations to realize that most of these publications are not representing contemporary society. For example, Istituto nazionale di statistica (ISTAT) figures show increasingly multiethnic families, single parents, childless couples, and same-sex couples in Italy (2021). Although there might be some references to gay males and lesbians, nonbinary, trans, and intersexed identities are symbolically annihilated in language textbooks. Why is this the case? Can queerness and diversity upset, offend, or scandalize some teachers, students, or potential textbook buyers? Despite some very recent, promising initiatives and independent inclusive experimentations,[6] more research and data in this direction could encourage publishing houses to engage more meaningfully with EDI themes in their books.

COMPREHENSIVE, INCLUSIVE, AND INTERSECTIONAL PRACTICES AND RESOURCES

If textbooks and commercially available resources do not offer inclusive materials, individual teachers are often left to their own devices to create their learning resources, and this is true in other languages and subjects too. As Dominique Carlini Versini suggests while talking of inclusive language: "In the absence of resources and of institutional standards on the issue, teaching [. . .] inclusively becomes a negotiation between tradition and innovation" (2022, p. 73). In this final section, I present some practical, day-to-day classroom strategies and discuss how to adapt some of the normative resources available and how to source and create bespoke Italian QLP resources for different levels.

Everyday Queer Class Strategies

A queer-informed language pedagogy is not only constructive for more proficient learners but could be infused at all levels, including ab initio. QLP could be applied in class even in the first few weeks of a complete beginner Italian course. For example, once the tutor has introduced the third person singular, teachers could invite learners to share their preferred personal pronouns and briefly explain their importance, encouraging students to use them in class and, if they wish, when submitting homework.[7] Among other classroom strategies, rather than mark students as incorrect when they get confused with their masculine and feminine endings, I tend to challenge their answers lightheartedly with open questions and without making assumptions: "Is this your boyfriend or girlfriend?" "Tell me about your spouse/significant other."

In Italian, this sort of questions would already require grammatical agreements and particular attention should be paid to using gender-neutral nouns such as persona or individuo.

To address the class, especially in welcoming them at the start, I have always used gender-inclusive language and new graphic conventions on my slides such as the -* or -з (e.g., benvenut*, benvenutз). Furthermore, I routinely question dominant, very often cis-hetero-patriarchal, models; for instance, when covering the world of work and professions at various levels, we discuss how in romance languages the grammar reflects traditional gender inequalities in power. I want students to be aware of the linguistic "glass ceiling" and the historically pervasive use of the masculine form for professional, institutional, and executive roles. With my intermediate class, for example, I revise irregular nouns and professions looking at the feminine forms such as amministratrice unica (CEO), ambasciatrice (ambassador), senatrice (senator), sindaca (mayor), avvocata (lawyer), ministra (MP), reminding learners that when the referent is a woman, they should use the feminine form. As Calamita (2018) suggests, to put this into practice, we use Robustelli et al.'s gender-inclusive guide (2014), and we work on newspaper articles and headlines that might still erroneously use masculine forms for women.

At beginner and post-beginner levels, tutors could resort to innovative and inclusive resources, even using gamification. While working on physical descriptions, rather than the traditional board game "Guess Who," in class, I use an alternative called "Who's She: A Guessing Game That Celebrates Accomplished Women Throughout History" (Kozerska, 2018). In this way, students can ludically practice their Italian language, vocabulary and agreements while learning about important transnational female figures from different eras and backgrounds, including STEM (science, technology, engineering, and mathematics), an area where women are often underrepresented, especially in universities and occupations.

Telling Queer Stories, "Transing" Resources, and Sourcing QLP Materials

Queering straight stories and commercially available resources is another useful teaching tactic. I often "twist" books' exercises regarding normative families by asking students to imagine a nontraditional structure or giving them the freedom to determine their own relationships in role-plays. I have realized that it is very difficult to find trans-inclusive teaching resources, but we can always adapt and infiltrate straight texts. The verb form "transing" is used to mean the practice of challenging and interfering with cis-normative texts and readings. For example, at intermediate level while revising the imperfect and pluperfect with vocabulary related to childhood and school, I have adapted a text in this way: "After a transition process, the person who once sat next to me at school is now Adele. She is a successful CEO and still one of my best friends." I am aware that this is a stretch to the praxis of working with authentic materials, but while we devise other types of resources, this might extend class discourses to productive and progressive possibilities.

I also employ broader understandings of "text," working, for example, with comics and, even if a little risqué, with the work of the popular Italian transgender cartoonist Josephine Yole Signorelli.[8] Alternatively, I used the work of important Italian singer-songwriters, such as Fabrizio De Andrè (1996) and his song "Princesa," inspired by Italo-Brazilian trans model Fernanda Farias de Albuquerque's autobiography (1994), which is also a prime example of how we can infuse a queer transnational approach to language lessons.

As per the "Princesa" example, it is crucial to tell queer edifying and constructive stories, prioritizing first-person accounts and in-community voices. Incorporating queer popular media in the classroom is perhaps the most feasible option, but this practice is often seen as reductive and "might not be enough" (Paiz, 2017, p. 358). Sole Anatrone and Julia Heim highlight how in Italian studies, for example, there is a tendency to rely on the same set of directors and queer-themed films (2021). My research on queer TV and films offers alternatives to this sort of "queer filmic canon" and includes productive and varied Italian BGILQT portrayals, for example, in talk shows, programs, TV series, soap operas, and social media (see Malici, 2014, 2020, 2021). Interviews and real biographies of Italian personalities can be also particularly valuable to offer first-person experience so that students can really put themselves in "others'" shoes. For example, Vladimir Luxuria became the first transwoman member of the European Parliament in 2006 and Gianmarco Negri the first elected transman mayor of an Italian city in 2019. While sourcing alternative materials, I have also found an excellent queer-friendly publishing house called Lo Stampatello.[9] They distribute children's books that could be easily readapted for lower levels (see, e.g., Pardi, 2014), or the Italian version of *Queer Heroes: Meet 53 LGBTQ Heroes from Past and Present* (Sicardi, 2019; Sicardi et al., 2020), which offer excellent materials for contrastive translation classes for Proficient learners. Although it is important to use successful narratives as well as coming-out stories of popular, wealthy people, such as gay male singer Tiziano Ferro, we should also remind students of the pervasive BGILQT-phobia routinely reported by news media and engage also with these problematic discussions in our teaching.

Devising QLP Resources

Creating alternative resources from scratch is language educators' ultimate option, and sometime the most productive one. Although the inclusion of decolonizing and EDI elements in the first semester of an ab initio Italian language course can be challenging, during the oral seminar, I dedicate some time to considering underrepresented identities through a tailored-made PowerPoint representing a queer family tree (Figure 12.1).

In the image, Giulio and Adele are divorced grandparents and Adele is now with Maria (representing same-sex relationships of older women). Their grandson Matteo happens to be in a wheelchair. Matteo's Uncle Marco is in a same-sex relationship with Kevin, whereas Auntie Marta is in an interracial relationship with Omar, and they have four biracial kids. Students discuss in Italian the degrees of kinship and identities that are often erased from commercially available language textbooks and resources. While doing this, we also introduce the more politically correct terms for "acquired," "step-," and "half-" family members, which in Italian historically take suffixes often perceived as pejorative (-igno/a, -astro/a). This graphic representation also allows students to learn a set of vocabulary that is not often introduced with traditional activities (compagno/a, divorziato/a, separato/a, stare con qualcuno/a). In this activity, however, I willingly left out—for now—some more controversial topics like same-sex couples with children, adoptions, and the ongoing "parent 1 and 2" debates in Italy.

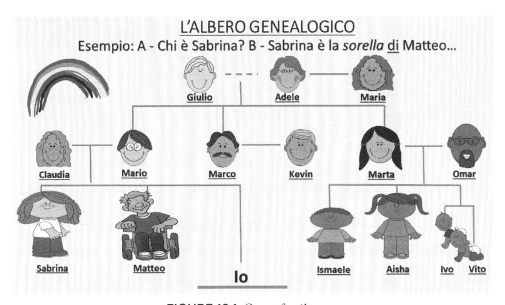

FIGURE 12.1. Queer family tree.

The students are always extremely engaged with this activity, and for example, I once heard some students enquiring about the relationships: "What's going on with the grandmother [Adele]?" "Is the other woman [Maria] her sister?" "Hang on, no . . . she's divorced Giulio and she's now with her, of course! It's 2021!" In one instance, at the end of a session, one student asked me to take a picture of this slide. In a subsequent email exchange, I tried to understand the reason for this request. They said that the reasons were many: "Firstly, the activity itself was challenging as it demanded lots of specific vocabulary and grammar, and it was fun and engaging." However, I was particularly pleased to read the rest:

> I was genuinely impressed to see my teacher take on such a progressive attitude towards the idea of the family, including things such as gay marriages, biracial children, relatives with disabilities etc. It was so refreshing to see more diversity and inclusion of all abilities in our learning in such a positive light; especially as this is something quite overlooked at university level teaching, in my opinion. I felt that the activity, whilst only a small part of the lesson, acted as an important reminder that when learning languages and studying different cultures, learning about minority groups within the wider world should have as much a priority as anything else that we learn. The activity also dissipated the idea of the stereotypically 'normal' nuclear family, encouraging inclusion and participation from everyone in the class, whilst also allowing the students to embrace their family dynamic in a comfortable and safe environment without judgement or prejudice. For example, being mixed-raced myself, it was so lovely to see a reflection of my familial situation on the screen, instead of constantly seeing diagrams of families of a single race and feeling outcast in that sense. (email, February 16, 2022)

I feel this testimony speaks volumes about the magnitude of a QLP approach and I do not wish to provide further commentary.

SOME CONCLUSIONS AND FURTHER OPENINGS

In conclusion, queer-informed language pedagogy productively challenges curricula, textbooks, and classroom practices that have historically been imbued with cis-hetero-patriarchal normative discourses and representations that have disregarded intersectionalities. This approach fosters inclusive, critically minded students and future citizens, while contrasting prejudice within the education system. Stonewall reported that 42% of our students hide their identity at university for fear of discrimination, and they recommend representing LGBT perspectives, history, and experiences in university curricula and teaching (2018). Far from being intended only for BGILQT identities, QLP also acknowledges and includes thick intersectionalities linked, for example, to ableism, gender, race, or decolonizing discourses. The present work provided an initial, small-scale study on language textbooks, which showed the need for further quali-quantitative analyses able to question the economic reasons, assumptions, and practices of publishing houses. More studies are also required on queering practices in the classroom to scrutinize attitudes of both teachers and students, particularly looking at new glocal and transnational avenues. Every teacher could potentially acquire QLP awareness regardless of their orientation; however, more consideration should be given to the role of policies, teacher training, and professional development offered by single institutions and external bodies. Further urgent work should be directed also toward trans, intersex, and nonbinary students and teaching resources. Teachers are increasingly asked to ensure curricula are inclusive, yet many are typically overburdened with teaching and admin while often being in precarious contracts, especially because of the pandemic and the unstable state of the education sector. Working collaboratively together, creating cross-university and cross-language online projects to share best practices and a database of adaptable and reusable resources might be one of the possible solutions.[10] In the meantime, it is vital to think about the pivotal role of languages in these uncertain times, as well as educators' responsibility as teachers and inclusive mediators. Crucially, we should all include and acknowledge queer narratives and intersectional possibilities even in the everyday delivery of our language classes, not just for abled, white, male, or BGILQT students but for all.

NOTES

1. Terms given by these groups to knowledge erroneously understood to erase the distinct male and female dichotomy, believed to arm and "convert" minors and students (see Bernini & Marcasciano, 2021, and for comparative Italo-French research, Garbagnoli & Prearo, 2018).
2. In most of my scholarship, I use this acronym in an alphabetical order to collectively represent marginalized sexualities and gender expressions while escaping hierarchical debates on which letter should go first.

3. Michela Baldo provides some examples of the "limitation encountered in neoliberal institutions that do not always foster the concepts promoted in queer and feminist thought," which also reveal a "paternalistic and colonial understanding of non-western countries, as somehow intrinsically un-queer" (2019, pp. 94–96).
4. The latter term describes people who identify their gender with their sex assigned at birth as opposed to trans/transgender people whose sex does not match their gender identity.
5. For a discussion of instructive and transformative queer moments, when individuals are unexpectedly confronted with queerness, see Malici (2014).
6. See for example, Francesca Calamita and Chiara De Santi, *DiversITALY* (2022); Stacy Giufre and Melina Masterson, *Tutt* a tavola! Volume 1* (2019) and *Volume 2* (2019).
7. As an example of good practice, some scholars suggest administering a private and voluntary survey even before the start of the course, and for this we could even use Google forms or video applications such as Flipgrid (see also Knisley, 2022).
8. "Fumettibrutti," accessed February 26, 2022, http://comics.feltrinellieditore.it/autore/josephine-yole-signorelli-fumettibrutti/.
9. "Lo Stampatello, accessed February 26, 2022, http://lostampatello.it/.
10. I am planning to apply for funding to develop this large project, and I would like to hear from interested parties and colleagues who can contact me via email: luca.malici@gmail.com.

BIBLIOGRAPHY

Anatrone, S., & Heim, J. (2021). Why LGBTQIA+ inclusivity matters for Italian studies. In S. Gibby & A. J. Tamburri (Eds.), *Diversity in Italian studies* (pp. 1–12). New York: John D. Calandra Italian-American Institute.

Atay, A., & Pensoneau-Conway, S. L. (2019). *Queer communication pedagogy*. Routledge.

Baldo, M. (2019). Queer(y)ing (im)possibilities in the British translation classroom. In M. De Marco & P. Toto (Eds.), *Gender approaches in the translation classroom: Training the doers* (pp. 83–102). London: Palgrave Macmillan.

Benetti, M., Murtas, C., Varchetta, C., & Di Napoli, R. (2016). *Foundations Italian 1* (3rd ed.). London: Palgrave Macmillan.

Bernini, L., & Marcasciano, P. (2021). *LGBTQIA+*. Rome: Treccani.

Bryson, M., & de Castell, S. (1993). Queer pedagogy: Praxis makes im/perfect. *Canadian Journal of Education / Revue canadienne de l'éducation*, 18(3), 285–305. https://doi.org/10.2307/1495388. http://www.jstor.org/stable/1495388

Calamita, F. (2018). Sexism and gender stereotypes in Italian language courses: Grazie! In L. Hipwell & D. Melucci (Eds.), *Teaching Italian Language and Culture annual* (Special issue, pp. 126–38).

Calamita, F., & De Santi, C. (2022). *DiversITALY*. Dubuque, IA: Kendall Hunt.

Calamita, F., & Trapè, R. (2021). Virtual exchanges and gender-inclusive language: An intercultural citizenship project to foster equality. In G. Carloni, C. Fotheringham, Λ. Virga, & B. Zuccalà (Eds.), *Blended learning and the global South* (pp. 115–30). Venice: Edizioni Ca' Foscari.

Carlini Versini, D. (2022). How can we teach French inclusively? Challenges and resistance. In N. Meyer & E. Hoft-March (Eds.), *Teaching diversity and inclusion: Examples from a French-speaking classroom* (pp. 68–76). London: Routledge.

De André, F. (1996). Princesa. *Anime salve*. Rome: Ricordi/BMG, Song.

De Vincenti, G., Giovanangeli, A., & Ward, R. G. (2007). The queer stopover: How queer travels in the language classroom. *Electronic Journal of Foreign Language Teaching*, 4(1), 58–72. https://e-flt.nus.edu.sg/v4sp12007/ward.pdf

Djavadghazaryans, A. (2020). "Please don't gender me!" Strategies for inclusive language instruction in a gender-diverse campus community. In R. Criser & E. Malakaj (Eds.), *Diversity and decolonization in German studies* (pp. 269–87). London: Palgrave Macmillan, Cham.

EHRC. (2014). What equality law means for you as an education provider—Further and higher education. https://www.equalityhumanrights.com/sites/default/files/what_equality_law_means_for_you_as_an_education_provide_further_and_higher_education.pdf

Ellis, V. (2007). Sexualities and schooling in England after Section 28: Measuring and managing "at-risk" identities. *Journal of Gay & Lesbian Issues in Education*, 4(3), 13–30. https://doi.org/10.1300/J367v04n03_03

Farías de Albuquerque, F., & Jannelli, M. (1994). *Princesa—Fernanda Farías de Albuquerque*. Rome: Editrice Sensibili alle Foglie.

Fumettibrutti. Accessed February 26, 2022. http://comics.feltrinellieditore.it/autore/josephine-yole-signorelli-fumettibrutti/

Garbagnoli, S., & Prearo, M. (2018). *La crociata "anti-gender." Dal Vaticano alle manif pour tous*. Turin: Kaplan.

Giufre, S., & Masterson, M. (2019). *Tutt* a tavola! Volume 1*. University of Massachusetts Amherst, 2019. http://openbooks.library.umass.edu/tutt-a-tavola-vol-1/

Giufre, S. (2019). *Tutt* a tavola! Volume 2*. University of Massachusetts, Amherst. http://openbooks.library.umass.edu/tutt-a-tavola-vol-2/

Gray, J. (2013). LGBT invisibility and heteronormativity in ELT materials. In J. Gray (Ed.), *Critical perspectives on language teaching materials* (pp. 40–63). London: Palgrave Macmillan UK.

ISTAT. (2021). *Matrimoni, unioni civili, separazioni e divorzi.* https://www.istat.it/it/files/2021/02/Report-matrimoni-unioni-civili-separazioni-divorzi_anno-2019.pdf

Knisley, K. A. (2022). A starter kit for rethinking trans representation and inclusion in French L2 classrooms. In N. Meyer & E. Hoft-March (Eds.), *Teaching diversity and inclusion: Examples from a French-speaking classroom* (pp. 22–33). London: Routledge.

Kozerska, Z. (2018). Who's she: A guessing game that celebrates accomplished women throughout history. Warsaw: Playeress. [Board game].

Lo Stampatello. Accessed February 26, 2022. http://lostampatello.it/

Malici, L. (2014). Queer TV moments and family viewing in Italy. *Journal of GLBT Family Studies, 10*(1–2), 188–210.

Malici, L. (2020). An all Italian *Game of Thrones*: A social media investigation of Maria De Filippi's gay male version of the trash, dating show *Uomini E Donne*. In S. Anatrone & J. Heim (Eds.), *Queering Italian media* (pp. 97–132). New York: Lexington Books.

Malici, L. (2021). Hixstory repeating? Italian trans televisibility through realism, family, Catholicism and violence. In D. G. Gonzalez (Ed.), *Trans* time. Projecting transness in European (TV) series* (pp. 81–108). Frankfurt: Campus Verlag.

Marin, T., Ruggieri, L., & Magnelli, S. (2019). *Nuovissimo Progetto Italiano 1: Corso di lingua e civiltà Italiana: A1.* Rome: Edilingua.

Mezzadri, M., & Balboni, P. E. (2019). *Ls. Corso interattivo di lingua Italiana per stranieri. A1.* Turin: Loecher/Bonacci.

Naddeo, C. M., & Orlandino, E. (2019). *Dieci. Lezioni di Italiano. A1.* Florence: Alma.

Nelson, C. (2006). Queer inquiry in language education. *Journal of Language, Identity & Education, 5*(1), 1–9. https://doi.org/10.1207/s15327701jlie0501_1

Nelson, C. (2018). Queer thinking about language learning: Current research and future directions. In K. Hall & R. Barrett (Eds.), *The Oxford handbook of language and sexuality.* Oxford: Oxford University Press.

Nemi Neto, J. (2018). Queer pedagogy: Approaches to inclusive teaching. *Policy Futures in Education, 16*(5), 589–604. https://doi.org/10.1177/1478210317751273.

Paiz, J. (2017). Queering ESL teaching: Pedagogical and materials creation issues. *TESOL Journal, 9,* 348–67. https://doi.org/10.1002/tesj.329.

Pardi, F. (2014). *Perchè Hai Due Mamme?* Milan: Lo Stampatello.

Robustelli, C., Manuelli, M. T., & Maraschio, N. (2014). *Donne, grammatica e media: Suggerimenti per l'uso Dell'italiano.* Rome: Gi.U.Li.A. Giornaliste.

Rossi Massimi, L. (2014). L'editoria Italiana per stranieri. Guerra, Bonacci, Alma Ed Edilingua. *Italica, 91*(1), 43–58.

Sicardi, A. (2019). *Queer heroes: Meet 53 LGBTQ heroes from past and present!* London: Wyde Eyed Editions.

Sicardi, A., Tanat-Jones, S., & Pardi, N. (2020). *Queer heroes: 53 eroi arcobaleno di tutti i tempi.* Milan: Lo Stampatello.

Stonewall. (2018). *LGBT in Britain—University report.* https://www.stonewall.org.uk/lgbt-britain-university-report.

Tondo, L. (2021, October 27). "Disgraceful": Italy's Senate votes down anti-homophobic violence bill. *The Guardian.* https://www.theguardian.com/world/2021/oct/27/italy-senate-votes-down-anti-homophobic-violence-bill.

Yep, G. A. (2016). Toward thick(er) intersectionalities: Theorizing, researching, and activating the complexities of communication and identities. In K. Sorrells & S. Sekimoto (eds.), *Globalizing intercultural communication: A reader* (86–94). Thousand Oaks, CA: Sage.

Ziglio, L., & Rizzo, G. (2014). *Nuovo Espresso 1: Corso Di Italiano A1.* Florence: Alma.

13

ADOPTING AND ADAPTING A LANGUAGE MOOC

Learning from Students' Experience
in Intermediate Italian Blended Courses

Daniela Bartalesi-Graf and Luisa Canuto

The overall decline in language course enrollment across North America in recent years has caused major disruptions to a number of academic programs. It has also encouraged a conversation among educators on how to best maximize resources and collaboration, promote curricular innovation, and share practices and initiatives that support their teaching as well as students' learning (Littlejohn & Hood, 2017; Pulker & Kukulska-Hulme, 2020).[1]

The experience discussed in this chapter—the integration and adaptation of the language massive open online course (LMOOC) AP® Italian Language and Culture (AP Italian hereafter) in classroom-based language blended courses[2] at the intermediate to advanced level in two institutions, the University of British Columbia (UBC hereafter) and Wellesley College (WC hereafter)[3]—constitutes one such attempt.

In this study we first identify the main features of AP Italian as well as the opportunities it affords, with particular reference to students' academic and personal purposes and gains, outside and inside the classroom. We then examine the challenges of the integration of AP Italian into blended language courses and the solutions that we adopted. Finally, the quantitative and qualitative data we present and analyze show the validity, from students' perspectives, of adopting and adapting well-structured online materials in blended courses.

While the motivations to develop, adopt, and adapt an LMOOC in conjunction with a university language course may differ depending on the specific teaching and learning context (Conde Gafaro, 2020; Mizza & Rubio, 2020; Orsini-Jones et al., 2017), the experiences presented in this chapter provide a model for other institutions to follow. The process whereby materials are adopted, adapted, and tested, and results are shared with the course developer(s) and with other stakeholders, also creates a compelling cycle for the continuous improvement of academic programs, which can be applied to different settings including K–12, university, and extended learning.

AP ITALIAN: CONTENT AND ORGANIZATION

AP Italian was created at WC in 2017 and came on the heels of three other Italian language and culture LMOOCs for beginner, intermediate, and advanced learners also developed by the WC Italian program for the edX platform.[4] The objective of AP Italian's authors was to create a strong base of Italian learners coming directly from high schools into low and upper intermediate university language courses,[5] anticipating that a motivating and easily accessible AP Italian online course could provide an incentive to high schools to offer Italian.[6]

Like other LMOOCs, AP Italian is a dedicated web-based online course that provides open access to language learning activities, regardless of learners' geographical location and educational level (Bárcena et al., 2014; Jitpaisarnwattana et al., 2021) and presents well-structured and engaging content in a variety of media formats (Margaryan et al., 2015).

More specifically, AP Italian can be described as a nonlinear LMOOC, or an online learning experience that gives learners—and instructors who adopt the course in their face-to-face classes—maximum flexibility in creating a personalized learning and teaching path. In fact, while the content follows a clearly defined progression, learners can approach the course material according to their interest and complete the activities in any sequence. Each cultural topic is presented through different media and in multiple formats. For example, videos include timed transcripts, closed captions, and embedded interactive activities; articles and literary excerpts are accessible in HTML with embedded annotation and hyperlinks, as downloadable PDF documents, or as audio files. Pre- and post- activities, which are integrated with each video, podcast, reading, realia, or infographic, help learners test their comprehension skills, activate their prior knowledge, and better relate to the new information or concepts. Finally, grammar reviews are also integrated within each module through machine-graded exercises, tables, and downloadable PDF documents.

TABLE 13.1. AP Italian Contents

Cultural topics	Linguistic topics	Multimedia tools
1. Vita Contemporanea 2. Identità Privata e Pubblica 3. Famiglia e Società 4. Scienza e Tecnologia 5. Sfide Globali e Nazionali 6. Arte Italiana e Made in Italy	1. Articles, adjectives, and present tense of regular, irregular verbs 2. Past tenses (passato prossimo, imperfect, pluperfect, passato remoto) 3. Direct and indirect object pronouns, relative pronouns, imperative, future, present and past conditional, imperative 4. Subjunctive moods in all tenses, If clauses 5. Gerunds, impersonal "si," passive voice 6. Fare + infinitive, present and past infinitive, past participles	• Original video interviews • Articles (from newspapers, magazines, and blogs) • Literary pieces (short stories, excerpts from novels, graphic novels, and poetry) and songs • Realia (TV spots, advertisements, radio programs, infographics) • Machine-graded exercises for formative and summative assessment • Questions and subjects for discussions and compositions • Downloadable audio programs especially designed for the practice of interpersonal communicative skills

Moreover, thanks to the affordances offered by the edX online platform, AP Italian course authors can promptly respond to feedback from users, edit the content, and add new material that better reflects changes or emerging issues in contemporary Italian society with each new annual course edition.[7] To provide an example of the immediacy of the AP Italian course, the 2020 and 2021 editions include new infographics, video interviews, and images that provide a clear picture of the impact of COVID-19 on different aspects of Italian society. The regular and ongoing update of AP Italian would be inconceivable with traditional textbooks (Anning, 2019; Jenkins et al., 2020).

Table 13.1 summarizes the cultural and linguistic topics included in each module of the course and provides an overview of the variety of multimedia tools to help learners practice and reflect on their learning.

RATIONALE FOR ADOPTION OF AP ITALIAN

In 2018, one year after the successful launch of AP Italian,[8] instructors at WC decided to adopt it in lieu of a textbook for their intermediate courses, first in their in-person classes and then when switching to remote teaching in the spring of 2020 during campus closure caused by the COVID pandemic. The integration of AP Italian encouraged instructors to completely revisit their intermediate curriculum, implement a new blended format, and reduce the number of weekly synchronous classes from five to three, thus offering students a more manageable schedule with no added cost for materials.

The decision to adopt AP Italian for UBC intermediate language courses, starting from 2019, stemmed from the need to respond to students' demands for increased opportunities to learn about and discuss broader cultural, historical, and artistic topics while also continuing to provide high-impact practices such as group projects and service-learning opportunities. After running an extensive search of all the largest online learning platforms, the course instructor decided that edX AP Italian offered the ideal combination of relevant and engaging learning materials at the appropriate level for her students. With the integration of selected cultural and linguistic sections from the LMOOC, a flipped approach to learning was also implemented. Students were now assigned the task of independently exploring the course content, deepening their understanding by watching original videos, listening to podcasts, reading articles and literature excerpts, and responding to comprehension questions before further expanding their linguistic and cultural skills with revisions, group projects, and discussions in class.

The instructors at WC and UBC looked at the integration of AP Italian as the opportunity to implement their teaching goals. Irrespective of the more distinctive reasons behind the adoption of AP Italian, both institutions shared some wide-ranging teaching and learning objectives, such as giving students access to high-quality, up-to-date, motivating cultural material while also strengthening the development of their linguistic and intercultural skills. The richness and relevance of the online material furthered the decision to implement a blended and flipped mode of instruction whereby students are exposed to the course content multiple times and in different ways: a first time when they are asked to explore the content on their own before class; a second time when they practice their learning in class; and finally, at the end of each lesson, when they are tested. As highlighted in much educational literature (Alley & Jansak, 2001; Crouch & Mazur, 2001; Muñoz-Merino et al., 2016; Orsini-Jones et al., 2018), this flipped, scaffolded approach to learning, which includes pre-, during, and post- activities, promotes students' deep learning and discovery and helps them build the confidence to succeed in their language learning goals.

So far, we have presented the many benefits of using an LMOOC like AP Italian in blended courses with regard to its impact on students' motivation and the practice of their linguistic and cultural skills. The next section will examine the challenges of integrating an LMOOC as part of a standard academic course and how those challenges were met.

CHALLENGES AND SOLUTIONS OF INTEGRATING AN LMOOC INTO BLENDED LANGUAGE COURSES

The adoption of AP Italian presented a number of challenges derived from a few fundamental differences between an LMOOC and academic language courses in general. These differences are summarized in Table 13.2 and then discussed in the section that follows.

AP Italian is organized in six modules, each one based on a specific cultural theme and each requiring between 20 to 25 hours to be completed. Within each module a substantial quantity of cultural and linguistic material, such as three to four readings, six to eight videos and podcasts, and several computer-graded exercises, is distributed over two to three lessons. Moreover, writing assignments such as discussions and speaking practice quizzes encourage learners to develop their productive skills and collaborative skills. By comparison, standard academic courses at UBC and WC span a period of 12 to 14 weeks for a total of 35 to 37 hours of instruction, to which students are expected to add at least as many hours for assignments and learning outside class.

In consideration of this "quantitative" difference, the UBC and WC language instructors opted to select only some of the AP Italian modules and lessons for their own blended courses. They also decided to develop new activities

TABLE 13.2. Summary of Comparison between AP Italian and F2F Academic Courses

LMOOC, AP Italian	UBC & WC, Intermediate courses
• 20–25 hours of learners' engagement per module for six modules • 120–150 total hours of learners' engagement to complete the course	• 35–37 hours of instruction + 35–37 hours for individual study • 70–74 total hours of learners' engagement

Limited involvement of instructors: this consists of supporting learners and managing:
  ○ Discussion Q&A forum
  ○ Designated email account
	Extensive involvement of instructors:
	  ○ Teaching and managing class
	  ○ Developing in-class activities to build on online work
	  ○ Creating formative and summative assessment methods
	  ○ Providing ongoing individual feedback on all activities
	  ○ Monitoring students' progress

Learners with very diverse educational backgrounds	Learners with similar educational background and (some) common knowledge
Learners with strong intrinsic motivation (personal enrichment)	Learners with both instrumental and intrinsic motivations (i.e., fulfilling a requirement and personal enrichment)

to expand on the online material and further support learning during face-to-face classes with the use of slide presentations, in-class activities, formative and summative assessment techniques, and discussions in class and online.

A second, well-reported issue of many LMOOCs is the limited level of learner-learner interaction (Martin-Monje et al., 2017; Rubio, 2015) and, to a lesser degree, of learner-instructor interaction (Decker, 2014; Israel, 2015; Littlejohn & Milligan, 2015; Orsini-Jones et al., 2015). Like other LMOOCs, AP Italian attracts thousands of participants who plan to take the course at their own pace and is not designed to accommodate a high level of collaborative learning or of ongoing instructor intervention. The UBC and WC Italian intermediate courses instead provided students with numerous possibilities to interact with their instructors and with other students. For example, discussions were regularly graded and moderated online first and then rehashed with the whole class or in small groups; synchronous instructional interactions and oral exams were used repeatedly to develop learners' speaking skills while also providing support and encouragement; and finally, asynchronous group projects served to further promote collaborative learning and practice.

As already discussed, LMOOCs are designed to attract a large and diverse learner base with students from all over the world. Since no entry tests or prior academic achievements are required to enroll in these courses (Conde Gafaro, 2020; Wiley, 2015), LMOOCs are structured in ways to appeal to most participants. As an example, in AP Italian grammatical concepts are each presented with worksheets in English and summarized in user-friendly tables with exercises in different formats, from matching to multiple-choice to the fill-in-the-blank variety, following each topic. Grammatical concepts in UBC and WC Italian intermediate courses are instead contextualized by using authentic texts and focusing on concrete applications. Learners who enroll in our face-to-face courses are expected to have already been exposed to most of the grammar topics and can therefore be asked to recall their knowledge through more complex, contextualized sentence practice and compositions. In other words, for UBC and WC Italian language instructors, the integration and use of grammar concepts from AP Italian in their courses involved the development of additional teaching and learning materials, which better responded to their students' specific needs and course learning objectives. For example, students could use individual editing checklists to identify and correct grammar errors in their own essays and then submit their second draft, and peer-writing feedback was also used to help students identify recurring areas for improvement and refine their writing skills.

Students who enroll in LMOOCs have strong intrinsic motivations to learn an additional language. Whether for their own professional development or for personal enrichment (Littlejohn et al., 2015), LMOOC learners choose to participate (Downes, 2012) and are therefore expected to self-regulate their learning, navigate the course material on their own, evaluate their own progress, and ultimately decide whether they wish to complete the course. As documented in the literature (Hone & Said, 2016; Jordan, 2015), these motivations may not necessarily involve a successful completion of the course (Chiappe & Castillo, 2020). On the contrary, students who enroll in a university language program bring varying motivations to taking a course, from an intrinsic interest in the subject, to instrumental or practical reasons, to integrative motivations. Regardless of their motive, in general, university students expect to complete their courses, be supported in their learning through achievable objectives and related assignments, receive specific and guiding feedback, and develop their linguistic and cultural competencies while engaging in a variety of learning activities. The integration of a well-organized, clearly articulated, and engaging content-based LMOOC into an academic face-to-face language course where teachers can support students' self-regulated learning by providing different cognitive, metacognitive, and social strategies (Conde Gafaro, 2020; Ellis & Shintani, 2013) can significantly add value to the overall learning experience and heighten students' motivation to learn an additional language.

As discussed in the next section, these researchers decided to collect and analyze extensive qualitative and quantitative data from 107 students' exit surveys and comments to illustrate the affordabilities of the integration of an LMOOC into academic language courses from the students' perspective.

After describing the AP Italian, delineating the reasons to use it in conjunction with intermediate language courses in two different academic institutions, and sharing the challenges as well as the opportunities that adopting this LMOOC offered, in the following pages we present data that unequivocally show students' positive feedback on the integration of AP Italian into our language courses, as well as their reported substantive gains in linguistic, intercultural, and metacognitive skills.

ANALYZING THE INTEGRATION OF AP ITALIAN IN BLENDED LANGUAGE COURSES: RESEARCH QUESTIONS, RESEARCH METHODS, AND DISCUSSION

After using AP Italian in conjunction with intermediate Italian language courses for two to three years, these researchers decided to systematically survey the students and then analyze the data related to their learning experience. More specifically, this study is guided by the following research questions:

In learning Italian, what aspects do students value the most? (RQ1)
What are the advantages and disadvantages of the blended and flipped learning models in a language course according to students? (RQ2)
From students' perspective and experience, what learning outcomes were achieved through the integration of AP Italian into a face-to-face, blended academic course? (RQ3)

Research Methods

In order to answer the research questions, a total of 107 anonymous student evaluations (43 from UBC and 64 from WC) from intermediate (second year) and advanced (third year) levels were collected. Only responses to more general questions on students' overall experience with their course and on its most valuable aspects were included, while comments that related to instructors' quality of teaching were disregarded.

First, we identified all the positive and negative comments relating to different aspects of the course included in each evaluation. A total of 223 comments (approximately 2 on average per evaluation) were identified. Following this, we conducted the following three types of data analysis:

General categorization based on recurrent students' comments and observation (RQ1)
Categorization of students' comments specifically related to the "flipped" and "blended" aspects of the course (RQ2)
Categorization of students' comments related to overall Student Learning Outcomes (SLO hereafter) (RQ3)

Research Data Description

General categorization based on recurrent students' comments and observation (RQ1)

The following five categories emerged from students' comments:

- ◇ pedagogy (students' experience in learning the Italian language);
- ◇ culture (students' experience in learning Italian culture);
- ◇ platform navigation (students' experience in navigating the online platform edX);

⋄ course organization (students' experience with syllabi, assignments, assessment, in-class activities versus at-home assignments, etc.);
⋄ emotional growth (students' personal experience in the course, i.e., feeling more/less confident, motivated, unmotivated, etc.).

Table 13.3 and Figure 13.1 illustrate the same results in two different formats.

Figure 13.2 shows the keywords (i.e., "online," "speaking," "discussion," etc.) that describe each category and that were mentioned at least two times in each category. For example, in the categories Platform Navigation and Course Organization, only two keywords appear more than once. Under Pedagogy and Culture there are six to eight different keywords and only one in Course

TABLE 13.3. Numbers of Comments for Each Major Category

Pedagogy	90
Culture	81
Course organization	26
Emotional growth	16
Platform navigation	10
Total number of comments	223

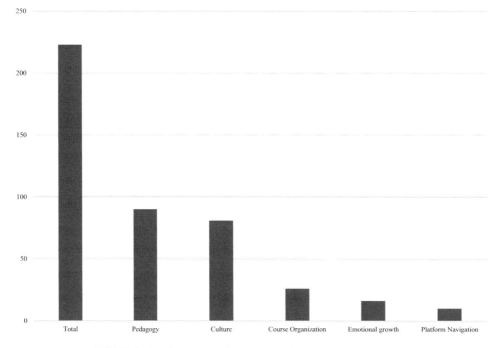

FIGURE 13.1. Number of comments for each major category.

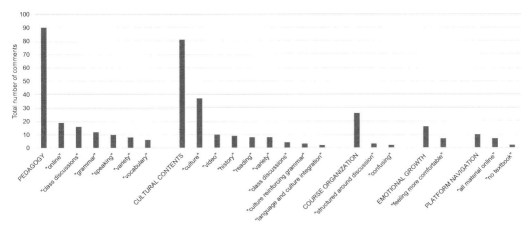

FIGURE 13.2. Categories and recurring keywords.

Organization. It's important to note that the only two negative comments were included in this last category to indicate "confusion" in the course format.

Categorization of students' comments specifically related to the flipped, blended, and online aspects of the course (RQ2)

As a second type of analysis, we looked at recurring themes that focused on the flipped and/or on the blended format of the courses. We identified six of such themes. The following are a small representative selection of students' comments under each of the themes. The number next to each category indicates how many unanimously positive comments related to those specific elements of the courses. For example, we identified 34 comments on the complementarity of the use of AP Italian in conjunction with in-class work, while 16 comments are relating to the variety of online materials. Figure 13.3 summarizes the number of comments in each of the six categories.

CATEGORY 1: COMPLEMENTARITY OF ONLINE AND IN-CLASS WORK (34 COMMENTS)

"The online component was where most of the actual instruction took place, so class was a great place to practice being put on the spot and speaking or writing."

"I liked how the online content was used to introduce concepts and information, and the classes were mostly used to present the ideas through verbal communication. This helped improve my abilities and comfort level of communicating in Italian."

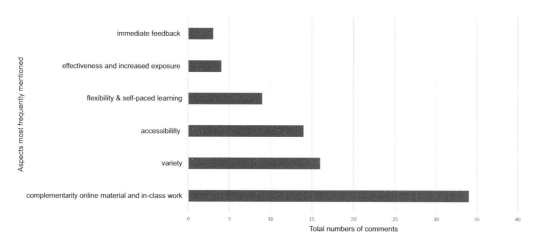

FIGURE 13.3. Comments on the flipped, blended, and online aspects of the course.

"I appreciated how the platform allowed me to work ahead in the material, so I could always come to class already knowing what was going to be covered. This allowed me to use class time to solidify knowledge I had already gained as opposed to struggling to wrap my mind around something completely new."

CATEGORY 2: VARIETY OF ONLINE MATERIALS (16 COMMENTS)

"I really enjoyed reading and interacting with real news articles, statistics, and interviews because it helped me put the course material into perspective."

"The extensive resources that were available to us [. . .] enabled me to [. . .] explore multiple ways of learning until I found one that worked well for me."

"The various modes of delivery (grammar charts, videos, articles, stories, etc.) kept the course really interesting and I think catered to different learning styles."

CATEGORY 3: ACCESSIBILITY OF ONLINE MATERIAL (14 COMMENTS)

"The most valuable feature of this course was the ability to have all of the information organized online. I was able to study the material at any point.

The online course was easily accessible, and the materials were compiled, which made studying more efficient."

"I really loved that all the material was online and we could access the material without a textbook."

"I REALLY loved the use of edX, because it facilitated easier homework completion and accessibility at any point in the day and at any location. It made reviewing all the easier and I have just learned so much."

CATEGORY 4: FLEXIBILITY AND SELF-SPACED ASPECTS OF THE COURSE (9 COMMENTS)

"The most valuable part of this course was being able to complete many of the assignment through an online platform. This contributed to my learning because it provided me with more flexibility to be able to complete and submit assignments and allowed me to focus more on learning and appreciating the language."

CATEGORY 5: INCREASED EXPOSURE TO THE LANGUAGE (4 COMMENTS)

"Watching online videos and finishing online exercises enabled me to learn and practice Italian more frequently."

CATEGORY 6: IMMEDIATE FEEDBACK (3 COMMENTS)

"I liked that all the assignments were online because I knew right away whether my answers were right or wrong."

Categorization of students' comments related to Student Learning Outcomes (SLO) (RQ3)

For this third analysis, we focused on comments related specifically to learning outcomes [Student Learning Outcomes (SLO)]. Similar to what we did with our second analysis, we identified the most frequently recurring themes (which in this case amounted to a total of three) in students' evaluations. The numbers in parentheses indicate how many comments relate to each theme. As an example, 46 students' comments relate to their linguistic and cultural gains ("knowledge"); progress in one or more "skills" (speaking, reading,

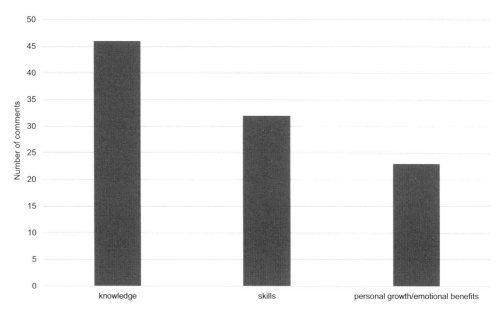

FIGURE 13.4. Student Learning Outcome (SLO).

writing, and listening) was noted in 32 comments. Finally, "personal growth," reflected in attitudinal changes toward learning a foreign language and confidence, appeared in 23 students' comments.

As done previously, this section too provides some representative students' comments under each theme. Alongside the comments, Figure 13.4 summarizes the number of comments in each of the three categories.

CATEGORY 1: KNOWLEDGE (43 COMMENTS)

"Learning about the culture of the country in the Italian language made me want to learn Italian even more and renewed my commitment to dedicating myself fully to mastery of the course material."

CATEGORY 2: SKILLS (32 COMMENTS)

"This course forced me to evaluate how I work best and how I can learn the best, which is very important for a college student. It gave me multiple ways to interact with the subject material which I appreciated."

"The online material strengthened my reading comprehension in Italian and class really made me a lot more comfortable with my conversational skills."

CATEGORY 3: PERSONAL GROWTH (23 COMMENTS)

"This course made me really start to hold learning above grades because the way the tests and exercises were formatted felt very low pressure."

"[This course] opened my eyes to the essential purpose of learning a new language."

ANALYSIS OF RESULTS

It is useful to look at the results of each of the RQs presented before summarizing and synthesizing them to draw conclusions.

RQ1: In learning a foreign language, what aspects do students value the most?

The majority of students' comments are found in the Pedagogy category showing that progress in language skills is very much valued by students at the intermediate and advanced levels, even in courses that center on Italian culture, rather than on the teaching and learning of language structures. Within the Pedagogy category, students appreciate the online component of the course (14 comments) and the focus on oral proficiency (shown by the two subcategories of class discussion (16) and speaking (10).

The high number of positive comments in the subcategories online, class discussion and speaking, suggests a connection between these three elements. The web-based learning and blended format, whereby students are exposed, prior to each class, to engaging and relevant content (videos, readings, self-corrected activities, etc.) and a variety of assessment methods, stimulate students to practice their language and cultural acquisition outside of class, therefore allowing for more in-class discussion time and meaningful speaking practice.

Students particularly appreciated the emphasis on cultural and intercultural topics in the course with 81 positive comments in this category. History (9 comments) is the most frequently mentioned cultural topic, perhaps reflecting a lack of attention in this area in beginner and intermediate language courses, which often focus on the exploration of regions, cuisine, school system, art, cinema, and so on, bypassing the historical foundation of contemporary Italian culture (Antenos-Conforti & Colussi, 2007). The focus on

Italian history in AP Italian may instead represent a refreshing and welcome novelty. The quality of the videos, which are used throughout the course to introduce and discuss history and other cultural topics, was also much valued (10 comments), confirming the findings of other studies (Luo & Ye, 2021; Martín-Monje et al., 2017).

Course organization is the only category that received two negative comments (out of a total of 26). The criticisms referred to the initial use at UBC of two different platforms (the university platform Canvas and edX) with the expectation that students would need to access both platforms, depending on the assignment. After the first course iteration, AP Italian content was integrated within the UBC upper intermediate Canvas course and learning goals and assignments were better aligned. The attention that students pay to the organizational aspect of their learning experience points to the importance of providing extreme transparency in assignments by eliminating possible ambiguities (Winkelmes, 2019). This also calls for increased attention to the drafting of the syllabus, which, if possible, should contain internal links to all assignments so that students know exactly what they are expected to cover in preparation for each class.

The relatively high number (16) of comments under the subcategory Emotional Growth tells us that students consider this an important aspect of their education. Feeling more comfortable (7 comments) is the most frequently cited emotion. Other comments such as improved confidence; feeling happy, grateful and proud; feeling involved, and feeling motivated reveal that students need to be supported in these areas in order to succeed academically (Mendez Lopez & Pena Aguilar, 2013). Our data is particularly relevant considering that these comments are spontaneous and were not provided in answer to any specific questions.

Finally, students also consider the accessibility aspect of Platform Navigation (10 comments) as an important element of their overall learning experience as they appreciate that all material is online (7 comments), hence available everywhere there is internet, and free, with no need for a textbook (2 comments).

RQ2: From students' perspective and experience, what are the advantages and disadvantages of the blended and flipped learning models?

Our study shows that a successful blended course must be based on a seamless integration of online work and in-class activities with the objective to devote in-class time to the reinforcement of what students already learned online (34 comments in the category Complementarity of online and in-class work).

Students also greatly valued the variety in content and delivery of materials (8 comments both in Pedagogy and Cultural Content) that the authors of AP Italian deliberately established as one of their guiding principles. For example, each module explores a different cultural topic by introducing it first with a reading and related vocabulary and comprehension exercises and then through a series of video interviews, articles, and infographics. Moreover, and unlike traditional textbooks, the online environment allows us to implement the principles of Universal Design for Learning by providing multiple methods for navigation since each item within the different modules can be accessed differently, either as a PDF or as an audio file, with or without annotation, or with timed transcripts and embedded comprehension activities.

Accessibility (14 comments) and Flexibility (9 comments) also received numerous positive appreciations from the students. The blended model better serves learners' busy schedules and complicated lives, increases language exposure, and provides immediate feedback (Rubio, 2012), which, as documented in the literature, can in turn stimulate students to become independent, self-regulated learners (Krystalli & Avarnits, 2018).

Based on the considerable number of students' comments compiled under Course Organization, the flipped approach to learning that we adopted with the integration of AP Italian was particularly appreciated. As mentioned in the literature (Muñoz-Merino et al., 2016; Orsini-Jones et al., 2018) this approach encourages learners to cover the materials (video interviews, readings, statistical information, etc.) and check their understanding on their own before coming to class, therefore leaving time in class to carry out interactive group learning activities.

Similar to what we noted above in relation to RQ2, we would like to point out that evaluation forms did not ask students to comment specifically on the online, blended, and or flipped portions of the course; rather, students spontaneously mentioned these.

RQ3: From students' perspective and experience, what learning outcomes were achieved through the integration of an LMOOC into a face-to-face, blended academic course? (RQ3)

A large number of comments (46) confirmed considerable progress in students' knowledge of Italian language and culture, and consequently of motivation to continue to study Italian. More specifically, students commented very favorably on the variety of media and learning tools that were available to them thanks to the integration of AP Italian into their face-to-face course.

In their evaluations, students reported in 32 comments considerable progress in their metacognitive and cross-cultural skills. Students' comments as reported under Category 2: Skills, well summarize how the course allowed them to "learn how to learn." Other researchers (Anderson, 2002) have recognized the importance of developing metacognitive and self-awareness skills to deepen one's overall language-learning skills. As expressed by a number of students (23 comments), the course encouraged them to reflect on their approach to and motivation for learning. For example, two students commented: "[This course] opened my eyes to the essential purpose of learning a new language" and "This course made me really start to hold learning above grades."

Based on our data and discussion, a language blended course that integrates an LMOOC into a face-to-face academic program positively affects several fundamental learning skills and results in overall gains in cultural knowledge, language skills, as well as attitudinal changes and personal and emotional growth.

CONCLUSIONS

Our study explores the experience of teaching Italian using an LMOOC in blended courses in two institutions: Wellesley College and the University of British Columbia. Following the principles of the scholarship of teaching and learning (SoTL), this study was conducted as a systematic inquiry into student learning. We have used qualitative and quantitative data that emerged from students' evaluations, separating and categorizing each comment, with the objective of understanding the viability of using an LMOOC in blended courses from students' perspective and verifying its validity and viability in different educational contexts, such as a large research university and a small liberal arts college.

Our data analysis has confirmed that our models of integration of online materials had a consistently positive impact on students' cognitive and metacognitive skills and on their motivation to learn the language, which is a major factor in the acquisition process (Anjomshoa & Sadighi, 2015). In addition, our results unequivocally point to some unique features of blended learning, such as overall increased exposure to the target language, affordability, flexibility, more opportunities for independent learning, and access to culturally rich, relevant, and up-to-date material.

For the instructors, adopting online open resources like AP Italian into their blended courses added value to the overall content of the course and to the variety of the learning activities students were able to engage with. It also represented a much welcomed opportunity to save time, effort, and money.[9] Moreover, the integration of open educational online resources into a blended language course can have a broader impact by encouraging a productive collaboration between course developers and instructors and by implementing a dynamic cycle whereby resources are adopted, adapted, and revised on a regular and timely basis.

In this study, we discussed two distinct, yet quite successful, models of adoption of online materials in two academic settings. At Wellesley College, AP Italian was used in lieu of the textbook, while at UBC it was used as the main curriculum for asynchronous classes. Our findings, as presented in this chapter, as well as other studies on the successful integration of LMOOCs in face-to-face courses (Conde Gafaro, 2020; Motzo & Proudfoot, 2017; Rubio, 2012), encourage us to assert that the adoption and adaptation of well-organized and clearly articulated material (Margaryan et al., 2015) can be very effectively applied to different contexts. Based on the results of our experience, we can safely conclude that an LMOOC could be successfully used in remote asynchronous and/or synchronous courses, in intensive summer courses, as well as in study abroad programs. Future research on language learning and educational technology could investigate whether similar results can be also discerned at the beginner level and in other languages. Moreover, while our study has not attempted to measure learning outcomes, it would be interesting to investigate whether students learning Italian in blended courses that use an LMOOC perform better than students who study in a more traditional setting.

The recent COVID crisis has motivated many of us to share resources, discuss best practices, develop new teaching and learning activities, and promote more affordable educational options for our students. The remote teaching experience of these last few months has taught us that technology can enable virtual learning in many extraordinary ways: It has helped us develop new skills and different perspectives (Borup et al., 2022); it has accelerated the need to put students at the center of instruction and make our courses accessible and flexible; it has prompted us to teach relevant, motivating, and up-to-date cultural content. The pandemic has also provided educators with unprecedented opportunities to share educational content and form new and reimagined collaborations within and outside our institutions with colleagues and students alike.

Our experience is an example of how educators can collaborate effectively to create language programs that can better meet today's students' demands and needs. Adopting blended teaching approaches will encourage educators to redefine their role and more fully embrace the challenges and the opportunities of working with online resources.

NOTES

1. For data on decline in enrollment in foreign language courses see the MLA report available at mla.org/content/download/110154/2406932/2016-Enrollments-Final-Report.pdf. For examples and information on practice and resource sharing, see COERLL (Center for Open Educational Resources and Language Learning) at https://www.coerll.utexas.edu/coerll/).
2. Throughout this chapter we adhere to the definition of "blended course" given by Mizza and Rubio (2020, p. 12): "a formal teaching and learning experience that includes a multiaccess, balanced, guided, and monitored instructional environment in which course design allows for: 1) reducing but not eliminating face-to-face meetings; 2) asynchronous and synchronous Web-based components to complement and reinforce face-to-face components and vice versa, 3) collaboration and interaction to take place between student-instructor, student-student, and student-content."
3. The University of British Columbia is a large public research university located in Vancouver, Canada. Wellesley College is a small, liberal arts college for women located in Wellesley, Massachusetts, United States.
4. edX is a MOOC provider founded in 2012 by Harvard and MIT.
5. According to the latest MLA report (2016), Italian has one of the lowest percentages of enrollments at the advanced level (10:1) indicating that for every 10 introductory enrollments there is only one enrollment in an advanced course at the undergraduate level. See the MLA report available online: https://www.mla.org/content/download/110154/2406932/2016-Enrollments-Final-Report.pdf
6. Italian is being taught in 821 high schools (period 2014–2021) in the United States (data available on the website of of the Italian Embassy in Washington, DC: https://ambwashingtondc.esteri.it/ambasciata_washington/it/italiaeusa/cultura/scuole-in-cui-si-insegna-l-italiano.html), corresponding to 3.1% of all US high schools.
7. The development of AP Italian is made possible thanks to a generous grant the main course author receives yearly since 2015 from the Italian Ministry of Foreign Affairs and International Cooperation.
8. The 2017–2018 edition of AP Italian counted more than 15,000 participants.

9. In his *Teaching in a Digital Age,* Tony Bates provides some details on the financial resources needed to create online materials. He also clearly outlines the substantive costs related to the development, delivery, maintenance, and overheads of a fully online master's course as an example (Bates, 2015).

BIBLIOGRAPHY

Alley, L. R., & Jansak, K. E. (2001). The ten keys to quality assurance and assessment in online learning. *Journal of Interactive Instruction Development, 13*(3), 3–18. https://www.learntechlib.org/p/93748/

Anderson, N. J. (2002). The role of metacognition in second language teaching and learning. *ERIC Digest.* Accessed November 6, 2022. http://educ7006.pbworks.com/w/file/fetch/50749087/Anderson%20on%20metacogntiion-1.pdf

Anjomshoa, L., & Sadighi, F. (2015, February). The importance of motivation in second language acquisition. *International Journal on Studies in English Language and Literature* (IJSELL), *3*(2), 126–37. http://citeseerx.ist.psu.edu/viewdoc/download?doi=10.1.1.680.6071&rep=rep1&type=pdf

Anning, R. (2019, May 2). Are textbooks becoming obsolete? *ELearning Industry.* elearningindustry.com/textbooks-becoming-obsolete

Antenos-Conforti, E., & Colussi, A. G. (2007, Spring). Beginners' level textbooks for Italian in North America: Ten years later. *Italica, 84*(1), 5–21. http://www.jstor.org/stable/27669123

Bárcena, E., Read, T., Martín-Monje, E., & Castrillo, M. D. (2014). Analysing student participation in foreign language MOOCs: A case study. *European MOOCs Stakeholders Summit,* 11–17. file:///Users/luisa/Downloads/Analysing_student_participation_in_Forei.pdf

Bates, A. W. (2015). *Teaching in the digital age.* Vancouver, BC: Tony Bates Associates. https://opentextbc.ca/teachinginadigitalage/

Borup, J., Graham, C. R., Short, C., & Kang Shin, J. (2022, January 11). Designing the new normal: Enable, engage, elevate, and extend student learning, *Educause Review.* https://er.educause.edu/articles/2022/1/designing-the-new-normal-enable-engage-elevate-and-extend-student-learning

Chiappe, A., & Castillo, B. D. L. (2020). Retention in MOOCS: Some key factors. *Ensaio Avaliação e Politicas Públicas em Educação, 29*(110), 1–23. https://doi.org/10.1590/S0104-40362020002802667

Conde Gafaro, B. (2020). MOOCs in the language classroom: Using MOOCs as complementary materials to support self-regulated language learning. In

A. Alberto (Ed.), *Recent tools for computer- and mobile-assisted foreign language learning* (pp. 194–211). Hershey, PA: IGI Global. https://doi.org/10.4018/978-1-7998-1097-1.ch009

Crouch, C. H., & Mazur, E. (2009). Peer instruction: Ten years of experience and results. *American Journal of Physics*, 69(9), 970–77. https://doi.org/10.1119/1.1374249

Decker, G. (2014). MOOCology 1.0. In S. Krause & C. Lowe (Eds.), *Invasion of the MOOCs: The promises and perils of massive open online courses* (pp. 3–13). Anderson, SC: Parlor Press.

Downes, S. (2012). *Connectivism and connective knowledge*. EdTech Books. https://edtechbooks.org/connectivism/

Ellis, R., & Shintani, N. (2013). *Exploring language pedagogy through second language acquisition research*. London: Routledge. https://doi.org/10.4324/9780203796580

Hone, K. S., & Said, G. R. (2016, July). Exploring the factors affecting MOOC retention: A survey study. *Computers & Education*, 98, 157–68. https://www.sciencedirect.com/science/article/pii/S0360131516300793

Israel, M. J. (2015). Effectiveness of integrating MOOCs in traditional classrooms for undergraduate students. *International Review of Research in Open and Distance Learning*, 16(5), 102–18. http://www.irrodl.org/index.php/irrodl/article/view/2222

Jenkins, J., Sánchez, L. A., Schraedley, M. A. K., Hannans, J., Navick, N., & Young, J. (2020). Textbook broke: Textbook affordability as a social justice issue. *Journal of Interactive Media in Education*, 1(3), 1–13. https://jime.open.ac.uk/article/10.5334/jime.549/

Jitpaisarnwattana, N., Reinders, H., & Darasawang, P. (2021, August). Learners' perspective on interaction in a language MOOC. *JALT CALL Journal*, 17(2), 158–82. https://www.castledown.com/journals/jaltcall/article/?reference=472

Jordan, K. (2015). Massive open online course completion rates revisited: Assessment, length and attrition. *International Review of Research in Open and Distributed Learning*, 16(3), 341–58. https://doi.org/10.19173/irrodl.v16i3.2112

Krystalli, P., & Arvanitis, P. (2018, November). *Self-assessment and immediate feedback in language learning*. Eleventh Annual International Conference of Education, Research and Innovation. Seville, Spain. https://doi.org/10.21125/ICERI.2018.1446

Littlejohn, A., & Hood, N. (2017). How educators build knowledge and expand their practice: The case of open education resources. *BJET British Journal of Education Technology*, 49(2), 499–510. https://berajournals.onlinelibrary.wiley.com/doi/10.1111/bjet.12438

Littlejohn, A., Hood, N., Milligan, C., & Mustain, P. (2015, December). Learning in MOOCs: Motivations and self-regulated learning in MOOCs. *The Internet and Higher Education*, 29, 40–48. https://doi.org/10.1016/j.iheduc.2015.12.003

Littlejohn, A., & Milligan, C. (2015). Designing MOOCs for professional students: Tools and patterns to encourage self-regulated learning. *eLearning Papers*, 42, 38–45. https://doi.org/10.6084/m9.figshare.1428569.v2

Luo, R., & Zixuan, Y. (2021, March). What makes a good-quality language MOOC? An empirical study of criteria to evaluate the quality of online language courses from learners' perspectives. *ReCALL*, *33*(2), 177–92. https://doi.org/10.1017/S0958344021000082

Margaryan, A., Bianco, M., & Littlejohn, A. (2015). Instructional quality of massive open online courses (MOOCs). *Computers & Education*, 80, 77–83. http://dx.doi.org/10.1016/j.compedu.2014.08.005

Martín-Monje, E., Castrillo, M. D., & Mañana-Rodríguez, J. (2017). Understanding online interaction in language MOOCs through learning analytics. *Computer Assisted Language Learning*, *31*(3), 251–72. https://doi.org/10.1080/09588221.2017.1378237

Mendez Lopez, M. G., & Peña Aguilar, A. (2013, April). Emotions as learning enhancers of foreign language learning motivation. *Profile*, *15*(1), 109–24. http://www.scielo.org.co/scielo.php?script=sci_arttext&pid=S1657-07902013000100008&lng=en&nrm=iso

Mizza, D., & Rubio, F. (2020). *Creating effective blended language learning courses*. Cambridge: Cambridge University Press. https://doi.org/10.1017/9781108355285

Motzo, A., & Proudfoot, A. (2017). MOOCs for language learning—Opportunities and challenges: The case of the open university Italian beginners' MOOCs. In Q. Kan & S. Bax (Eds.), *Beyond the language classroom: Researching MOOCs and other innovations* (pp. 85–97). Research-publishing.net. https://files.eric.ed.gov/fulltext/ED574805.pdf

Muñoz-Merino, P. J., Ruipérez-Valiente, J. A., Delgado Kloos, C., Auger, M. A., Briz, S., de Castro, V., & Santalla, S. N. (2016, November). Flipping the classroom to improve learning with MOOCs technology. *Computer Applications in Engineering Education*, *25*(1), 15–25. https://doi.org/10.1002/cae.21774

Orsini-Jones, M., Conde Gafaro, B., & Altamimi, S. (2017). Integrating a MOOC into the postgraduate ELT curriculum: Reflecting on students' beliefs with a MOOC blend. In Q. Kan & S. Bax (Eds.), *Beyond the language classroom: Researching MOOCs and other innovations* (pp. 71–83). Research-publishing.net. https://doi.org/10.14705/rpnet.2017.mooc2016.672

Orsini-Jones, M., Conde, B., Borthwick, K., & Zou, B. (2018). B-MELTT: Blending MOOCS for English language teacher training. *ELT Research Papers*, *18*(2), 1–41. https://www.teachingenglish.org.uk/sites/teacheng/files/Pub_J121_Blending%20MOOCs%20for%20English%20language%20teacher%20training_FINAL_Web.pdf

Orsini-Jones, M., Pibworth, L., Cribb, M., Brick, B., Gazeley-Eke, Z., Leinster, H., & Lloyd, E. (2015). Learning about language learning on a MOOC: How massive, open, online and "course"? In *Proceedings of the 2015 EUROCALL Conference* (pp. 450–57). Research-publishing.net. https://doi.org/10.14705/ rpnet.2015.000374

Pulker, H., & Kukulska-Hulme, A. (2020). Openness re-examined: Teachers' practices with open educational resources in online language teaching. *Distance Education*, *41*(2), 1–14. https://doi.org/10.1080/01587919.2020.1757412

Rubio, F. (2012). The effects of blended learning on second language fluency and proficiency. In F. Rubio & J. Thoms (Eds.), *Hybrid language teaching and learning: Exploring theoretical, pedagogical and curricular issues* (pp. 137–59). Boston: Heinle Cengage Learning.

Rubio, F. (2015). The role of interaction in MOOCs and traditional technology-enhanced language courses. In E. Dixon & M. Thomas (Eds.), *Researching language student interaction online: From social media to MOOCs* (pp. 63–88). San Marcos, TX: CALICO monograph.

Wiley, D. (2015). The MOOC misstep and the open education infrastructure. In C. J. Bonk, M. M. Lee, T. C. Reeves, & T. H. Reynolds (Eds.), *MOOCs and open education around the world* (pp. 43–51). New York: Routledge. https://doi.org/10.4324/9781315751108-2

Winkelmes, M.-A. (2019). Why it works: Understanding the concept behind transparency in learning and teaching. In M.-A. Winkelmes, A. Boye, & S. Tapp (Eds.), *Transparent design in higher education and leadership* (pp. 17–35). Sterling, VA: Stylus.

14

TEACHING ITALIAN USING LMOOCS

The Target Audience and New Operational Models

Matteo La Grassa and Andrea Villarini

CAN YOU LEARN LANGUAGES THROUGH MOOCS?

Our contribution begins with the question at the base of any didactic discussion concerning MOOC language courses.[1] Although used in a clearly provocative manner on our part, the query addresses an issue that is currently widely debated: the possible relationship between the teaching of foreign languages and massive online courses, and, to further expand the debate, between language teaching and technology.

We are, in fact, living in a historical moment when all of us, essentially all over the world, are being forced to deal with forms of distance learning. Since the first few months of 2020, albeit with some slight variations from country to country, we have all had to grapple with online teaching due to public health restrictions caused by the COVID-19 pandemic. But the pandemic did not "invent" the use of technologies; if anything, it resulted in accelerating a process whose signals were already clearly present.

Language teaching has always been attentive to the teaching potential of what, over time, could have been defined as "new" technology. If there is one teaching approach that has always welcomed the use of aids in the classroom (tape recorders, computers, VCRs), it is, almost exclusively, the teaching of languages.

Therefore, it would be incorrect to say that the use of technology in language teaching is only recent. The truth is that foreign languages and technology have always had a very close and mutually beneficial relationship.

The real novelty, however, which did not previously exist, not even recently, is the utilization of the internet—the possibility of bringing people at distant locations together and of creating virtual classes where anyone can connect, from anywhere, and interact with other learners and the teacher. The interactions can be both synchronous and asynchronous. Although, with e-learning, it is mainly the latter that helps unlock individual potential, which is not as common in the traditional classroom, that in itself contains positive and, naturally, negative aspects.

MOOCs for languages (hereinafter also LMOOCs) fit into a context that is already widely used within language teaching (as previously mentioned that of teaching a foreign language using technological support). However, they have specific features, which not only differ from those of classroom teaching but also from other types of online courses.

They could almost be considered the most extreme form of e-learning, an uncharted territory that does, however, enable us to experiment and to find solutions, which may then be adopted in more traditional educational contexts, both online and in person.

What makes LMOOCs so unique and so different from other forms of distance learning is inherent in the second letter of the acronym: M for massive, namely their ability to target thousands of people or in any case an unlimited and undefined number of learners. Numbers that can reach dizzying heights and that effectively turn our notion of the classroom, as we have known it, upside down.[2]

This takes us back to our initial query and in some ways justifies its existence: With this number of participants can we even begin to conceive being able to teach a foreign language? Put this way, the answer would seem obvious: no, we cannot. But if instead we consider a different idea of class group and, consequently, of the tutoring relationship between teacher and learner, we see that, even in the presence of these large numbers of extremely heterogeneous students, teaching is possible.

MANAGING PUBLIC HETEROGENEITY

The most characteristic element of LMOOCs is therefore its high number of attending students, a number that can easily exceed thousands. Closely linked to such high student numbers is inevitably the mode of course attendance that may not only be rather inconsistent but can also begin at different and unpredictable times, which is precisely what allows MOOCs to expand the offer on such a large scale.

These aspects that highlight the most evident differences between LMOOCs and other online language courses should be taken into account in the various stages of planning, both macro, largely related to defining the general outline of the learning process, and micro, related to the specific didactic activities.

When designing a course, identifying the target audience is key; however, in the case of LMOOCs, correctly determining a specific target group proves more difficult. A language course (online or in person) is usually addressed to a group of students with defining characteristics such as age, motivational profile, previously known and studied languages, and above all their linguistic-communicative skills. With regard to this last aspect, the successful outcome of the educational program is closely related to the possibility of having direct contact with the students who will then form the classes within the courses. It is rare that students attend a course not suited to their level, as they will have had the opportunity to test their skills in advance through input tests developed by the institution offering the course.

The design of an LMOOC, however, follows a different logic and cannot move beyond a precise definition of target learners. It is certainly advisable to design it for and direct it to a specific audience: in the case of Introduction to Italian, examined in this chapter, a target audience of elementary-level learners was chosen. Unlike other online and in person courses, the target audience in this case is only potential, as the enrollment and participation, for longer or shorter periods, is open to absolutely anyone. It is therefore a choice that students tend to make on their own, based on personal assessment, but which is not determined in any way by the educational institution. Nor could it be, without denying the fundamental element of openness (Open, in the acronym) that characterizes all MOOCs.

Looking at the characteristics of the Introduction to Italian students, although their level of linguistic-communicative competence was broadly in line with the course contents and activities, it was evident that a significant proportion of students had very different skills. The choice of attending the course was often dictated by a general interest in Italian language and culture with the aim of consolidating skills that had been previously acquired but, perhaps, not used for a long time.

In addition, a portion of students, although a minority, were native speakers who attended the course to aid student interactions and provide language explanations. The inability to define an LMOOC audience in advance and to control the mode of attendance are aspects that should undoubtedly guide the didactic planning phase. Hence the choice to design a course with objectives that are suitable for students with different characteristics.

From data collected on the Introduction to Italian students, which will be discussed later, it was clear that there is no predominant age group; with a slight percentage difference, the young adult and more mature adult groups are equally represented (Villarini, 2016). In addition, contrary to what was expected, the group of students aged over 55 proved just as relevant.[3] Therefore, considering the lack of direct correlation between target learners and the learners that actually attend the course, it seemed only appropriate when presenting the contents to limit them to the macro areas of personal and public communication (according to the Common European Framework of Reference for Languages categorization), in which nonspecialist daily communication takes place. Instead, educational and professional domains were avoided: in that way, the course would have appealed to an audience with sector-specific interests and needs.

We can then consider a group of students attending an LMOOC by definition a group with partially mixed abilities (Caon & Tonioli, 2016; Şalli-Çopur, 2005; Ur, 1996), where students differ in initial skill sets, learning styles, motivation, and all other "internal factors" (Villarini, 2021) that characterize the process of language acquisition. Nevertheless, it is not possible to implement the same activities in an LMOOC as those adopted in common mixed-ability classroom settings. Due to the extremely high number of students, it is not possible to respond as freely to the diversity of goals or scaffolding techniques of students with differing characteristics. Likewise, it is unrealistic to set up collaborative activities within fixed heterogeneous groups that are established at the beginning and remain the same throughout the activity. It is also important to note that LMOOC attendance is characteristically inconsistent, which effectively hinders the proposal of fully structured activities or in any case with predetermined start and end dates.

In order to efficiently manage students' varying levels of competence, which is inevitable given their high numbers and free enrollment, the best solution has been to make the contents available at different levels of complexity. In Introduction to Italian, besides seeing the input content (always an audiovisual text), students can activate various tools that aid comprehension: subtitles in Italian; subtitles in English; the entire transcript of the text both in Italian and in English. There is also the option of slowing down the speech and, of course, watching the video an unlimited number of times. It is important to emphasize that these tools are freely accessible to all students, who can choose to use them or not depending on their ability. Therefore, effort has been made to render the input understandable (Krashen, 1985) and motivating, with varying levels of difficulty that can be managed autonomously by the student from an entirely student-centered perspective. Tutors can, of course, recommend ways of using the texts without making them compulsory. Students are required to take greater responsibility for their own learning process, thus acquiring more autonomy and following less externally directed methods.

There is no attempt to simplify the input by directly altering the structure of the text, an action that would have been unrealistic and of dubious effectiveness; however, students are guaranteed a variety of possibilities to make use of the text itself, thus responding to the needs of individual students with differing skill levels.[4]

Introduction to Italian also provides for progression in the content covered. However, in view of the number of students enrolled and their inconsistent attendance, it seemed appropriate to make the entire course accessible immediately. In this way, students who, as previously mentioned, form a mixed-ability group are able to independently choose to follow one or more segments of the course even in a nonconsecutive manner, since attendance during the previous weeks is not required.

THE OPERATIONAL MODEL

One of the most important things to consider when designing a course is the choice of an operational model as a reference point. An operational model is a structure that provides the guidelines for the organization of specific contents and activities that characterize the language teaching process. Choosing a correct model therefore represents a methodological choice that clearly impacts application. In regard to the teaching of Italian L2, there has been lively debate on the various operational models and particularly their suitability to various learning contexts.[5] Based on the didactic unit (Freddi, 1999), a model called the acquisition unit (Balboni, 2014) was subsequently developed that includes the phases of globality, analysis and synthesis, and reflection.[6] It is common knowledge that these three stages are reflected, in terms of language pedagogy, in theories of learning, with particular reference to the perception of input, which should be studied first on a global level and only subsequently processed in a more analytical form. With specific reference to language learning, this theory finds further support in the neurolinguistic principles of bimodality and directionality (Danesi, 1998), which claim that both cerebral hemispheres play a role in learning. Linguistic input is initially processed globally by the right hemisphere and then analytically by the left hemisphere.

As an operational model based on the theoretical principles mentioned above, the phased acquisition unit should be the framework for implementing language pedagogy activities consistent with these principles.[7] Language input should therefore be presented in context, in a form that can be processed globally at first and then analytically; while activities to analyze sociopolitical, linguistic, and cultural aspects identified as learning objectives should be included at a later stage.

The choice of an operational model is equally important when developing online language courses. In this case, however, it will not be possible to blindly imitate a model designed for teaching in person. Just as methodological approaches to in-class and distance learning should clearly be different, likewise the operational models cannot be replicated in the two different contexts.

As regards formal online language courses, one proposal that has proved to be particularly effective is that developed by Troncarelli (2011), here represented graphically (see Figure 14.1). For a course divided into units, the author proposes an integration of two different design types: one based on objectives attainable through didactic activities carried out mainly through self-study and subject to evaluation, and one based on tasks,[8] activities carried out in a collaborative manner with a communicative goal, which generally results in a piece of work developed by groups and subgroups of students.

It is important to note that the design of any language course founded on this model is aimed at achieving communicative goals, based on the idea of language primarily as a communication tool. The model strongly opposes the widespread idea that an online language course is limited to being simply a repository of materials; on the contrary, its design must include forms of interaction between students, mainly in asynchronous and written form, without excluding (if and when possible) synchronous and oral interaction.

That being said, it should be noted that the validity of the model is strongly linked to the type of courses it has been designed for. In fact, these courses are implemented on an e-learning platform (Learning Management System) and envisage the creation of class groups (10–12 students), a time schedule divided into weeks, a set deadline for the duration and consignment of activities, and continuous tutoring (including video conference meetings) throughout the course. In reference to the part of the model that draws inspiration from a design based on objectives, Troncarelli's proposal incorporates and adapts an already familiar structure of in-class language teaching to the e-learning context. This involves a contextualized presentation of an input text that becomes the focus of a variety of activities of both global and analytical understanding, as well as reflection on pragmatic, phonetic, morpho-syntactic, lexical, and

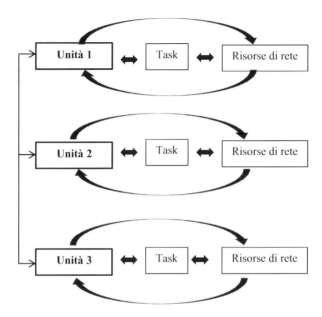

FIGURE 14.1. Operational model for online language courses (taken from Troncarelli, 2011).

text-based aspects. All the activities are organized along a learning pathway and should ideally be carried out sequentially.[9] It is worth highlighting the effort to develop tasks for collaborative work on the basis of constructivist and connective principles (Downes, 2007), which claim that in order for learning to be effective and meaningful, it must translate into a process that calls for the active collaboration of members of the learning community.

As mentioned above, LMOOCs have introduced other new elements in the panorama of online language teaching, above all with regard to the number of students and their mode of attendance that are both inconceivable in regular settings. Moreover, due to the unavoidable consequences of these aspects, the possibility of providing synchronous interactions is almost zero.[10] These features that differ from other online courses have required some adjustments to the model previously shown,[11] due to the distinct design of the tasks.

A commonly defined task with introduction, implementation, and evaluation phases, which involves prolonged collaboration over time, was of course not feasible. Our chosen solution has therefore been to propose much shorter tasks similar to those carried out in microlearning experiences, focused on communicative functions, that could also result in nonguided interactions between peers.

Studente 1
Ciao a tutti! How do you say British? Does inglese mean English or British? I am British but not English ☺ Help! ☺ Grazie mille xx

Studente 2
sei brittanico, scozzese o gallese o forse irlandese

Studente 1
Gosh, you are good, Lynda!! ☺ Grazie infinite x

FIGURE 14.2. Mixed-language interactions during a task.

The tasks given in Introduction to Italian do not require learners to take part in a group project, but to carry out an individual activity that is then shared with the other participants on a dedicated forum. This sharing can generate unpredictable communicative exchanges that may arise for a variety of reasons. In the example in Figure 14.2 the reason is given by an explicit request for support.

In this case, the explicit request for language support from a learner who is trying to perform the assigned task (a brief personal presentation) is likely to be answered by a more competent student. It is interesting to note that interactions can also take place in mixed-language form, where the exchange goes ahead even if the interlocutors do not have the capacity to manage it fully in Italian.

In addition to the different structure of the tasks, another element that distinguishes the operational model chosen for Introduction to Italian was the creation of short self-contained learning units centered around a single text. Every week during the course there were three units, based on a single audiovisual input text, that gave learners the opportunity to delve deeper into the linguistic and communicative aspects. Each of these was then given a dedicated forum with the aim of increasing learner interaction and not limiting it exclusively to task sharing.

THE NEW IDEA OF CLASS

As anticipated, teaching a large number of students is possible as long as we completely abandon the idea of the traditional class and the opportunities it provides for communicative exchange. Rather, we should prepare ourselves to manage entirely different communication flows and entirely different exchange networks, which, when well managed, are capable of producing effective learning.

The approach taken here is to abandon the idea of class as a replica, albeit with much larger numbers, of what we have always known, and which takes place within four walls, and to instead adopt a new idea of class based on the presence of large and even larger numbers of learners, as a complex system that involves the use of instruments specific to complex systems (Puglisi, 2021).

Starting, as always, from the data collected by analyzing the Introduction to Italian LMOOC, we see how dynamics are created within an LMOOC class that are similar to those on a social network, mediated by a digital platform and the tools it makes available. Of course, the traditional class should also be seen as a social network, but the difference between the two networks is not simply a difference in size (traditional = small, LMOOCs = enormous) but also the completely different rules, behaviors, and roles assumed by the participants on the network. These changes are primarily in the roles that LMOOC participants (including tutors) can adopt on the basis of their position within the social network, defined by interactions that take place on the course forum.

These roles cannot be predefined systematically, as is often the case in the traditional classroom where a teacher is a teacher, a student is a student, and so on. Instead, they emerge spontaneously on a multifactorial basis that comprises (Puglisi, 2021) the type of input provided during the course, the learning tasks designed for the participants, and the way opportunities provided by the comment functions are handled to the individual course pages.

In this way, a participant assumes different roles within the same LMOOC, from being a mere spectator who simply logs in to take a look at the contents of the course pages and then logs out, to building subnetwork relationships with other learners within the general macro-network formed by all participants, up to the most extreme and productive case of the learner who takes on the role of a guide. That person could be defined as a "star" learner, as is the case on certain social platforms for comments on and reviews of some businesses, where specific followers are identified as extremely reliable thanks to their strong presence on the platform and previous comments deemed useful by the rest of the community.

There is clearly a positive correlation between the placement of the learner within the social network (How many nodes can they activate? How many relationships can they maintain during the course weeks?) and the results in terms of language learning and level of satisfaction from participating in the LMOOC (Puglisi, 2021).

WHO CHOOSES TO STUDY A LANGUAGE THROUGH AN LMOOC?

Given how the network of learners is set up, we would like to take a closer look at who is choosing to turn to an LMOOC to improve their language skills.

We found that our experience as curators of the Italian LMOOC does not reflect the initial assumptions of a certain interchangeability between learners in class and online. Those choosing to attend an online course of this kind represent a specific type of learner, with specific motivations and specific learning objectives. That is why knowledge of the characteristics of this new learner-figure could be useful for the development of such courses in the future.

When it comes to gender, the data we gathered show nothing new: The majority of LMOOC participants, just like in traditional language courses, are women. What we found more interesting, however, is the data on the average age of course attendees.

Generally, we tend to think that those who choose online courses (especially anyone choosing an LMOOC among other online courses) must surely be young and therefore used to "moving around" and "doing things" on the internet. Our data (see Figure 14.3), however, show us that the opposite is true. More specifically, those choosing this type of course are mature students of postschool age with a not insignificant percentage of students in their later

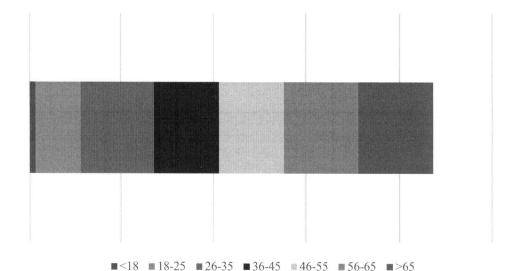

FIGURE 14.3. Average age of course attendees.

years. More than 50% of students are in fact over 36 years old. Our impression, from reading the data, is that the online audience is composed of mature learners, who most likely choose this type of course precisely thanks to its flexible timetable and the absence of attendance requirements.

In addition to the age factor, it was interesting to see the ways LMOOC participants intend to continue on their L2 learning journey.

The data (see Figure 14.4) reveals an audience that chooses online learning not as an occasional alternative to classroom courses, but rather, as a new and almost definitive method of learning. From data analysis, it might seem that anyone turning to an LMOOC does not want (or more likely, cannot) go back to in-class, fixed-timetable courses. This is made clear, for example, in the answers students gave to the question "What do you want to do to improve your competence once you have completed the MOOC?" These showed that the majority of them do not intend to abandon online learning modes; some would like to do another LMOOC, some would choose another online course, not necessarily an LMOOC, and others would surf the web for new materials and/or resources. Only 5% of our students would opt for an in-class course.

As previously mentioned, this is a group of adults (with some elderly participants) who have turned to online courses, yet, contrary to what one might expect, are still fond of traditional teaching methods.

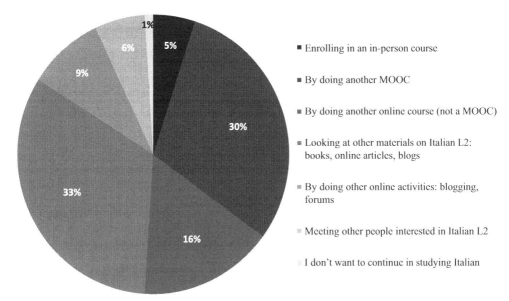

FIGURE 14.4. What do you want to do to improve your competence once you have completed the MOOC?

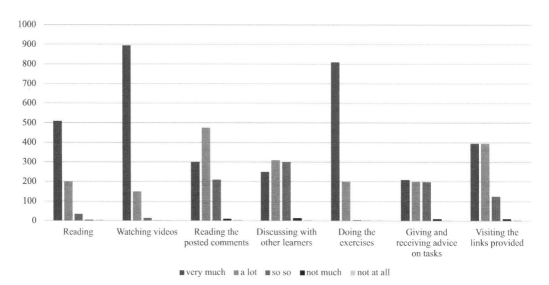

FIGURE 14.5. Favorite activities of Introduction to Italian.

From the data shown in Figure 14.5, we see that the participants of our LMOOC enjoyed, above all, the more traditional and less interactive of the activities proposed. Watching the videos, in fact, perhaps the most passive of the learning activities, proved to be the most appreciated, followed by self-correcting exercises (another activity with very little interaction), compared to, for example, the possibility of interacting with other students through a forum. As LMOOC creation is still in its infancy, this data could be used to develop future initiatives by seeking to limit the more advanced interactive activities in favor of more passive and self-correcting ones.

It appears that LMOOC participants are not yet ready for high-innovation digital education and prefer the more traditional forms. This is a particularly interesting fact that we believe should be analyzed in more detail and, if possible, confirmed by other surveys with different and even broader samples of followers. This would further widen the gap between classroom learners (now almost universally taught through innovative forms of education) and digital learners (MOOCs and other courses) that remain behind in this regard, in addition to what has already been said about age, attendance, and time constraints.

Another important matter of discussion regarding LMOOC courses is that of dropouts, a frequent occurrence in all LMOOCs (not only Italian or languages in general) that are available online. This could lead to hasty conclusions on the rating of such courses that dismiss them as unnecessary. But the data should be analyzed in greater depth.

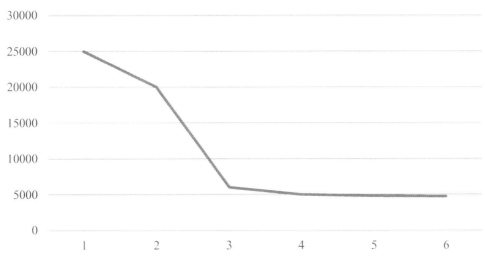

FIGURE 14.6. Active learners in Introduction to Italian.

Our Introduction to Italian course recorded a dropout rate that can be defined "physiologically" close to 70% of enrolled students. Put this way, it would appear a complete failure. However, to say that 70% of followers did not finish the course means, first of all, that in order to drop out they would have enrolled and attended a number of lessons and thus come into some contact with our language, even if not for the entire duration of the course. And more importantly, it means that 30% of them, about 30,000 (based on our total number of participants of about 100,000 people overall) completed the activities. Impressive numbers, which would require decades for the most successful in-class learning programs.

Moreover, if we observe the trend of these dropouts (see Figure 14.6), we see how it gains strength after the first week of the course, with a sharp increase between the first and the second weeks. Once over the hurdle, the upward trend becomes much gentler, reflecting that of any learning initiative, both in the classroom and in other forms of online teaching.

We believe that the reason for these dropouts, leaving out the justification of content shortage, is first and foremost because there are no registration fees for an MOOC, which consequently leads to an explosion in the initial number of participants. After the first week, those attracted merely by the free enrollment drop out, leaving only those truly motivated to learn.

For this very reason LMOOCs are diversifying from their initial offer that was entirely free of charge with a view to increasing the financial sustainability of the implementation costs as well as those of managing their hosting platform;

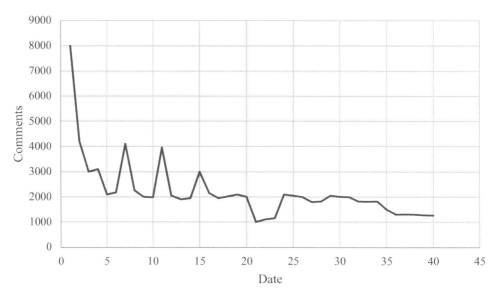

FIGURE 14.7. Trend in attendance by week.

a move also aimed at keeping students connected, reducing the number of dropouts, by including commercial offers within the course. The most frequent shift is allowing free access to only a part of the course instead of the whole thing, reserving any additional content to anyone willing to pay a small fee. Although this is partly reducing enrollment, it has a stabilizing effect on the numbers, albeit lower. Low, but with numbers that nevertheless remain high when compared with those attainable in a single edition of an in-person course.

Through further investigation, we can observe the fluctuation in numbers not only in relation to the overall course, but within the individual weeks.

Looking at Figure 14.7, even in this case, we can once again see small drops in participation with peaks in attendance at the beginning of each new course week. This leads us to another useful conclusion: The most significant and relevant activities for the development of the course syllabus should be placed at the beginning of the week when the number of participants is at its maximum, leaving the second part of the week for supplementary activities.

In conclusion, thanks to our experience as curators of the Italian LMOOC, and on the basis of data we have gathered and analyzed of its outcomes, we can confirm that learning languages through this type of course is not only possible but in some cases even desirable; especially, as we have shown, when the target audience are elderly and mature learners who have already left the traditional classroom behind. These are learners who have less time available for in-person courses and who cannot afford to stay in our country for long or medium-length periods to learn our language spontaneously. The purpose of our contribution is to enrich the general debate with these possible intervention strategies for operational models and the management of LMOOC-born social networks developed to further improve the offer of available educational programs in this field.

NOTES

For Italian academic purposes only: This contribution is the result of a joint collaboration between the authors. Andrea Villarini is responsible for the drafting of the sections "Can You Learn Languages through MOOCs?," "The New Idea of Class," and "Who Chooses to Study a Language through an LMOOC?" Matteo La Grassa is responsible for the drafting of the sections "Managing Public Heterogeneity" and "The Operational Model."

1. For further information on the teaching of Italian L2 with MOOCs, see Villarini (2020).
2. MOOC Introduction to Italian, created by the authors (with the contribution of colleagues at the University for Foreigners of Siena) and dedicated to Italian language for beginners, has reached more than 100,000 followers in its various editions, with peaks of more than 50,000 subscribers for a single edition. It should be noted that there are MOOCs for the English language, whose volume of users is of course incomparable to that of Italian MOOCs, which travel at a rate of more than 400,000 followers per edition.
3. A very similar composition is found in LMOOC Move-Me classes, specifically targeted at university students (Troncarelli, 2018). In this case, the significant presence of adult and older learners is even more surprising.
4. Of course, reference is made to differences that may be present in any case among elementary Level A learners, for example among students of Pre-A1 to A2 level, according to the *Companion Volume* (Council of Europe, 2020).
5. Furthermore, if we consider the complexity of the framework in which the language learning/teaching process takes place, the factors at play, and the characteristics of the participants involved, it is clear why several operational models have been developed and described over the years, not to mention the variability of these factors over time (for example, the changes that have taken place in the context of language pedagogy methods). Specifically in regard to some contexts of online learning, we have been talking about a digital didactic unit (La Grassa, 2021) for some years now.

6. For a detailed description of these phases and of the steps involved in teaching, see Balboni (2014).
7. There is no reference here to the methodologies that, although undoubtedly related to the adopted operational model, may vary according to the decisions made by the teacher.
8. For the purposes of this work, there is no need to discuss the advantages, shortcomings, and methods of a teaching approach based on tasks, as there is already extensive literature on these topics. For the description of the characteristics of a task and its possible applications in the classroom, we refer mainly to Skehan (1988) and Willis and Willis (2007). For task-based experiences in teaching Italian L2 we refer, among others, to Paternostro and Pellitteri (2014).
9. As confirmation of this, consider that on the e-learning pages where this model has been applied, there are instructions such as "Before doing the task, read the information provided" or "We recommend . . . ." These specifications are necessary to effectively provide the learner with the possibility of following alternative routes with greater ease than in an in-class setting.
10. This is further confirmed by the installation of the MOOC platforms where the only interactive tools are the forums, by definition instruments of asynchronous and predominantly written communication.
11. For a detailed analysis of the elements that differentiate online courses on LMS and LMOOC, please refer to La Grassa (2020).

BIBLIOGRAPHY

Balboni, P. E. (2014). *Didattica dell'italiano come lingua seconda e straniera*. Torino: Bonacci-Loescher.

Caon, F., & Tonioli, V. (2016). La sfida delle classi ad abilità linguistiche differenziate (CAD) in Italia e in Europa. In C. M. Rodríguez (Ed.), *Le lingue in Italia, le lingue in Europa: Dove siamo, dove andiamo* (pp. 137–54). Venezia: Edizioni Ca' Foscari—Digital Publishing.

Council of Europe. (2020). *Common European framework of reference for languages: Learning, teaching, assessment. Companion volume with new descriptors*. https://rm.coe.int/cefr-companion-volume-with-new-descriptors-2018/1680787989

Danesi, M. (1998). *Il cervello in aula! Neurolinguistica e didattica per le lingue*. Perugia: Guerra.

Downes, S. (2007). *What connectivism is*. https://www.downes.ca/post/38653

Freddi, G. (1999). *Psicolinguistica, sociolinguistica e glottodidattica*. Torino: UTET Libreria.

Krashen, S. (1985). *The input hypothesis: Issues and implications*. London: Longman.

La Grassa, M. (2020). E-learning e massive learning nella didattica dell'italiano L2: Metodologie a confronto. In A. Villarini (Ed.), *Insegnare l'italiano con i MOOC* (pp. 37–59). Pisa: Pacini.

La Grassa, M. (2021). Un modello operativo per la didattica delle lingue online: l'Unità Didattica Digitale. *EL.LE*, *10*(1), 29–52.

Paternostro, G., & Pellitteri, A. (2014). Insegnare attraverso i task. Anatomia di una lezione. *Italiano a stranieri*, 18, 3–7.

Puglisi, A. (2021). *Le interazioni didattiche nei corsi di italiano online*. Pisa: Pacini.

Şalli-Çopur, D. (2005). Coping with the problems of mixed ability classes. *The Internet TESL Journal*, *10*(8). http://iteslj.org/

Skehan, P. (1988). *A cognitive approach to language learning*. Oxford: Oxford University Press.

Troncarelli, D. (2011). Percorsi per l'apprendimento dell'italiano L2 online. In T. Minerva & L. Colazzo (Eds.), *Connessi! Scenari di innovazione nella formazione e nella comunicazione. Atti del VIII Congresso Nazionale Società Italiana di E-learning* (pp. 885–93). Milano: Ledizioni Ledi Publishing.

Troncarelli, D. (2018). L'internazionalizzazione del sistema terziario di istruzione e l'uso di MOOC per lo sviluppo della competenza in L2: Il progetto MOVE-Me. In L. I. McLoughin & A. Villarini (Eds.), *E-learning, MOOC, e lingue straniere: Studi ricerche e sperimentazioni. E-learning, MOOCs and foreign languages: Research, studies and experiences* (pp. 17–26). Napoli: Unior Press.

Ur, P. (1996). *A course in language teaching: Theory and practice*. Cambridge: Cambridge University Press.

Villarini, A. (Ed.) (2020). *Insegnare l'italiano con i MOOC*. Pisa: Pacini.

Villarini, A. (2021). Le caratteristiche dell'apprendente. In A. De Marco (Ed.), *Manuale di glottodidattica* (pp. 71–86). Roma: Carocci.

Willis, D., & Willis, J. (2007). *Doing task-based teaching*. Oxford: Oxford University Press.

CONTRIBUTORS

Valentina Abbatelli is an assistant professor and language coordinator in Italian Studies at the University of Warwick (UK), where she teaches Italian language and cultural modules. She holds a PhD in Historical Linguistics and History of Italian Language from Università degli Studi di Roma "La Sapienza" and a second PhD in Italian Studies from the University of Warwick. Abbatelli is very much interested in the pedagogy of teaching and learning in modern languages, with a particular focus on the development of intercultural competence and empathy through a transnational and glocal approach. She also works within digital pedagogy, particularly in digital assessment, to develop transferable skills and language virtual exchange projects.

Pietro Amadini is currently an associate professor at Jilin International Studies University in Changchun, China, where he teaches Italian as a second language and Latin and cultural comparative studies. He has produced several scientific articles on the artistic relations between Italy and East Asia, and in 2012 he earned a PhD in East Asian Studies from Ca' Foscari University of Venice. He has recently oriented his studies toward online teaching strategies.

Riccardo Amorati is a teaching and research associate at the School of Languages and Linguistics of The University of Melbourne, Australia. Following university studies at the University of Bologna, he completed his doctoral degree in applied linguistics at the University of Melbourne. His research focuses primarily on the psychological factors that influence second language learning (motivation, anxiety, well-being) and on novel approaches to second language teaching. Other research interests include student recruitment and retention in language studies and intercultural communication.

Daniela Bartalesi-Graf is senior lecturer in the Department of Italian Studies at Wellesley College. Her research interests are in Italian language pedagogy and twentieth-century Italian cultural studies. She is the author of three textbooks: *L'Italia dal fascismo ad oggi: Percorsi paralleli nella storia, nella letteratura e nel cinema*; *Voci dal Sud: A Journey to Southern Italy with Carlo Levi and his* Christ Stopped at Eboli; and *Caleidoscopio, an Italian Language and Culture Intermediate Textbook* (co-authored with Colleen Ryan, Professor of Italian, Indiana University). Daniela has also developed four Italian Massive Open Online Courses for the edX platform that, since 2016, have served well over 100,000 students worldwide.

Paola Bernardini is a sessional lecturer at the University of Toronto Mississauga. She completed her PhD in Italian Studies at the University of Toronto. Her research investigates Italian novels by installments (*feuilleton*) published in the nineteenth and twentieth centuries. Her major areas of interest include contemporary literature and culture, women writers, literary journalism, and contemporary Italian cinema. She is an award-winning journalist and co-editor of *Federico Fellini. Riprese, riletture, (re)visioni* (Cesati, 2015) and *Offstream: Minority and Popular Cultures* (Cesati, 2019). She has served as assistant editor of *Italica* (journal of the American Association of Teachers of Italian) from 2015 to 2021.

Rosalba Biasini is a lecturer in Italian at the University of Liverpool (UK), where she teaches Italian language and culture at all levels. She graduated in Lettere Classiche (L'Aquila, Italy, 2004) and completed an MA in Translation Studies (Manchester, UK, 2005) and a Master ITALS (Ca' Foscari, Venezia, Italy, 2013). She holds a PhD/DPhil in Italian literature (Oxford, UK, 2010). Her research interests and publications span from the works of partisan writer Beppe Fenoglio (1922–1963) to the didactics of Italian as a foreign language, with a focus on the use of literature and translation in foreign language learning. For a detailed list of publications, see https://www.liverpool.ac.uk/languages-cultures-and-film/staff/rosalba-biasini/publications/.

Silvia Carlorosi is an associate professor of Italian at Bronx Community College of the City University of New York. She received a Laurea in Lingue Straniere from the University of Urbino, an MA in Mass Communications at Miami University of Ohio, and a PhD in Italian at the University of Pennsylvania. She published various articles on Italian cinema, literature, pedagogy, and translation. She is the author of *A Grammar of Cinepoiesis: Poetic Cameras of Italian Cinema* (Rowman and Littlefield, 2015), which analyzes the interaction between cinema and poetry and evaluates the modes of a poetic camera. She also co-edited the volume *Il secondo occhio di Ulisse: Saggi di letteratura italiana attraverso lo sguardo del forestiero* (Pisa: Pacini Editori, 2019).

Luisa Canuto is the language director of the UBC Italian Program and an associate professor of teaching at the French, Hispanic, and Italian Studies department, where she has been teaching language and culture courses since 1994. Her research interests and publications include the use of educational technologies in the classroom, the impact of evidence-based strategies and techniques, the integration of experiential learning opportunities, and curriculum program renewal and development. An invited speaker for workshops and seminar presentations, she regularly presents at national and international conferences on the topics of the scholarship of teaching and learning, intercultural competence, educational technologies, and pedagogy.

Julia M. Cozzarelli is a professor of Italian at Ithaca College. She holds PhD and MA degrees from Yale University and has published on language, literature, and pedagogy. She is the author of the elementary Italian textbook *Sentieri: Attraverso l'Italia contemporanea* and a co-author of the student activities manual for the intermediate textbook *Da capo*, for which she was also a contributing author. She has published journal and book articles on medieval and Renaissance literature and on teaching Dante, Boccaccio, and Calvino to undergraduates. At Ithaca College, she serves as the chair of the School of Humanities and Sciences' Curriculum Committee.

Domenica Diraviam holds a PhD in Comparative Studies (Italian American Studies and Digital Humanities) from Florida Atlantic University. Her research focuses on the art and legacy of Tom DiSalvo within the scope of diasporic and transnational Italian studies. Her area of expertise also includes oral history and public digital humanities. She has collaborated on the creation of the digital archive *Italian American Memories*, has curated art shows of Tom DiSalvo's art both locally and virtually, and has produced scholarship on the topic of pedagogy and migration. Her scholarly contributions appeared on *Voices of Italian America*, *Park Times*, and *Strade Dorate*. She holds a master's degree in French from the University of South Florida and is a senior instructional designer, Italy study abroad faculty leader, and French and Italian instructor at Broward College.

Marella Feltrin-Morris has published articles on translation, paratext, and pedagogy, as well as on modern and contemporary Italian literature. Among her publications are "Welcome Intrusions: Capturing the Unexpected in Translators' Prefaces to Dante's *Divine Comedy*" (*Tusaaji: A Translation Review*, 2018) and "A First Taste of Translation: Introducing Context" (forthcoming in *Spunti e riflessioni per una didattica della traduzione e dell'interpretariato nelle SSML*, edited by Valeria Petrocchi). Her translations of short stories by Luigi Pirandello and Massimo Bontempelli have appeared in *North American Review*, *Two Lines*, *Exchanges*, and *Green Mountains Review*, among other journals. Her translation of Paola Masino's novel *Birth and Death of the Housewife* was published by SUNY Press in 2009. She is a contributor to the collaborative digital edition *Stories for a Year*, an ongoing project that will provide the first complete English translation of Pirandello's short stories. She is a professor of Italian at Ithaca College.

Elisabetta Ferrari is a lecturer in Italian studies in the School of Languages and Linguistics at the University of Melbourne. She has worked in tertiary education in Australia for the past two decades in various capacities. Following university studies in languages and literature at the Università degli Studi di Parma she completed a BA with Honors at Monash University and a master of arts in Cinema Management at the University of Melbourne. Her research interests include teaching innovation and pedagogy, the contemporary Italian detective novel, Italian cinema, and twentieth-century Italian visual art.

Giulia Guarnieri received a PhD in Romance languages and literatures and is a professor of Italian language and literature at Bronx Community College of The City University of New York. She is the author of *Narrative di viaggio urbano: Il mito e l'antimito della metropoli americana* and has published several articles on Calvino, translation studies, travel literature, instructional technology, and urban studies. She also leads the Writing Intensive Faculty Development program and is also a mentor of the Advanced Online Faculty Development at her college.

John Hajek is professor of Italian studies and director of the Research Unit for Multilingualism and Cross-cultural Communication (RUMACCC) at the University of Melbourne. He completed his university studies in Australia, Italy, and the UK and has held research fellowships at the Universities of Oxford and Melbourne. He has a wide range of research interests including language education and pedagogy, and multilingualism.

Louise Hipwell is a teaching professor and coordinator of the Italian language program at Georgetown University and is a recent recipient of the College Dean's award for teaching excellence. She has a PhD in Italian from Rutgers University and before joining the faculty at Georgetown she served as coordinator of third and fourth semester language courses at the University of Pennsylvania. Her pedagogical interests include teaching with technology (hybrid courses), integrated performance tasks, and integrating telecollaboration and experiential learning (internships) into the curriculum. She has participated for the last few years as a reader/table leader at the annual AP reading. She is co-organizer of the biennial Italian Language and Culture Conference at Georgetown and has worked as co-editor of two volumes based on papers presented at this conference.

Matteo La Grassa is a researcher at the University for Foreigners of Siena. His main research topics are teaching Italian vocabulary to foreign students, educational use of new technologies, and analysis of models for distance learning and innovative methodologies for the teaching of Italian L2. On these topics, he has monographs and numerous scientific publications to his credit.

Shuang Liang is a teacher of Italian language and literature at Beijing International Studies University, Beijing, China. She holds a PhD in Italian Studies from the Ca' Foscari University of Venice and received her master's degree in Italian literature at the Beijing Foreign Studies University. She also studied at the University of Pisa as a visiting student during her master's. Her research focuses on Eugenio Montale, twentieth-century Italian poetry, and the reception of Italian literature in China. She worked as a teaching assistant for an Italian contemporary literature course, mainly aimed at Chinese students studying at the Ca' Foscari University of Venice. She is also the translator of various published literary books and scientific articles from Italian to Chinese.

Alessandro Macilenti is a translator, independent researcher, and author. He graduated in foreign languages at the University of Milan and completed a master's in Italian language teaching at the Ca' Foscari University of Venice.

He holds a PhD in Italian studies from the Victoria University of Wellington. In his doctoral thesis, he applied the analytical methods of third-wave ecocriticism to selected twenty-first-century Italian literary works, demonstrating that these works offer an opportunity to communicate meaningfully and accessibly the discomforting truths of global environmental change. In 2018 the monograph was published by Peter Lang in the series Studies in Literature, Culture, and the Environment.

Luca Malici is Italian assistant professor (Education) in the School of Modern Languages and Cultures at the University of Durham, UK. He has taught Italian language, translation, and culture at all levels at the Universities of Birmingham, St. Andrews, and Sheffield. His principal research interests lie in the fields of equality, diversity, and inclusion (EDI) as well as communication, cultural, and media studies with a special focus on the ways in which individuals engage with and are affected by means of communication. On the one hand, this greatly feeds into his inclusive and technology-enhanced language teaching practice and research. On the other hand, in his doctoral research and subsequent scholarly publications, he investigated the portrayal of LGBTIQ (Lesbian, Gay men, Bisexual, Transgender, Intersex, and Queer) subjects and issues on Italian film, television, and social media.

Patrizia Palumbo is currently working as a lecturer of Italian at Columbia University, where she got a PhD in 1996. She has written a number of articles on medieval culture and on Italian colonialism in Africa, which she has presented at international conferences and published in academic journals. Her current research focuses on the history of the capitals of Italian culture and on Italian stardom from silent film to the present.

Viviana Pezzullo is a lecturer of French and director of undergraduate studies of French at the University of Miami. In 2021 she earned a PhD in comparative studies (French, Francophone, and Italian studies) from Florida Atlantic University (FAU). Additionally, she holds a master's degree in philology and a bachelor's degree in modern arts from the University of Naples Federico II. Her contributions on pedagogy appeared in *Teaching Higher Ed*, *ACUE Community*, and *Inside Higher Education*. Viviana's areas of expertise include twentieth- and twenty-first-century literature (with a special emphasis on women writers), visual culture, and translation. She published articles on these topics in *The French Review*, *Gender/Sexuality/Italy*, and *NeMLA Italian Studies*. Her interest in digital humanities (DH) and transnational identities led her to co-found several DH projects, such as FAU's digital archive "Italian American Oral History Collection" and the website "Italian American Memories," which has received internal and external grants and has developed into a formal partnership with the John D. Calandra Italian American Institute.

Francesca Raffi is a senior research fellow in English language and translation at the University of Macerata (Italy) where she has been teaching English language and translation at undergraduate and postgraduate levels since 2015. She holds a PhD in English for special purposes and audiovisual translation from the University of Naples Federico II, and she is a Chartered Linguist of the Chartered Institute of Linguists (UK). She is Honorary Fellow at the Department of Languages, Cultures and Film, University of Liverpool (UK). She is the author of more than thirty publications on re(translation); linguistic and sensorial accessibility to texts, media, arts, and culture; and in the field of reception studies, focusing on translated products/services and their audiences. The detailed list is available here: http://docenti.unimc.it/f.raffi #content=publications.

Alessandra Saggin is a senior lecturer in the Italian Department at Columbia, where she has been working since 2010. She has a laurea and a master's in classics from the University of Pisa, Italy. She teaches all levels of language courses, from elementary to advanced. For the advanced level she recently created a content-based course about Italian art. Her research interests are second language acquisition, Italian cinema, Italian art, and the use of technology in learning and teaching.

Tatiana Selepiuc is a sessional lecturer at the University of Toronto Mississauga. She earned a PhD in Italian studies at the University of Toronto. Her research focuses on Italian literature of the Cinquecento, specifically Pietro Aretino's contributions to the chivalric tradition. Her major areas of interest include Italian Renaissance literature and foreign language (FL) teaching. She has served as assistant editor of *Italica* (journal of the American Association of Teachers of Italian) from 2016 to 2021.

Barbara Spinelli is a senior lecturer in Italian at Columbia University. She worked as a researcher in educational linguistics at the University for Foreigners in Perugia, Italy. She collaborated with the Centre for Language Assessment and Certifications as a teacher trainer and language tester. She was involved in research projects promoted by the European Commission and the Council of Europe as a language expert. She has published book chapters as well as articles in international research journals. She is the co-author of the *Profilo della lingua Italiana: Livelli A1, A2, B1, B2 del QCER* (Rizzoli Education). Her main research areas are network-based language learning, curriculum design, and plurilingual and intercultural education.

Andrea Villarini is a full professor of modern languages teaching at the University for Foreigners of Siena and he is the head of the Postgraduate School of Teaching Italian as a Foreign Language. He deals with issues related to teaching of Italian as L2 with Information and Communication Technologies and Italian sociolinguistics. He coordinates research units for national and international projects on languages less widely used and less taught. He has been part of the scientific committees of international conferences, and he has been invited to give lectures and training courses in Italy and abroad. He has numerous publications in books and magazines, both national and international.

INDEX

Note: Information in figures and tables is indicated by page numbers followed by *f* and *t*.

ACTFL. *See* American Council on the Teaching of Foreign Languages (ACTFL)
advanced level, 83–86
advanced placement (AP), 235–37, 236*t*
Affricot, Johanne, 206
ages, of LMOOC students, 266–67, 266*f*
alignment, 94
Amadini, Pietro, 155
American Council on the Teaching of Foreign Languages (ACTFL), 61, 176–77
Anatrone, Sole, 226
Anderson, Benedict, 113n1
anxiety, 139, 159
AP. *See* advanced placement (AP)
Art of Tom DiSalvo, The, 42–43, 49–52
audio guides, 67, 72, 76*t*
audiovisual translation (AVT), 118–29
autonomy, 176
AVT. *See* audiovisual translation (AVT)

Badia, Patricia, 44
Baldo, Michela, 230n3
Banks, James, 16
Bates, Tony, 253n9
Bellamy, 201, 213n4
belonging, 100
Belt and Road Initiative (BRI), 154, 171n2
Bertan, Giorgio, 88, 90n4
Black Lives Matter (BLM), 197–208
blended learning (BL), 79–80, 87–89, 238–240, 238*t*, 240–247, 242*f*–244*f*, 242*t*, 246*f*, 252n2
BLM. *See* Black Lives Matter (BLM)
Bologna, 64

Bronx Community College (BCC), 8–9
Bundu, Antonella, 201

Calamita, Francesa, 221
CALL. *See* computer-assisted language learning (CALL)
Cavatorta, Giuseppe, 61
CEFR. *See* Common European Framework of Reference (CEFR)
cheating, online learning and, 13–14
China, exchange students from, in Italy, 153–64, 157*t*–158*t*
Chiodo, Carol, 43
cinema, 36–37
cities, Italian culture and, 62–65
CLIL. *See* content and language integrated learning (CLIL)
ClipFlair, 121
CLL. *See* communicative language learning (CLL)
Columbia University, 60
Common European Framework of Reference (CEFR), 96, 113n3, 119
communicative language learning (CLL), 138–139
community : engagement, 41–53; of feeling, 100; imagined, 94; learning, 10
computer-assisted language learning (CALL), 176
content and language integrated learning (CLIL), 199
conversation courses: assignments in, 32–34; background on and rationale for, 26–27; classroom activities in, 32–34; design and planning of, 29–31; grammar in, 31–32; as models for

283

conversation courses (*continued*)
   curricular innovation, 25–38; pedagogical foundation for, 27–29
COVID-19 pandemic, 1–2; cheating and, 13–14; educational toll of, 7–8; writing assignments and, 11–15, 11*f*–13*f*
cultural scripts, 101–10, 113n2
culture: capitals of, 60–76, 69*f*, 70*f*, 72*f*, 73*f*, 76*t*; cities and, 62–65; cultural narrative of place, 95; digital humanities and, 41–53; third culture space, 93
Curtis, Sandra, 51

Dagli inviati sul campus, 135–150
Danesi, Marcel, 86
DCT. *See* dual coding theory (DCT)
De André, Fabrizio, 226
decolonization, 202
DH. *See* digital humanities (DH)
digital humanities (DH), 41–53, 57n3, 79
Diraviam, Domenica, 50
DiSalvo, Tom, 43, 49–50
diversity, 16, 197–206, 216
dual coding theory (DCT), 120
Dweck, Carol, 20n1

EDI. *See* equality, diversity, and inclusion (EDI)
EL. *See* experiential learning (EL)
engagement, 94
equality, diversity, and inclusion (EDI), 216
equity-oriented activities, 15–16
Erasmus Program, 153
exchange students, from China, in Italy, 153–64, 157*t*–58*t*
experiencing, in multiliteracies approach, 98
experiential learning (EL), 79–89, 135

Farias de Albuquerque, Fernanda, 226
Ferreira, Michael, 175, 194n1
film subtitles, as activity, 85–86
Florence, 64

games, 86
Genoa, 63
Georgetown University, 175, 177, 194n1, 194n6
globalization, 92, 171n6
glocalization, 93–94
Goldoni, Carlo, 88–89

Google Arts and Culture, 68
grammar, in conversation courses, 31–32
group work, 147–48
growth mindset, 7, 11–14, 19–20, 20n1

H5P, 67
Hall, Crystal, 43
Heim, Julia, 226
high-impact practices (HIPs), 79–89
HIPs. *See* high-impact practices (HIPs)

identity, language and, 218–19
imagined communities, 94
inclusivity, 197–98, 203–4, 208–9, 216, 222*t*
Initiative on Technology-Enhanced Learning (ITEL), 175
interconnectedness, 92
intermediate level, 80–83
Italian American Memories (ITAMM), 42, 44, 49, 50
Italian Studies, digital humanities and, 43–44
Italicity, 96, 98, 99–101
ITAMM. *see* Italian American Memories (ITAMM)
ITEL. *see* Initiative on Technology-Enhanced Learning (ITEL)
Ithaca College, 25–38

Joseph, Hristo, 46

language, first: writing and, 14–15
language massive open online course (LMOOC), 234–52, 236*t*, 238*t*, 242*f*–244*f*, 242*t*, 246*f*, 257–71, 263*f*, 264*f*, 266*f*–270*f*
learning: blended, 79–80, 87–89, 238–40, 238*t*, 240–47, 242*f*–244*f*, 242*t*, 246*f*; communicative language, 138–39; experiential, 79–89, 135; project-based, 135; tandem, 175–88, 179*t*, 181*t*–182*t*, 185*f*–187*f*
learning community, 10
learning to write (LW), 199
Leone, Paola, 177
linguistic landscape, 95
LMOOC. *See* language massive open online course (LMOOC)
ludolinguistica, 86
Luxuria, Vladimir, 226
LW. *See* learning to write (LW)

Macilenti, Alessandro, 155
Manca, Elena, 177, 194n7
massive open online course (MOOC), 234–52, 236*t*, 238*t*, 242*f*–244*f*, 242*t*, 246*f*, 257–71, 263*f*, 264*f*, 266*f*–270*f*
meaning-making, 93
medieval period, 81
metadata, 48–49
Milan, 63
Mocchiutti, Michela, 88
Mollica, Anthony, 86
MOOC. *See* massive open online course (MOOC)
multilevel classrooms, 28–29
multilevel structuring, courses suitable for, 34–37
multiliteracies approach: Critical Framing in, 97, 98; cultural scripts and, 101–110; experiencing in, 98; glocalization and, 93–94; imagined communities and, 94; Italicity and, 99–101; linguistic landscape and, 95; Overt Instruction in, 97–98; pedagogical project of, 96–101, 97; scaffolding in, 98; semiotic landscape and, 95; Situated Practice in, 97, 98; Transformed Practice in, 99
Musti, Fulvia, 177, 194n3

Naples, 64–65
Negri, Gianmarco, 226
New York City, 101–110
New York University, 60

Omeka, 44, 48, 57n5
operational models, 261–64, 263*f*

Palermo, 65
pandemic. *See* COVID-19 pandemic
PBL. *See* project-based learning (PBL)
PDH. *See* public digital humanities (PDH)
performance indicators (PI), 185
Picciano, Anthony G., 89n1
place, cultural narrative of, 95
place-based learning, 90n5
podcasting, 135–50
Pouzergues, Paul, 29
project-based learning (PBL), 135, 137*f*, 138–39
public digital humanities (PDH), 42–43, 45, 51

Queer Language Pedagogy (QLP), 216–99, 222*t*, 227*f*

reading comprehension, 45–47, 47*f*, 48*f*
reciprocity, 176
Rome, 64

scaffolding, in multiliteracies approach, 98
Scego, Igiaba, 201
schwa (ə), 203, 205, 210–11
Sciorra, Joseph, 44
semiotic landscape, 95
Shuang Liang, 156
Signorelli, Josephine Yole, 226
spatial understanding, 95
stacked course model, 30
subtitles: as activity, 85–86, 118–29; interlingual, 118–23; intralingual, 118–19; reverse, 131n4

tandem learning, 175–88, 179*t*, 181*t*–182*t*, 185*f*–187*f*
Teaching in a Digital Age (Bates), 253n9
Teletandem, 175–77, 186–88, 194n6
Telles, João, 176, 194n1
textbooks, bias in, 221–23, 222*t*
third culture space, 93
Tortora, Christina, 44
transing, 225–26
translations, as activity, 118–29; of books, 85; of film subtitles, 85–86
Trapè, Roberta, 221
Trieste, 63–64
Turin, 62–63

University of Arizona, 61
University of British Columbia (UBC), 234, 238
University of Liverpool, 123, 129
University of Melbourne (Australia), 135
University of Salento, 177
University of Toronto Mississauga (UTM), 79, 87–89
Uyangoda, Nadeesha, 206

Venice, 63
Versini, Dominique Carlini, 224
Victoria University, Wellington, New Zealand, 122
Vivo, Giuseppina, 45
Vivo-Fruttauro Letters, 42–45

Wass, Gerry, 29
Wellesley College (WC), 234, 235, 238

WLL. *See* writing to learn language (WLL)
WordPress, 67
World-Readiness Standards, 176
writers' workshops, 84–85
writing assignments: equity-oriented, 15–16; exploratory, 14, 20n7; low-stakes, 14–15; pandemic and, 11–15, 11*f*–13*f*; sample, 16–18
writing to learn content (WLC), 199
writing to learn language (WLL), 199

Yu Xiaoping, 154